Contesting the French Revolution

Paul R. Hanson

WILEY-BLACKWELL
A John Wiley & Sons, Ltd., Publication

This edition first published 2009

Blackwell Publishing was acquired by John Wiley & Sons in February 2007. Blackwell's publishing program has been merged with Wiley's global Scientific, Technical, and Medical business to form Wiley-Blackwell.

Registered Office
John Wiley & Sons Ltd, The Atrium, Southern Gate, Chichester, West Sussex, PO19 8SQ, United Kingdom

Editorial Offices
350 Main Street, Malden, MA 02148-5020, USA
9600 Garsington Road, Oxford, OX4 2DQ, UK
The Atrium, Southern Gate, Chichester, West Sussex, PO19 8SQ, UK

For details of our global editorial offices, for customer services, and for information about how to apply for permission to reuse the copyright material in this book please see our website at www.wiley.com/wiley-blackwell.

Library of Congress Cataloging-in-Publication Data

Hanson, Paul.
Contesting the French Revolution / Paul Hanson.
p. cm.
Includes bibliographical references and index.
ISBN 978-1-4051-6083-4 (hardcover : alk. paper) – ISBN 978-1-4051-6084-1 (pbk. : alk. paper) 1. France–History–Revolution, 1789–1799–Historiography. 2. France–History–Revolution, 1789–1799–Causes. 3. France–History–Revolution, 1789–1799–Influence. I. Title.

DC147.8.H34 2009
944.04072–dc22

2008038601

A catalogue record for this book is available from the British Library.

Set in 10/12.5pt Photina
by SPi Publisher Services, Pondicherry, India
Printed and bound in Malaysia by Vivar Printing Sdn Bhd

01 2009

Contesting the French Revolution

Contesting the Past

The volumes in this series select some of the most controversial episodes in history and consider their divergent, even starkly incompatible representations. The aim is not merely to demonstrate that history is 'argument without end', but to show that study even of contradictory conceptions can be fruitful: that the jettisoning of one thesis or presentation leaves behind something of value.

Published

Contesting the Crusades
Norman Housley

Contesting the German Empire 1871–1918
Matthew Jefferies

Vietnam: Explaining America's Lost War
Gary R. Hess

Contesting the French Revolution
Paul R. Hanson

In preparation

European Renaissance
William Caferro

Witch Hunts in the Early Modern World
Alison Rowlands

Reformations
C. Scott Dixon

The Rise of Nazism
Chris Szejnmann

Origins of the Second World War
Peter Jackson

The Enlightenment
Thomas Munck

For my students, past, present, and future

Contents

Acknowledgements

I would like first to thank Tessa Harvey, who invited me to write this book back in the autumn of 2005, at a moment when I had both the opportunity and the time to undertake the project. It has been a pleasure throughout working with Tessa, Gillian Kane, Kitty Bocking, Ian Coombes, and the other professional staff at Wiley-Blackwell, as well as David Williams at The Running Head, who took charge of the copy-editing process.

I have been teaching and writing about the French Revolution for more than a quarter century, but my first opportunity for sustained reflection about this book came at the home of John Merriman in Balazuc, a small village in the Ardèche, where I spent three weeks in March 2006 reading new scholarship and digesting the eight reviews of the prospectus I had submitted, which helped me give structure and shape to the manuscript. At the beginning of my stay John and I paid a visit to the château of Balazuc, a massive structure looming above the village. It had been sold during the Revolution as a *bien national* and then remained in the hands of the same family for more than two centuries; in 2006 it had just been sold again to an entrepreneur who was in the process of converting it into bed and breakfast accommodation. That visit made me ponder the many small ways in which the legacy of the Revolution lives on in the cobblestone streets and terraced fields of villages all over France.

A number of colleagues have read portions of the manuscript, and their feedback has been enormously helpful to me in reshaping and revising the text. I should like to thank in particular Laura Mason, whose early critique and encouragement gave me confidence to forge ahead, Colin Jones, Marisa Linton, Peter Campbell (and his students), and my colleague here at Butler, Scott Swanson, as well as the anonymous readers for Wiley-Blackwell. Their input helped me to correct a number of errors, to reorganize the text at some points, and to sharpen and refine my analysis and argument. I would also like to thank Butler University for a sabbatical leave in the fall of 2007, during which time I completed a draft of the book.

History is a dialogue – a sometimes contentious one, as the title to this series suggests – between the historian and the past, among historians of the same and different generations, between a writer and his readers, between a teacher and her students. As I have tried to suggest in this slim volume, the history of the French Revolution is not fixed. It is a work in progress, an argument or debate that has raged now for more than two centuries and will continue for many years to come. It is also vast in its scope. Recent historiography has not only challenged traditional interpretations of the Revolution, it has added new areas of inquiry that have expanded and enriched our understanding of the period. In writing this volume I have had to make choices about what to include, because not every issue or event could be addressed in a short text. I have also tried to engage the debates in as evenhanded a manner as I could. But there will be those who feel I have neglected topics that merited inclusion, and others who will disagree with my reading of interpretive debates. If this book does not generate debate it will indeed have failed in its prime objective. In the spirit of history as dialogue, therefore, I would like to close here by inviting readers to send me comments, suggestions, and criticisms at this e-mail address: contestingpaulhanson@butler.edu. This book is done, but there will be another to write, and your responses to this effort may help to make the next a better one.

Chronology

22 February–12 May 1787	Assembly of Notables
8 August 1788	King convokes Estates General
25 September 1788	Parlement of Paris issues ruling on Estates General
5 May 1789	Opening of Estates General
17 June 1789	Third Estate calls itself the National Assembly
20 June 1789	Tennis Court Oath
11 July 1789	Dismissal of Necker
14 July 1789	Fall of the Bastille
20 July–6 August 1789	The Great Fear
4 August 1789	Constituent Assembly abolishes feudalism
26 August 1789	Assembly votes the Declaration of the Rights of Man
5–6 October 1789	Women of Paris march to Versailles
2 November 1789	Church lands nationalized
January–February 1790	First municipal elections
12 July 1790	Assembly votes the Civil Constitution of the Clergy
25 November 1790	Slave uprising in Saint-Domingue
20–21 June 1791	Flight to Varennes
17 July 1791	Champ de Mars massacre
30 September 1791	Legislative Assembly convenes
20 April 1792	France declares war on Austria
24 April 1792	Rouget de Lisle composes "La Marseillaise"

20 June 1792	Failed assault on Tuileries Palace
10 August 1792	Invasion of Tuileries/Fall of the monarchy
21 August 1792	First use of the guillotine
2–6 September 1792	Massacre of Paris prisoners
20 September 1792	Victory at Valmy/National Convention convenes
22 September 1792	National Convention declares the Republic
11 December 1792	Trial of Louis XVI begins
21 January 1793	Execution of Louis XVI
1 February 1793	France declares war on Great Britain and Holland
7 March 1793	France declares war on Spain
10 March 1793	Vendée rebellion begins
5 April 1793	Committee of Public Safety established
4 May 1793	Grain "maximum" decreed
31 May–2 June 1793	Parisian uprising ousts Girondin deputies
June–August 1793	Federalist revolts
13 July 1793	Assassination of Marat
26 July 1793	National Convention votes death penalty for hoarders
4–5 September 1793	Uprising in Paris following surrender of Toulon to the British
17 September 1793	National Convention votes the Law of Suspects
29 September 1793	National "maximum" fixed for prices and wages
5 October 1793	National Convention adopts revolutionary calendar
16 October 1793	Execution of Marie-Antoinette
31 October 1793	Execution of the Girondin deputies
October–November 1793	De-Christianization campaign
4 February 1794	National Convention abolishes slavery in French colonies
24 March 1794	Execution of Hébert and his supporters
5 April 1794	Execution of Danton and his supporters
7 May 1794	Robespierre institutes the Cult of the Supreme Being
8 June 1794	Festival of the Supreme Being
27 July 1794	Fall of Robespierre
19 November 1794	Government closes Jacobin clubs
20–22 May 1795	Government defeats last great Paris uprising

22 August 1795	National Convention votes Constitution of Year III
5 October 1795	Napoleon suppresses royalist uprising in Paris
26 October 1795	Directory regime replaces National Convention
27 May 1797	Gracchus Babeuf condemned to death
4 September 1797	Fructidor coup
11 May 1798	Floréal coup
19 May 1798	Napoleon sails to Egypt
18 June 1799	Prairial coup
10 November 1799	Napoleon's coup d'état/18 Brumaire
1801	Napoleon signs Concordat with the Catholic Church
2 December 1804	Napoleon crowns himself Emperor

Introduction

The French Revolution has inspired debate ever since Thomas Paine wrote *The Rights of Man* in response to Edmund Burke's highly critical *Reflections on the Revolution in France*, first published in 1790.[1] Some, like Paine, have seen in 1789 an assertion of individual freedom, a declaration of human rights, an enduring beacon for all those around the globe who have challenged repressive regimes over the past two centuries. Others, following Burke, have viewed the French revolutionaries as rending asunder the very fabric of society by attacking the traditions of Christian morality and hierarchy, and promoting an egalitarian ideal that would lead inexorably to mob violence and revolutionary terror; indeed, to a despotism far worse than that which some had ascribed to the Old Regime monarchy. Yet embedded in this polarity of views is an important point of agreement: the French Revolution was a momentous event, one that continues to influence the course of world history down to the present day.

This book will focus principally on the historical debates about the French Revolution, but it is worth noting here at the outset that historical interpretation of the Revolution has itself been influenced by the political and social currents of the nineteenth and twentieth centuries. The three revolutionary upheavals in France over the course of the nineteenth century, for example – in 1830, 1848, and 1871 – each had an impact on the way that historians in France viewed 1789. On a more global scale, the Russian Revolution of 1917 raised a whole new set of questions about the French Revolution, as did the Chinese Revolution of 1949. One might

---

1 E. Burke, *Reflections on the Revolution in France* (New York, Oxford University Press, 1999), and T. Paine, *The Rights of Man* (New York, Oxford University Press, 1998).

assert a kind of dialectical relationship here. Each of those revolutions was in some sense a product of 1789, and each, in turn, influenced contemporary understanding of that first modern revolution.

It is not only historians, however, who have debated the significance of the French Revolution. The celebration of the Bicentennial in France in 1989 was a hugely contentious affair, much unlike its counterpart in the United States in 1976. The cover of the 14 July 1989 issue of the French magazine *L'Express* posed the question, "Is Robespierre Guilty?," and readers were polled not only on his responsibility for the Terror, but also in regard to their views on the execution of Louis XVI and whether the Terror of the 1790s could legitimately be compared to the Soviet Gulag of the twentieth century. Earlier in the bicentennial year the wife of President François Mitterrand suggested that it might be time to rewrite the lyrics of the *Marseillaise*, the French national anthem, in order to emphasize national unity rather than violent conflict, a proposal that was vigorously debated and ultimately rejected by the French public.[2]

Similarly, when the Berlin Wall came down later in 1989 and the Soviet bloc collapsed in the early 1990s, some saw this as an end to the "totalitarian" ideology that had originated with Jean-Jacques Rousseau and the French Revolution, while others viewed those events as the final realization in Eastern Europe of the ideals of 1789: Liberty, Equality, and Fraternity. In that same bicentennial year, Chinese students and workers occupied Tiananmen Square in Beijing for more than a month, protesting government policies and calling for democratic reform. Toward the end of the protest the students erected a statue of Lady Liberty on the square. Americans tended to see in this a Chinese version of their own Statue of Liberty and interpreted the student protest as a call for American-style democratic elections. Europeans more likely thought of the French Revolution and its female liberty, Marianne, and saw in the student calls for democracy a desire to end official corruption and return to the egalitarian ideals of the Chinese revolution of 1949. All of this suggests the degree to which debates about the French Revolution extend far beyond the halls of academe, and points as well to the continuing resonance and relevance of 1789 around the globe.

The historical debates about the French Revolution have been many and varied, and it would be well to summarize them here and to outline a structure for the book before plunging into the midst of the fray. Over the course of the nineteenth century one might characterize those debates as

2 See S. L. Kaplan, *Adieu 89* (Paris, Fayard, 1993), for a spirited recounting of the Bicentennial controversies in France. The book was later published in English as *Farewell Revolution: The Historians' Feud, France, 1789/1989* (Ithaca, Cornell University Press, 1996), a title which exaggerates the degree to which the book focuses on historical debates.

pitting those who were sympathetic to the aspirations and achievements of the revolutionaries against those who viewed the revolutionaries as little more than a violent mob. Among the former one might note in particular Jules Michelet, a liberal historian who wrote a highly romanticized history of the Revolution at mid-century, and Jean Jaurès, whose socialist history of the Revolution appeared near the end of the century.[3] Among the latter one might mention the work of Hippolyte Taine.[4]

Two other nineteenth-century intellectuals, more than any others, have continued to shape the ways that we think about the French Revolution. The first was Alexis de Tocqueville, a landowning aristocrat who served both in the Chamber of Deputies under the July Monarchy and in the Constituent Assembly under the Second Republic. Best known for his two-volume *Democracy in America*, de Tocqueville later published a short study of the Old Regime and the Revolution, in which he argued that the most important contribution of the revolutionary era was to continue the modernizing and centralizing work that had begun in the French state under Louis XIV, and that the failure of the Revolution was largely due to the political inexperience of the deputies, who tried to follow the abstract ideals of Enlightenment philosophes.[5] De Tocqueville was a classic liberal, an advocate of parliamentary government, but skeptical of popular democracy, even a bit fearful of the politics of the crowd.

Karl Marx, like de Tocqueville, was an eyewitness to the events of the 1848 revolution in Paris. Just prior to that revolution he had published, along with Friedrich Engels, the work for which he is best known, *The Communist Manifesto*. Marx wrote very little about the first French Revolution, but published lengthy essays on the revolutions of 1848 and 1871, which he saw as extensions of the first. For Marx, unlike de Tocqueville, revolution was a positive force. 1789 had marked the triumph of the bourgeoisie over the aristocracy, an end to feudalism, and the emergence of a capitalist economy. Economic change, then, underlay political change. The industrial bourgeoisie controlled the parliamentary regimes of nineteenth-century Europe, Marx argued, and future revolutions would bring the victory of the proletariat (the working class) and the emergence first of a socialist economy and then a communist society. Whereas de Tocqueville had emphasized the contribution of the 1789 revolution to an

---

3 J. Michelet, *Histoire de la Révolution française* (Paris, Chamerot, 1847–50), 5 vols.; J. Jaurès, *Histoire socialiste de la Révolution française* (Paris, Editions de la Librairie de l'humanité, 1922–27), 8 vols. This was the first definitive collection, edited by Albert Mathiez, of the works originally published by J. Rouff between 1895 and 1905.

4 H. Taine, *Les Origines de la France contemporaine* (Paris, Hachette, 1876–94).

5 A. de Tocqueville, *L'Ancien régime et la révolution* (Paris, Lévy frères, 1856), trans. by S. Gilbert as *The Old Regime and the French Revolution* (Garden City, NY, Doubleday, 1955).

increasingly powerful, centralized state, Marx predicted that a communist revolution would eventually bring the withering away of the state, an end to class conflict, and the development of a society in which individual liberties would flourish.[6]

The appointment, in 1889, of Alphonse Aulard as the first Chair of the History of the French Revolution at the Sorbonne, a position in which he has been followed by a series of distinguished historians of the Revolution, signalled the beginning of academic historiography of the Revolution. Aulard's contributions were several: he published his own general history of the French Revolution, and a work on de-Christianization during the Revolution, but also edited two important documentary collections that have served historians ever since: the first on the Paris Jacobin Club and the second on the Committee of Public Safety, which functioned as the executive branch of the government during the year of the Terror. With Aulard, then, began the tradition of serious archival research that has characterized French revolutionary studies ever since.[7]

The Russian Revolution of 1917 had a profound impact on the historiography of the French Revolution. Many saw the Bolsheviks as a twentieth-century version of the Jacobins, while others saw Vladimir Lenin as a modern-day Robespierre. The importance of Marxist theory to the Russian revolutionaries prompted historians to apply Marxist analysis and categories to the study of 1789, so much so that by mid-century what some would characterize as a "Marxist orthodoxy" had come to dominate the field. Beginning with Albert Mathiez, a student of Aulard, and continuing most prominently in the work of Georges Lefebvre and Albert Soboul, both holders of the Chair of the History of the Revolution at the Sorbonne, this interpretation viewed 1789 as a "bourgeois revolution," first pitting the bourgeoisie against the aristocracy in a struggle for political ascendancy, and then pitting the bourgeoisie against the *sans-culottes*, viewed by these historians as a nascent proletariat.

Class struggle lay at the heart of this interpretation, which emphasized economic and social factors in its analysis of both the causes and the dynamic of the Revolution. The protagonists of the story were the rising bourgeoisie, growing in numbers and wealth in the eighteenth century, but

---

6 See R. C. Tucker, ed., *The Marx–Engels Reader* (New York, W. W. Norton, 1979, 2nd ed.), for most of these works, which have also been published many times in separate editions.

7 A. Aulard, *Histoire politique de la Révolution française* (Paris, A. Colin, 1903); *La Révolution et les congrégations* (Paris, E. Cornely, 1903); *La Société des Jacobins: recueil de documents pour l'histoire du Club des Jacobins de Paris* (Paris, Jouaust, 1889–97), 6 vols.; *Recueil des actes du Comité de salut public* (Paris, Imprimerie Nationale, 1951), 27 vols. For excerpts from a number of the nineteenth-century histories of the Revolution see M. R. Cox, ed., *The Place of the French Revolution in History* (Boston, Houghton Mifflin, 1998).

long denied social status and political power by the privileged aristocracy. When the monarchy faced a fiscal crisis in 1787–88, the aristocracy saw an opportunity to defend, even enhance, its traditional position of political primacy, while the bourgeoisie pressed for constitutional and political reform. The crown, frustrated in its own efforts at reform over the last half of the century, initially supported the demand of the Third Estate (led by the bourgeoisie) for a convocation of the Estates General, but when that body convened in the spring of 1789 King Louis XVI quickly came to see the interests of the monarchy as more closely aligned with those of the aristocracy and took measures to stymie the growing popular movement for radical reform. It was too little, too late. The bourgeoisie was now joined by two powerful allies: the peasantry, long oppressed by the vestiges of the old feudal system, especially the array of seigneurial dues that many of them paid to noble landowners, and additionally burdened in 1789 by the first serious crop failure since early in the century; and the *sans-culottes* – the artisans, workers, and shopkeepers of urban France – who, like the peasantry, bore the brunt of the tax burden under the Old Regime, and whose livelihood was similarly jeopardized by rising grain prices. A wave of rural protests in the summer of 1789, along with urban uprisings (most notably in Paris), prevented the king from stifling the burgeoning reform movement and allowed the radical deputies of the Third Estate to transform the Estates General into a National Assembly. With the fall of the Bastille in Paris on 14 July 1789 the French Revolution had begun.[8]

As the Revolution progressed, following the Marxist interpretation, the bourgeoisie asserted the rights of private property and capital, thereby alienating in some measure both the peasantry and urban workers. The peasants soon developed into a conservative, even counterrevolutionary, force. But so long as the king and the aristocracy remained a threat to the Revolution, the bourgeois deputies maintained their uneasy alliance with the *sans-culottes*. By 1793, however, following the trial and execution of Louis XVI, a division emerged in the leadership of the National Convention between moderate Girondin deputies and the more radical Montagnards. Prominent Girondin leaders began to call for an end to the Revolution and a return to the rule of law. They were uncomfortable, in particular, with the influence of the Paris crowd on national politics. The Montagnards, by

---

8 The classic expression of this interpretation is G. Lefebvre, *The Coming of the French Revolution*, trans. R. R. Palmer (Princeton, Princeton University Press, 1947). Other seminal works in the Marxist interpretation include A. Mathiez, *La Vie chère et le mouvement social sous la Terreur* (Paris, Payot, 1927); G. Lefebvre, *Les Paysans du Nord pendant la Révolution française* (Lille, O. Marquant, 1924); G. Rudé, *The Crowd in the French Revolution* (Oxford, Clarendon Press, 1959); and A. Soboul, *Les Sans-culottes parisiens en l'an II: mouvement populaire et gouvernement révolutionnaire, 2 juin 1793–9 thermidor an II* (Paris, Clavreuil, 1958).

contrast, saw the work of the Revolution as incomplete and cultivated the support of the *sans-culottes*, ultimately emerging victorious in their rivalry when the Girondin leadership was proscribed from the National Convention on 2 June 1793, following a massive street demonstration.

In the months that followed, the revolutionary government responded to the demands of the urban populace by introducing price controls and taking measures to ensure the supply of grain to the cities. But the Jacobin government was now faced with counterrevolution in the west of France, with rebellion in the four federalist cities and their hinterlands, and with war against the European monarchies. The result was the Terror. In the name of defending the Republic, the Committee of Public Safety moved resolutely against suspected enemies of the Revolution and also took steps toward an increasing centralization of state power. This came at the expense of the popular democracy of the Paris sections and clubs, so that when moderates challenged Robespierre and his closest supporters in the summer of 1794, claiming that the Terror had gone too far, the *sans-culottes* of the capital were either not inclined or not capable of defending their erstwhile champion. Following Thermidor the moderate bourgeoisie, the rising capitalist class, reclaimed political power, which it held until the coup of Napoleon Bonaparte in 1799.

Thus, the fragile alliance between the bourgeois revolutionaries and the *sans-culottes* broke down, in the Marxist interpretation, in large part because the bourgeoisie came to realize its own social and economic interests. On the other side, the *sans-culottes*, not yet constituting a true working class, lacked the class consciousness that might have enabled them to create a more organized and resolute political force. That task would be left to their heirs in the nineteenth and twentieth centuries – not until the Bolsheviks in 1917 would the proletariat succeed in carrying out a successful communist revolution.

This, in broad strokes, is the Marxist, or classical, interpretation that dominated the field in France and Great Britain, and to a lesser degree in the United States, throughout the middle decades of the twentieth century. But as with all orthodoxies (some, at least, claimed that it achieved that status), it came under increasing scrutiny and eventually challenge. Alfred Cobban presented the first major critique, arguing that the revolutionary deputies were *not* in fact drawn from the commercial or capitalist bourgeoisie, but were instead predominantly lawyers and professionals, many of them local officeholders in the final years of the Old Regime. The French Revolution may have been a social revolution, in Cobban's view, but it was not an attack on feudalism led by a new capitalist bourgeoisie.[9]

9 A. Cobban, *The Social Interpretation of the French Revolution* (Cambridge, Cambridge University Press, 1964).

Across the Atlantic, George Taylor added his voice to the critique in two important scholarly articles. If the French Revolution were a bourgeois revolution, Taylor argued, then one should find evidence of capitalist economic activity among those who led it. Instead what he found in his research was that the investment patterns of prominent figures in the Third Estate, the so-called bourgeoisie, were strikingly similar to those of the French aristocracy. Most individuals with disposable income preferred to invest in land. Far from being the result of class conflict, Taylor asserted that the Revolution of 1789 was essentially an accident, one that could have been avoided by a more astute and capable monarch.[10] In the 1970s a revisionist line of argument began to emerge, represented most notably in Great Britain by the work of Colin Lucas and William Doyle.[11]

In France, Denis Richet and François Furet were the most important critics of what Furet characterized as the old Marxist "catechism."[12] Their work shifted the focus away from class analysis, from the social history that had dominated the field over the previous twenty years, back toward the realm of ideas and language. It was not an economic crisis that caused the Revolution, not a social clash between a rising bourgeoisie and a declining aristocracy, but rather a constitutional crisis that paralyzed the Old Regime monarchy, creating a void in which competing discourses vied for political supremacy. In the midst of that upheaval both monarchical authority and civil society collapsed, Furet argued, leaving discourse and language supreme, particularly that discourse shaped by the political philosophy of Jean-Jacques Rousseau. The goal of the revolutionaries was transparency on the one hand, an end to the politics of courtly intrigue, and on the other the creation of a new political order reflecting the general will of the people. To aspire to political unity was not to achieve it, however, and in the often bitter debates of the 1790s, which tended to spill out beyond the national assemblies onto the streets of Paris and provincial cities, those who dissented from the dominant discourse came to be seen as counterrevolutionaries, as plotters against the general will, and this ideological confrontation led inexorably toward the Terror.

---

10 G. V. Taylor, "Types of Capitalism in Eighteenth-Century France," *English Historical Review* 79 (1964), 478–97; and "Noncapitalist Wealth and the Origins of the French Revolution," *American Historical Review* 72 (1967), 469–96.

11 C. Lucas, "Nobles, Bourgeois, and the Origins of the French Revolution," *Past and Present* 60 (August 1973), 84–126; W. Doyle, "Was There an Aristocratic Reaction in Pre-revolutionary France?," *Past and Present* 57 (November 1972), 97–122.

12 D. Richet, "Autour des origines idéologiques lointaines de la Révolution française: élites et despotismes," *Annales: Economies, Sociétés, Civilisation* (hereafter, *Annales E.S.C.*) xxiv (1969), 1–23; F. Furet, "Le catéchisme de la Révolution française," *Annales, E.S.C.*, xxvi (1971), 255–89; F. Furet, *Penser la Révolution française* (Paris, Gallimard, 1978), trans. by Elborg Forster as *Interpreting the French Revolution* (Cambridge, Cambridge University Press, 1981).

Revisionist historiography did not present a new paradigm to replace the Marxist interpretation. Nor did Marxist-influenced work disappear from the scene. Albert Soboul, then Chair of the French Revolution at the Sorbonne, offered a spirited response to François Furet, pointedly suggesting by the very book title that he chose that one must *understand* the Revolution before one can *interpret* it.[13] Michel Vovelle, Soboul's successor at the Sorbonne, also continued to work in a Marxist vein and was prodigious in both his scholarly output and his global travels through and beyond the Bicentennial commemorations.[14] In Great Britain, Colin Jones has defended a social interpretation of the Revolution.[15]

Many other historians, however, have focused their research in recent years on political and cultural factors. Prominent among these, in the United States, have been Keith Baker and Lynn Hunt. Baker, following François Furet, has emphasized discourse and ideology in his work on the origins of the Revolution.[16] Hunt's work, while influenced by Furet, emphasizes the impact of culture on revolutionary politics and does not abandon attention to social factors.[17] They have led the way in fashioning an argument that rather than ushering in a new era of capitalism and bourgeois politics, the French Revolution was most important for introducing democracy in the modern world.

Rather than ending debate, then, the demise of the Marxist interpretation, if one can call it that, has instead opened up the terrain for an array of new approaches to the study of the Revolution, and a host of new arguments, which we will explore in the chapters ahead. The aim is both to engage the controversies and to introduce the reader to the history of the Revolution. The book will adopt a mostly chronological structure, to facilitate navigation through what was an enormously complicated and

---

13 A. Soboul, *Comprendre la Révolution française: problèmes politiques de la Révolution française, 1789–1797* (Paris, F. Maspero, 1981).

14 M. Vovelle, *La Mentalité révolutionnaire* (Paris, Editions Sociales, 1985); *La Révolution française* (Paris, Messidor, 1986), 5 vols.; *La Révolution contre l'Eglise: de la Raison à l'Etre suprême* (Bruxelles, Editions Complexe, 1988); ed., *Paris et la Révolution* (Paris, Publications de la Sorbonne, 1989); *Les Colloques du Bicentenaire* (Paris, Editions La Découverte, 1991); *Combats pour la Révolution française* (Paris, Editions La Découverte, 1993).

15 C. Jones, "Bourgeois Revolution Revivified: 1789 and Social Change," in C. Lucas, ed., *Rewriting the French Revolution* (Oxford, Clarendon Press, 1991), 69–118; "The Great Chain of Buying: Medical Advertisement, the Bourgeois Public Sphere, and the Origins of the French Revolution," *American Historical Review* 101 (February 1996), 13–40.

16 K. Baker, *Inventing the French Revolution* (Cambridge, Cambridge University Press, 1990).

17 L. Hunt, *Politics, Culture, and Class in the French Revolution* (Berkeley, University of California Press, 1984); *The Family Romance of the French Revolution* (Berkeley, University of California Press, 1992).

confusing decade of upheaval, but the heart of the text will be bracketed by two thematic chapters. We will begin with a lengthy chapter addressing the causes and origins of the French Revolution, a broad and multifaceted topic that has generated much of the debate among historians in recent decades. Why did the French Revolution occur? Was it an accident, as George Taylor suggested? If it was not the work of a rising bourgeoisie, then who was responsible, and what motivated them? How important were social and economic factors? And how might one take into account discourse, ideology, and culture? For the practical-minded (or future political leaders), could the Revolution have been avoided? The historiography of the past three decades has not only raised new questions about the origins and causes of the Revolution, both long- and short-term, but has also blurred the line between Old Regime and Revolution. What began as an argument that the Old Regime monarchy was more reform-minded than most had long assumed has ended up with the somewhat startling proposition that the Revolution actually began before 1789.

A second major topic that has generated enormous controversy over the generations is violence. Why was the revolutionary decade so violent? This issue lies at the heart of what has long divided those who view the Revolution in a favorable light from those who condemn it. The focus in this debate has been on the year of the Terror, 1793–94, but violence erupted in the first year of the Revolution, with the taking of the Bastille and the Great Fear that followed in much of the French countryside; it broke out again in the uprising that toppled the monarchy in August 1792 and during the September prison massacres that followed in Paris; it characterized resistance to the revolutionary government in the Vendée uprising and the Federalist revolts of 1793; and it proved to be an endemic problem on a smaller scale through the years of the Directory. And one must not forget the violence of the revolutionary wars. How are we to understand that violence? Was it inherent in revolutionary ideology, or the product of circumstances or human nature? Can one separate revolutionary ideals from the violent means used to achieve them? And if not, can one legitimately celebrate the Revolution, or does its violence indelibly tarnish the whole project? These questions will be the focus of a penultimate chapter, before turning to the question of legacy.

Chapters at the heart of the text will focus on major topics or periods: 1789: The First Act; The Declaration of the Rights of Man and the end of Feudalism; The Constitutional Monarchy; The First French Republic; The Terror; Thermidor and the Directory; The Rise of Napoleon. All of these periods, or topics, contain within them a number of debates and controversies. Those debates have also been reshaped, or extended, by a substantial body of work over the past twenty years that has focused on questions of gender, slavery, and colonialism. Once confined to the periphery of French Revolutionary studies, that scholarship must now be seen as integral to our understanding of the Revolution and as such will be integrated into the chapters above rather than being dealt with as separate topics. In a final chapter on Legacy, we will consider not only the impact of the Revolution on French society, but its meaning in today's world and current directions in historiography.

Two major developments occurred in Europe as a result of the French Revolution: the first was the assertion of universal human rights, and the second was the emergence of the modern state. The agenda of the revolutionaries was to combine the two, to create a constitutional government that would secure and protect individual freedom. But as the events of the 1790s made amply clear, the two were not necessarily compatible. The increase in state power and centralization during the Terror, as an example, came at the expense of individual liberty. By contrast, under the regime of the Directory many French citizens looked to the government to strengthen its authority, to increase its policing ability, so that their freedom of movement and the liberty to enjoy the fruits of their labor might be secured. There is a paradox here, one that would endure up into the twentieth century, if not to the present day. For some (e.g. the Jacobins of the 1790s) a democratic state promised to be a vehicle for the achievement of individual liberty, whereas for others (both conservatives and anarchists in the nineteenth century) the state loomed as a vehicle of repression.

1

Origins: Inevitable Revolution or Resolvable Crisis?

Could the French Revolution have been avoided? At one level the answer to this question is a simple one: No historical event is inevitable, and certainly no revolution or war need have occurred at precisely the time it did. Our question is a bit more complicated, however, and we might put it in a different way. Could the Bourbon monarchy have survived the crisis that it faced in the 1780s? To be sure, there are monarchists in Paris today who fondly hope for a restoration of the Bourbon throne, but few would consider that hope to be realistic. On the other hand, the other great monarchies of Europe – the Habsburgs, the Hohenzollerns, the Romanovs – survived up until World War I, and the Bourbons returned to the French throne for a brief time after the defeat of Napoleon. So while the collapse of the monarchy in France may have been inevitable, eventually, it need not have happened when it did and as it did. This leaves plenty of room for debate about why the French Revolution occurred, and whether or not it could have been averted in 1789.

One of the striking things about the French Revolution, particularly as compared to other major revolutions in world history, is that it occurred in the most powerful, most prosperous, and most populous nation in Europe at the time. No one in the 1780s would have said that the Bourbon monarchy was on the verge of collapse. So what happened? Understanding the roots of the crisis that confronted the French state in 1789 is a crucial first step toward understanding the nature of the Revolution itself.

The tension between individual liberty and the growth of state power will be a theme running throughout this volume, and it points as well to a distinction we might make in considering the origins of the French Revolution. On the one hand we will find them in the aspirations for greater freedom and individual rights expressed by educated French people over the course of the eighteenth century, but we will also find causes of revolution in the challenges confronting the French state in the second half of the century, both internal and external, which in the end the monarchy proved unable to master. These two broad themes – the quest for individual freedom, and problems confronting the state – will be explored in this chapter in three sections. The first will discuss the cultural and ideological origins of the French Revolution. For many years the focus here among historians was on the Enlightenment, on the critique of absolute monarchy and the Catholic Church presented by philosophes such as Voltaire, Montesquieu, and Jean-Jacques Rousseau. This was not uncontested territory itself. Some argued that these thinkers were really not so revolutionary in their ideas, while others questioned the extent of their influence in the eighteenth century. More recently, however, scholars have begun to consider an expanding array of cultural developments and institutions, including religious currents (especially Jansenism), popular literature, the world of theatre, an emerging newspaper press, and the growing influence in the final decades of the Old Regime of the "public sphere" and public opinion.

The idea of the public sphere points us toward the second section of this chapter, dealing with the social and economic origins of the Revolution. In the Marxist interpretation the focus in this regard was on the rising bourgeoisie and a developing capitalist economy in France. That interpretation, as already noted, has come under serious criticism, and new arguments have been advanced regarding economic change in the eighteenth century and its impact on social categories and political attitudes. An expanding commercial sector was of particular importance, as was the pattern of gradual urbanization. Two major questions will draw our attention in this section: Was the Old Regime economy vibrant and capable of growth, or teetering on the brink of obsolescence? and, Were the elites of the Third Estate virtually indistinguishable from the nobility in their interests and political views, as some have suggested, or were there real tensions and differences between them? In addition, the role of the peasantry as a revolutionary force must be assessed.

The third section of the chapter will focus on structural and institutional origins of the Revolution, some of which are rooted in economic factors. It is clear, for instance, that a financial crisis forced the monarchy to convene the Estates General in 1789. Past scholarship focused largely on the inequality of taxation and an inefficient tax collection system as responsible for this, but very recent work has drawn our attention to the related issue of public debt and the financial institutions of the Old Regime. Some historians have argued that the monarchy made serious efforts to reform judicial and administrative structures in the second half of the eighteenth century, pointing (on the judicial side) to efforts by Chancellor Maupeou at the end of the reign of Louis XV and (on the administrative side) to reforms introduced by Turgot in the early years of Louis XVI's rule. Loménie de Brienne also attempted reforms on the very eve of the Revolution. All of these efforts failed, however, which has generated debate about the validity of the reforms themselves and the obstacles to their implementation. At the heart of the matter, some would argue, lay the system of privilege upon which the Old Regime monarchy rested.

I would make one final preliminary observation before moving ahead. It is common in the historiography to distinguish between long-term and short-term causes of the Revolution. The inefficiencies of the tax system would be an example of the former, the bad harvests of 1788 and 1789 an example of the latter. I have used the word "origins" more often than "causes" in these introductory remarks, and in the title to this chapter, quite intentionally. In thinking about the impact of Enlightenment thought, for example, it is difficult to see it as a cause of the Revolution, particularly since so few of the philosophes called for any kind of revolutionary upheaval. But there is no doubt that Enlightenment ideas contributed to the ferment of the 1780s and to the constitutional debates in the Constituent Assembly. Similarly, one would be wary of arguing that an expanding "public sphere" and the emergence of public opinion as an acknowledged force in the 1780s *caused* the Revolution, but these changes helped to create a social and cultural context within which political contestation became more possible than it was earlier in the century, and in this sense we must include these elements among the origins of the French Revolution.

Cultural and Ideological Origins

In nearly every textbook on European history or Western civilization a discussion of the Enlightenment precedes the section on the French Revolution, and in that juxtaposition the Enlightenment has come to be seen as a cause of the Revolution. The most celebrated proponent of a direct connection between the two is almost certainly Alexis de Tocqueville, who argued that the abstract ideas of the philosophes, who had no direct experience in government or administration, led to the impractical and ultimately failed experiments of the several revolutionary regimes, from the Constitutional Monarchy through the Jacobin Republic and Directory.[1] In the early twentieth century Daniel Mornet also made a case

1 A. de Tocqueville, *L'Ancien Régime et la révolution* (Paris, Lévy frères, 1856).

for the influence of Enlightenment ideas on revolutionary politics, and monarchist critics of the Revolution have long contended that the Enlightenment was to blame for the fiasco of 1789.[2]

It is easier to make a case for the philosophes as critics of the Old Regime than as advocates of revolution. One sees in Montesquieu's *Persian Letters* and *The Spirit of the Laws* a critique of royal absolutism, but the latter is more a call for aristocratic restraint on royal power than a call for democratic reform. Many of Voltaire's essays and literary works contained biting criticism of the Catholic Church and religious intolerance, but despite his own deist views he saw religion as essential to the preservation of public morals among the masses. The Revolution would attack both the monarchy and the Church, but not, most historians would agree today, at the call of either Montesquieu or Voltaire.

Jean-Jacques Rousseau went considerably further in his criticism of Old Regime monarchy and society. The *Second Discourse on the Origins of Inequality* argued that the existing social order was the product of an elaborate hoax played upon the weak by the powerful rather than being the fruit of celestial design, and went so far as to suggest that a despotic monarch could be turned out by his subjects. Rousseau carried this argument further in *The Social Contract*, in which he developed his concept of the "general will," asserting that sovereignty resided in the people rather than in the person of the king. In 1791 Louis-Sébastien Mercier published *De J. J. Rousseau considéré comme l'un des premiers auteurs de la Révolution*, clear evidence of the influence he attributed to the philosophe, and it is well-known that Rousseau's writings profoundly shaped the political thinking of Maximilien Robespierre.[3]

That Rousseau's thought was influential *during* the Revolution, however, does not necessarily mean that his writings were a *cause* of the Revolution. Joan McDonald argued, for example, that the *Social Contract* was not widely read before 1789 and that its limited audience was more likely to have included liberal monarchists than future revolutionaries.[4] James Miller took the opposite view in his elegant intellectual biography of

2 D. Mornet, *Les Origines intellectuelles de la Révolution française* (Paris, A. Colin, 1933); see also Lynn Hunt's entry on the French Revolution in A. Kors, ed., *Encyclopedia of the Enlightenment* (Oxford, Oxford University Press, 2003), vol. 2, 80–84, for a discussion of monarchist critics, as well as commentary on what some revolutionaries themselves had to say about Enlightenment influence.

3 See, for example, N. Hampson, *The Life and Opinions of Maximilien Robespierre* (London, Duckworth, 1974), and D. P. Jordan, *The Revolutionary Career of Maximilien Robespierre* (Chicago, University of Chicago Press, 1989).

4 J. McDonald, *Rousseau and the French Revolution, 1762–91* (London, Athlone Press, 1965).

Rousseau, pointing out that the key political concepts more fully explicated in the *Social Contract* were also sketched out, in abbreviated form, in his novels *Emile* and *La Nouvelle Héloise*, both of which were enormously popular in the final decades of the Old Regime. Miller credits Rousseau with rehabilitating the idea of democracy, long discredited among European political theorists: "In this respect, the French Revolution has played a major role in determining how we can read Rousseau. The event illuminates the text – for it was the Revolution, after all, which forced the idea of democracy onto the agenda of modern history."[5]

There has been no paucity of scholarly work on Rousseau over the years, but the ascendancy of the Marxist interpretation in the twentieth century and the turn to social history following World War II meant that, for a generation or two, historians of the French Revolution looked away from the Enlightenment toward social and economic causal factors. That trend changed due to the influence of François Furet, who particularly emphasized Rousseauist ideas as responsible not only for the upheaval of 1789 but also for drawing revolutionary politics ineluctably toward the Terror. In this Furet echoed an earlier argument of J. L. Talmon, who saw in Rousseau's philosophy the origins of twentieth-century totalitarianism.[6] Keith Baker has also recently reemphasized Enlightenment thought in exploring the origins of the Revolution, although focusing on lesser-known figures such as Jacob-Nicolas Moreau, Anne-Robert-Jacques Turgot, and the abbé Gabriel Bonnot Mably, in whose work Baker sees a virtual "script for a French revolution."[7]

The relationship between the Enlightenment and Revolution remains a contested one, however. In response to Furet's argument, Roger Chartier suggested that rather than the Enlightenment having caused the Revolution it was the revolutionaries who self-consciously created the Enlightenment as their intellectual precursor, a dialectical relationship also hinted at by James Miller in the passage quoted above.[8] Darrin McMahon has challenged both Furet and Chartier in *Enemies of the Enlightenment: The French Counter-Enlightenment and the Making of Modernity*.[9] As the title suggests, McMahon argues on the one hand that the Enlightenment existed as an intellectual force long before the Revolution occurred – its

---

5 J. Miller, *Rousseau: Dreamer of Democracy* (New Haven, Yale University Press, 1984), 203.

6 F. Furet, *Penser la Révolution française* (Paris, Gallimard, 1978); J. L. Talmon, *The Origins of Totalitarian Democracy* (London, Secker and Warburg, 1952).

7 K. M. Baker, *Inventing the French Revolution* (Cambridge, Cambridge University Press, 1990), 86–106.

8 R. Chartier, *Les Origines culturelles de la Révolution française* (Paris, Seuil, 1990).

9 D. McMahon, *Enemies of the Enlightenment: The French Counter-Enlightenment and the Making of Modernity* (Oxford, Oxford University Press, 2001).

enemies were in full voice by mid-century – and on the other that this opposition to Enlightenment ideas continued on into the decade of the 1790s, contrary to Furet's assertion that Jacobin ideology, the heir of Rousseau, created its own mythic enemies as justification for the Terror. This is a debate to which we will return in later chapters.

As we see, then, there have been those who have interpreted the Enlightenment as a cause of the French Revolution in a positive sense, others who viewed its influence more negatively as leading to the political excesses of the Revolution, and still others who have called any causal relationship into question. In recent years, post-modernist thinkers have interpreted the Enlightenment in a more broadly negative light, arguing that in its insistence on empirical truth the Enlightenment privileged European culture and paved the way for colonialism, imperialism, and the subjugation of non-European peoples. Daniel Gordon and others dispute that view in a recent collection of essays, in the conclusion to which Gordon writes that "One way to think about Enlightenment political thought is that it was an effort to bring about a double institutionalization of liberty – to proclaim liberty as a basic human right and to set its limits in practice."[10]

If one sees Enlightenment thought as central to the assertion of human rights, then certainly one must count the Enlightenment among the origins of the French Revolution, given the centrality of the *Declaration of the Rights of Man and of the Citizen* to the Revolution itself. Many years ago Georges Lefebvre argued that one might read the *Declaration* point by point, despite its claims to universality, as essentially a critique of the failings of the Old Regime.[11] Lynn Hunt has recently contributed two books focusing on the *Declaration of Rights* and the genesis of those rights in the eighteenth century on both sides of the Atlantic.[12] Given the importance of the *Declaration* both as an expression of revolutionary ideals and as a window into the abuses of the Old Regime, we will examine it at some length in Chapter Three.

In another important work, Dale Van Kley explored at length the religious origins of the French Revolution, paying particular attention to the Jansenist controversy within the French Catholic Church. Beginning with the papal bull *Unigenitus* (1713) and culminating with an order of the Archbishop of Paris in the 1750s denying them the sacraments,

---

10 D. Gordon, *Postmodernism and the Enlightenment: New Perspectives in Eighteenth-Century French Intellectual History* (London, Routledge, 2001), 210.

11 G. Lefebvre, *The Coming of the French Revolution*, trans. R. R. Palmer (Princeton, Princeton University Press, 1947). This book, still among the best introductions to the origins of the French Revolution, includes a chapter discussing the *Declaration*.

12 L. Hunt, ed., *The French Revolution and Human Rights: A Brief Documentary History* (Boston, Bedford Books, 1996); *Inventing Human Rights: A History* (New York, W. W. Norton, 2007).

Jansenists found themselves the targets of concerted royal persecution. The response of the Jansenist minority to that persecution focused criticism not only on the hierarchy of the Catholic Church (by appealing to the conciliar tradition within the church), but also on the sacred character of the monarchy itself. Since many Jansenists were members of the parlement of Paris, they became embroiled in the Maupeou controversy of the 1770s, when Louis XV's chancellor attempted to curtail the authority of the parlements. Maupeou's reforms elicited a wave of critical pamphlets, many of them written by Jansenist *parlementaires*.

Notable among these pamphlets was one published in Bordeaux by Guillaume-Joseph Saige, a young lawyer whose cousin sat on the parlement of Bordeaux. In his pamphlet, *Cathechisme du Citoyen*, Saige combined Jansenist and Rousseauist ideas, arguing, on the one hand, that the conciliarist tradition within the French Catholic Church represented a kind of republicanism, and, on the other, that the many communes of rural France represented "so many little republics within the great republic of the French nation." So incendiary was this pamphlet, with its direct challenge to monarchical despotism and its insistence that sovereignty was embodied not in the king but in the nation, that the parlement of Bordeaux itself ordered it to be burned. Van Kley argues that the Jansenist strain within French Catholicism was not only an essential influence on the Civil Constitution of the Clergy of 1790, but on the genesis of French republicanism: "religion as mediated by ideology entered into the very texture of revolutionary republicanism, making sense of many of its otherwise paradoxical traits."[13]

We are more accustomed to thinking of the Catholic Church as a target of revolutionary violence than as a contributor to revolutionary ideas. The church and the monarchy were intimately linked, and the church was among the largest landowners in France. Those lands would be confiscated in 1790 in order to repay the national debt, and by 1794 the church would come under direct attack from radical Jacobins. It seems counterintuitive, then, to think of religious thought among the intellectual origins of the French Revolution, but Van Kley makes a powerful case. Roughly a quarter of the delegates to the Estates General would be drawn from the clergy, of course, so their influence on the debates of the early years is hardly surprising. What is more remarkable, perhaps, is the number of priests, or ex-priests, who figured among the radical Jacobins of the Year II.

---

13 D. Van Kley, *The Religious Origins of the French Revolution: From Calvin to the Civil Constitution, 1560–1791* (New Haven, Yale University Press, 1996), 375. See also K. Baker, *Inventing the French Revolution*, Chapter 6, for a discussion of the Saige pamphlet. The quotation will be found on page 149.

Historians have broadened our understanding of the cultural origins of the French Revolution in a number of other ways as well over the past quarter century. David Bell has examined the emergence of nationalism and the idea of the nation, arguing that a "cult of the nation" emerged in the eighteenth century that, while it came to challenge the centrality of monarchy and the Church in the French polity, also had its roots in French religious thought.[14] Robert Darnton has produced a body of work extending back to the 1970s that has explored the "business" of the Enlightenment – the publishing houses and distribution networks by which clandestine works of all sorts circulated in France – while also stretching our definition of Enlightenment culture to include "Grub Street hacks" and "the forbidden bestsellers" of the final decades of the Old Regime. Some of those "Grub Street" journalists and pamphleteers, including Jacques-Pierre Brissot and Antoine-Joseph Gorsas, went on to become prominent journalists and deputies during the Revolution, and the shopkeepers and working people who stormed the Bastille in 1789 or the Tuileries Palace in 1792 were more likely to have been reading some of the libelous pornography targeting Marie-Antoinette than the plays of Voltaire or the political theory of Rousseau. Did such literature *cause* the French Revolution? Certainly not, but it did contribute to what Darnton calls the "common culture" of late eighteenth-century France that made revolution conceivable in 1789.[15]

The concept of a "common culture" can be seen as related to the idea of the "bourgeois public sphere," first introduced in the 1960s by the German philosopher Jurgen Habermas, and to the concept of "public opinion" that historians such as Keith Baker and Mona Ozouf have discussed in some of their writings.[16] Habermas situated the "public sphere" between the state and civil society, arguing that it emerged in the late seventeenth and early

---

14 D. A. Bell, *The Cult of the Nation in France: Inventing Nationalism, 1680–1800* (Cambridge, MA, Harvard University Press, 2001).

15 R. Darnton, "The High Enlightenment and the Low-Life of Literature in Pre-Revolutionary France," *Past and Present* 51 (May 1971), 81–115; "In Search of the Enlightenment: Recent Attempts to Create a Social history of Ideas," *Journal of Modern History* 43 (1971), 113–32; *The Business of Enlightenment: A Publishing History of the Encyclopédie, 1775–1800* (Cambridge, MA, Harvard University Press, 1979); *The Literary Underground of the Old Regime* (Cambridge, MA, Harvard University Press, 1982); *The Great Cat Massacre and Other Episodes in French Cultural History* (New York, Basic Books, 1984); *The Forbidden Best-Sellers of Pre-Revolutionary France* (New York, W. W. Norton, 1995). For critiques of Darnton's work, see H. T. Mason, ed., *The Darnton Debate: Books and Revolution in the Eighteenth Century* (Oxford, Voltaire Foundation, 1998).

16 J. Habermas, *The Structural Transformation of the Public Sphere: An Inquiry into a Category of Bourgeois Society*, trans. Thomas Burger (Cambridge, MA, MIT Press, 1992); K. Baker, "Public Opinion as Political Invention," in Baker, *Inventing the French Revolution*, 167–99;

eighteenth centuries in conjunction with the growth of a new commercial bourgeoisie in Europe. The "public sphere" found expression in a number of institutional settings: Masonic lodges, provincial academies, clubs, cafés, salons, and journals. Those who participated in those institutions or fora were generally critical of absolutist monarchy, advocating both increased economic and political liberty and a more open, democratic society. It is ironic that Habermas' ideas have gained currency over the past quarter century, as the revisionist assault on the Marxist interpretation of the French Revolution has achieved dominance, given that Habermas' analysis is quite consistent with Marxist philosophy and political theory.

While the concept of the "public sphere" is quite abstract and multifaceted, that of "public opinion" is more focused and tangible, if still somewhat vaguely defined. It is also a term that one finds in contemporary usage. Louis XVI himself made reference to public opinion early in his reign, and both Jacques Necker and Charles-Alexandre Calonne appealed to public opinion in their debate over their respective management of royal finances in the 1780s. It was not uncommon in the last decades of the Old Regime for members of the parlement of Paris to publish their remonstrances against royal edicts, implicitly appealing to "public opinion," and lawyers quite often published their legal briefs, written in narrative style, to present the cases of their more celebrated clients before the court of "public opinion." Sarah Maza has provocatively analyzed six such *causes célèbres*, including the "Diamond Necklace Affair" in which Marie-Antoinette was implicated, and an adultery case pitting Guillaume Kornmann against the playwright Beaumarchais. The *mémoires judiciaires* published by lawyers in these cases were not subject to the same censorship restrictions as other forms of literature, and as such could raise issues related to privilege and the exercise of power that more explicitly political writings could not, except clandestinely. They were enormously popular – hundreds of copies, sometimes thousands, circulated in Paris and throughout the realm. They were important, Maza argues, because they bridged the gap between the philosophical and literary concerns of the Enlightenment and the political concerns of the Revolution, on the one hand, and between the private sphere and the public sphere on the other; they raised questions, in the process, about the relationship between private and public virtue. The reputation of the monarchy was clearly tarnished by the "Diamond Necklace Affair," despite the innocence of the

---

M. Ozouf, "Public Spirit," in F. Furet and M. Ozouf, eds., *A Critical Dictionary of the French Revolution*, trans. Arthur Goldhammer (Cambridge, MA, Harvard University Press, 1989), 771–80; M. Ozouf, "L'Opinion publique," in K. Baker, ed., *The Political Culture of the Old Regime* (Oxford, Pergamon, 1987), 419–34; and "Public Opinion at the End of the Old Regime," *Journal of Modern History* 60 (September, 1988), S1–S21.

queen in the scandal, and many of these cases targeted prominent aristocrats. They represent a significant element in the social and cultural ferment that swept across France on the eve of the Revolution.[17]

Politics became public during the Revolution, publicized to an engaged populace through a burgeoning popular press. While there was no free press under the Old Regime, however, a growing body of work has made clear in recent years that the roots of that development lay in the decades before 1789 and that newspapers published along the borders of France circulated widely within the country.[18] They may not have been as bold as their revolutionary heirs, nor did they provide a forum for political debate as newspapers would in the 1790s, but they did educate the reading public regarding a range of national and international affairs, and as such constituted an important part of Habermas' "public sphere."[19]

Virtually all of the works discussed in the preceding pages have focused, in one way or another, on the written word: on Enlightenment texts, on religious texts, on lawyers' briefs, on newspapers, journals, and underground literature, on the Declaration of the Rights of Man. That focus begs the question, as Robert Darnton has put it, "Do Books Cause Revolutions?"[20] How does one make the connection between the written word, or words, of the Old Regime, and the political rhetoric and actions of the Revolution? In this regard, François Furet and Keith Baker have both drawn strong criticism for failing to place the discourse that they analyze in any sort of social context.[21] One historian who has tried to do precisely this in recent years is Arlette Farge, who in a series of books has guided

---

17 S. Maza, *Private Lives and Public Affairs: The Causes Célèbres of Pre-Revolutionary France* (Berkeley, University of California Press, 1993).

18 J. D. Popkin, *News and Politics in the Age of Revolution: Jean Luzac's "Gazette de Leyde"* (Ithaca, Cornell University Press, 1989); *Revolutionary News: The Press in France, 1789–1799* (Durham, Duke University Press, 1990); J. D. Popkin and J. R. Censer, eds., *Press and Politics in Pre-Revolutionary France* (Berkeley, University of California Press, 1987); D. G. Levy, *The Ideas and Careers of Simon-Nicolas-Henri Linguet* (Urbana, University of Illinois Press, 1980); N. R. Gelbart, *Feminine and Opposition Journalism in Old Regime France: The "Journal des Dames"* (Berkeley, University of California Press, 1987); R. Darnton and D. Roche, eds., *Revolution in Print: The Press in France, 1775–1800* (Berkeley, University of California Press, 1989); C. Bellanger et al., *Histoire Générale de la presse française* (Paris, Presses Universitaires de France, 1969).

19 See C. Jones, "The Great Chain of Buying: Medical Advertisement, the Bourgeois Public Sphere, and the Origins of the French Revolution," *American Historical Review* 101 (February 1996), 13–40, for a fascinating article making explicit through an analysis of provincial French newspapers the commercial aspect that is central to Habermas' concept of the public sphere.

20 R. Darnton, *The Forbidden Best-Sellers of Pre-Revolutionary France*, Section III.

21 See, for example, Marisa Linton, "The Intellectual Origins of the French Revolution," in P. R. Campbell, ed., *The Origins of the French Revolution* (New York, Palgrave Macmillan, 2006), 139–59.

her readers through the neighborhoods of Paris, describing and analyzing the rumors, plots, minor revolts, acts of violence, public threats, and private quarrels that characterized the daily lives of common people over the course of the eighteenth century. She is interested in both public opinion and the public sphere, though less with the bourgeois and aristocrats who filled the assemblies of the early revolution than with the ordinary folk who would storm the Bastille in 1789.[22]

While Farge has been concerned with the theater of the streets, three other scholars have written works in recent years that focus on the theater itself as a site of political contestation and cultural ferment in the eighteenth century. Jeffrey Ravel takes as his subject those who attended the theater in the seventeenth and eighteenth centuries, arguing that "the dynamics of the parterre . . . are central to understanding the passage from the world of kings, courtiers, and absolute sovereignty to our current regime of laws, citizens, and inalienable rights, a transition that took place most surprisingly and unsettlingly in eighteenth-century France." Paul Friedland, while pointing out that the audience often mingled with the actors on stage in French theaters until mid-eighteenth century, is concerned more with the actors themselves. He argues that the conceptual understanding of theatrical representation underwent a fundamental shift in the 1750s, and that this paralleled a similar change in the political world, one that made the Estates General of 1789 a much more volatile assemblage of delegates than it had been at its last meeting in 1614. This is a fascinating and provocative argument, more compelling, perhaps, than his final chapters which claim that theater and politics merged during the Revolution. Finally, Susan Maslan examines both theatrical texts and audiences, making a case that revolutionary theater reflected the demand for direct democracy made by the *sans-culottes* of Paris and other large cities. These three works together build a bridge between the question of origins and that of revolutionary politics, one that is seldom crossed by historians, and they also represent some of the more creative work of recent years bringing cultural and social history together.[23]

---

22 A. Farge, *The Vanishing Children of Paris: Rumor and Politics before the French Revolution*, trans. Claudia Miéville (Cambridge, MA, Harvard University Press, 1991); *Fragile Lives: Violence, Power and Solidarity in Eighteenth-Century Paris*, trans. Carol Shelton (Cambridge, MA, Harvard University Press, 1993); *Subversive Words: Public Opinion in Eighteenth-Century France*, trans. Rosemary Morris (University Park, Pennsylvania State University Press, 1995).

23 J. R. Ravel, *The Contested Parterre: Public Theater and French Political Culture, 1680–1791* (Ithaca, Cornell University Press, 1999), 227, for the quotation above; P. Friedland, *Political Actors: Representative Bodies and Theatricality in the Age of the French Revolution* (Ithaca, Cornell University Press, 2002); S. Maslan, *Revolutionary Acts: Theater, Democracy, and the French Revolution* (Baltimore, Johns Hopkins University Press, 2005).

Social and Economic Origins

A generation ago, social and economic factors lay at the very heart of historical analysis of the French Revolution and its origins. When Norman Hampson's *A Social History of the French Revolution* appeared in 1963, the review in the *Times Literary Supplement* offered this glowing assessment: "This account is clear and marvellously concise .... Likely to hold its own for a long time as the most accurate, most thorough and most measured account of the revolutionary crisis."[24] Indeed, most scholarly work on revolutions around the world at that time, when revolutionary upheaval still seemed more likely than terrorist attacks, focused on social and economic tensions as the major causes of revolution.[25] But within a decade of the appearance of Hampson's book the revisionist critique of the Marxist interpretation would be in full sway, and by the 1980s social interpretations had given way to an emphasis on political and cultural interpretations, which continue to dominate the scholarship on the Revolution today. Our task here, then, is to assess the revisionist critique of the Marxist social analyis, and to examine trends in quite recent scholarship aimed at revitalizing our understanding of the social origins of the French Revolution.

The Marxist interpretation, simply put, argued that a rising bourgeoisie, empowered economically by an emerging capitalist economy, but denied political influence by the landed aristocracy, rose up to challenge both monarchy and aristocracy in 1789, thereby launching a revolution that swept both aside in order to allow the creation of a new, constitutional political regime and a social order that would rest upon talent and merit rather than birth and privilege. The French Revolution, thus, had both social origins and consequences, and marked the transition from feudalism to capitalism. Revisionists challenged this interpretation on a number of scores. Alfred Cobban, as already noted, pointed out that one found very few bourgeois capitalists among the deputies of the Third Estate. George Taylor argued that there were very few signs of capitalist economic development in eighteenth-century France, and that the economy remained very much dominated by traditional agrarian patterns. Following up on this work, Colin Lucas made the case that there was very little

---

24 N. Hampson, *A Social History of the French Revolution* (London, Routledge and Kegan Paul, 1963). The *TLS* review is quoted on the back cover of the paperback edition, first issued in 1966 and reprinted up into the early 1980s.

25 See, for example, C. Johnson, *Revolutionary Change* (Boston, Little, Brown, 1966) and J. A. Goldstone, ed., *Revolutions: Theoretical, Comparative, and Historical Studies* (New York, Harcourt Brace Jovanovich, 1986), which offers an overview of scholarship from the previous two decades.

difference, either socially or economically, between the aristocratic and bourgeois elites of the late eighteenth century, and William Doyle challenged the view that there was an "aristocratic reaction" in the 1780s, a last-ditch effort on the part of the old "sword" nobility to defend their traditional position and prerogatives under the Old Regime monarchy.[26] Indeed, Doyle argued, the aristocracy and the bourgeoisie had far more in common than they did to divide them. If there was a "rising bourgeoisie" at century's end, they were rising into the ranks of the aristocracy itself, either through marriage or through the purchase of royal office.

Among the most spirited early responses to revisionist downplaying of the social origins of the Revolution was Colin Jones' article, "Bourgeois Revolution Revivified: 1789 and Social Change," which appears in at least two collections of essays.[27] Jones challenges the revisionist view that the French economy was stagnant in the eighteenth century and that the bourgeoisie was either moribund or composed largely of aspiring aristocrats. He points to a growing body of scholarship showing that, if anything, the French economy was more dynamic in this period than that of Great Britain, often cited as the paradigmatic example of early industrialization.[28] Most economic historians today would agree that France, rather than being backward or retarded in its economic development, pursued a more gradual path to industrial capitalism than Great Britain or, at a later date, Germany and the United States. Over the course of the eighteenth century, however, commercial trade grew quite dramatically, by as much as 400 percent, while manufacturing grew more modestly, by perhaps 75 percent. Cities such as Paris, Lyon, Bordeaux, and Marseille were particularly dynamic, and these would be the centers of revolutionary ferment in 1789. Jones emphasizes this growth in the French commercial economy and the spread of a consumer society, both of which

---

26 In addition to the works cited in the Introduction (footnotes 8–10), see W. Doyle, *Origins of the French Revolution* (Oxford, Oxford University Press, 1980); F. L. Ford, *Robe and Sword: The Regrouping of the French Aristocracy after Louis XIV* (Cambridge, MA, Harvard University Press, 1953), for the classic account of the division of the aristocracy between "robe" and "sword" nobility, and a case for an aristocratic reaction on the eve of the Revolution; and G. Chaussinand-Nogaret, *The French Nobility in the Eighteenth Century: From Feudalism to Enlightenment*, trans. William Doyle (Cambridge, Cambridge University Press, 1985), for a French perspective on the revisionist argument regarding the nobility.

27 C. Jones, "Bourgeois Revolution Revivified: 1789 and Social Change," in C. Lucas, ed., *Rewriting the French Revolution* (Oxford, Clarendon Press, 1991), 69–118; and in G. Kates, ed., *The French Revolution: Recent Debates and New Controversies* (London, Routledge, 1998), 157–91.

28 F. Crouzet, *Britain Ascendant: Comparative Studies in Franco-British Economic History*, trans. Martin Thom (Cambridge, Cambridge University Press, 1990); P. O'Brien and C. Keyder, *Economic Growth in Britain and France, 1780–1914: Two Paths to the Twentieth Century* (London, Allen and Unwin, 1978).

contributed to the emerging "public sphere" of which Habermas wrote, although Jones prefers the term "civic sociability." The merchants, shopkeepers, large landowners, professionals, and officeholders, in essence a bourgeoisie, were those who shaped that "civic sociability." Their numbers had grown over the eighteenth century from roughly 700,000 to as many as 2.3 million.[29] And it was this bourgeois elite, Jones argues, that led the Revolution of 1789.

This view is echoed by William Sewell in his book analyzing the Abbé Sieyès' *What Is the Third Estate?*, the most influential and celebrated pamphlet published on the eve of the French Revolution. In Sewell's words, "Sieyès gained his initial fame by expressing in a novel and brilliantly conceived rhetoric the aspirations and resentments of the French bourgeoisie – the diverse class of well-to-do officials, merchants, lawyers, professionals, rentiers, men of letters, and landowners who made up the politicized segment of the Third Estate."[30] Sieyès' pamphlet, still read today, at least in part, in most college courses on the French Revolution, appealed to its readers in clearly social terms, conveyed in stirring rhetoric. He posed three questions at the outset: "What is the third estate? Everything. What has it been heretofore in the political order? Nothing. What does it demand? To become something therein." Why, in Sieyès view, was the third estate "everything"? Because they performed virtually all of the productive and useful functions in society, whereas aristocrats were little better than parasites on the social order. This was a call to revolution, at least to dramatic political change, in social terms. Sewell accepts the critique of Furet and others directed against the classic Marxist argument that an entrepreneurial, capitalist bourgeoisie launched the revolution. He sees the French bourgeoisie in broader terms, as does Colin Jones, but insists that there was a social basis to their resentment that prompted them to rebel against the old political order.

Timothy Tackett has also weighed in on this issue in a recent book examining the deputies elected to the Estates General. To quote Tackett, "In the face of the 'convergent elites' hypothesis of the revisionists, it will be argued that the principal contending groups within the Estates, the Nobility, and the Third Estate were separated by a considerable gulf, a gulf

29 C. Jones, "Bourgeois Revolution Revivified," 94, and W. Doyle, *Origins of the French Revolution*, 231, cite P. Léon's contribution to F. Braudel and E. Labrousse, eds., *Histoire économique et sociale de la France* (Paris, Presses Universitaire de France, 1970), 607, for these figures.

30 W. H. Sewell, *A Rhetoric of Bourgeois Revolution: The Abbé Sieyès and "What Is the Third Estate?"* (Durham, Duke University Press, 1994), 185–86; excerpted passages from the book are reprinted under the title "A Rhetoric of Bourgeois Revolution" in G. Kates, ed., *The French Revolution*, 143–91.

created not by class *per se*, but by a combination of wealth, status, and culture." The nobility, Tackett argues, were substantially more wealthy than the delegates of the Third Estate, enjoyed marks of social privilege denied to commoners, and were the products of a strikingly different education than delegates of the Third; indeed, they tended to be considerably less well educated than their bourgeois social inferiors. Fully four-fifths of the noble delegates had had military experience, another trait that marked them apart from the delegates of the Third Estate. Tackett concurs as well in regard to the social resentment to which Sewell alluded: "The majority of the future Third deputies was clearly impatient if not openly hostile toward the nobility." "But to challenge a class explanation of the Revolution," Tackett concludes, "is not to put into question all social explanation – as the revisionists would seem to suggest."[31]

Many historians, then, continue to see the validity of a social interpretation of the French Revolution, both its origins and its impact, while abandoning the traditional Marxist schema. Not all are in agreement, however. In a recent book that is certain to spark renewed debate, Henry Heller argues that the Marxist view of the French Revolution as the product of an emergent capitalist economy, led by a capitalist bourgeoisie, is still the most compelling interpretation. Indeed, despite the revisionist trend toward cultural and political history, Heller claims that much recent economic and social history has leant new support to the classical Marxist thesis.[32]

Whether one accepts an interpretation of the French Revolution as a bourgeois revolution, or not, it is clear that the bourgeoisie did not make the Revolution alone. One thinks first, perhaps, of the taking of the Bastille, of the urban uprisings in Paris and other major cities in the summer of 1789 that prevented the king from ignoring or turning back the more radical demands for change emanating from the Estates General. But roughly 80 percent of French population remained rural at this time, and one must take into account conditions in the countryside in the final decade of the Old Regime in order to understand fully the social origins of the French Revolution. This is not to say that the deputies to the Estates General themselves had that picture in view. As Timothy Tackett has

31 T. Tackett, *Becoming a Revolutionary: The Deputies of the French National Assembly and the Emergence of a Revolutionary Culture, 1789–1790* (Princeton, Princeton University Press, 1996), 14, 107, 306.

32 H. Heller, *The Bourgeois Revolution in France, 1789–1815* (New York, Berghahn Books, 2006). As evidence that French historians have not lost their sense of humor in the midst of what has sometimes been a heated debate, William Doyle begins his H-France review of Heller's book with these words: "Henry Heller hates me." http://h-france.net/vol7reviews/doyle.html.

noted, fully 75 percent of the deputies were urban and had very little sense of the problems or concerns of country people.[33]

Pierre Goubert observed many years ago that "the quintessence of the ancien régime is confusion."[34] That is to say, given the many local dialects, the variations in patterns of landholding, the overlapping and competing judicial and administrative jurisdictions, the contrasts between *pays d'état* and *pays d'élection*, the greater or lesser weight of the seigneurial system from one province to another, it is very difficult to generalize about conditions in the French countryside at the end of the Old Regime. It is clear, however, that there was unrest among the peasantry as revealed by patterns of rural protest on the one hand, and by the content of the *cahiers de doléances* on the other.

Debate over the rural origins of the Revolution has generally centered on the so-called "feudal reaction," the claim that in the final decades of the Old Regime seigneurial lords made more onerous the dues and duties that they collected from peasants in order to enhance their incomes in the face of inflationary prices and declining rents. This argument, prominent in the work of Georges Lefebvre and C. E. Labrousse, was challenged both by Alfred Cobban and George Taylor, who asserted quite plainly that there was no evidence in rural *cahiers* of peasant hostility toward seigneurial exactions.[35] We are still not in a position to reach a definitive view in regard to the weight of seigneurial obligations in provincial France, despite the growing number of rural studies that have appeared in recent decades, but the magisterial work of John Markoff and Gilbert Shapiro on the content of the *cahiers* has made clear that the assertions of George Taylor were simply unfounded. Markoff and Shapiro found widespread demands in rural *cahiers* for the abolition of both seigneurial dues and ecclesiastical payments, which the peasants often had trouble distinguishing, whereas, by contrast, peasants commonly called for the reform, rather than the abolition, of royal taxes.[36]

---

33 T. Tackett, *Becoming a Revolutionary*, 22.

34 P. Goubert, *The Ancien Régime: French Society, 1600–1750* (New York, Harper Torchbooks, 1973), 17.

35 G. Lefebvre, *Les Paysans du nord pendant la Révolution française* (Paris, Armand Colin, 1972), and *The Coming of the French Revolution* (Princeton, Princeton University Press, 1947); C. E. Labrousse, *Esquisse du mouvement des prix et des revenus en France au XVIIIe siècle* (Paris, Librairie Dalloz, 1933), and *La Crise de l'économie française à la fin de l'Ancien Régime et au début de la Révolution* (Paris, Presses Universitaires de France, 1944); G. Taylor, "Revolutionary and Nonrevolutionary Content in the *Cahiers* of 1789: An Interim Report," *French Historical Studies* 7 (1972), 479–502.

36 G. Shapiro and J. Markoff, *Revolutionary Demands: A Content Analysis of the Cahiers de Doléances of 1789* (Stanford, Stanford University Press, 1998).

This evidence suggests that the peasantry, by and large, was coming to accept the emergence of the monarchical state while their resentment of the seigneurial system was growing. This was not universally the case, particularly in those areas where seigneurial exactions were light, nor would it be correct to assert that peasants never protested against taxes. Markoff and others emphasize the precariousness of rural life – when times were hard, peasants protested not only against taxes, but against dues and tithes as well, and they particularly resented perceived inequities. Among the most unpopular taxes was the *gabelle*, the salt tax, and resistance to it was greatest along the borders between those provinces that collected the *gabelle*, and those that were exempt from it, such as Brittany. Indeed, some 23,000 people were employed along the borders of Brittany to guard against smuggling.[37]

The most common form of peasant protest under the Old Regime was the food riot, which has long been interpreted as a veiled protest against the emergence of a centralized state.[38] The most serious wave of food riots in the late Old Regime occurred in 1775, the so-called Flour Wars, in which peasants throughout central France rose up to protest Turgot's reforms introducing free trade in grain. The protests forced the repeal of the reforms and the eventual dismissal of Turgot.[39] The incidence of rural unrest remained high over the final two decades of the Old Regime, culminating in the widespread riots and protests of 1788–89, when grain and bread prices reached their highest point of the eighteenth century. While historians following the Tillys have seen these protests as essentially reactionary, a defense of local needs against the encroaching demands of the modern state, Markoff has presented the intriguing argument that one might see in these food riots a kind of political tutelage, a moment of political empowerment that could be seen as leading to the demands for direct democracy that were so common among both the peasantry and the urban *sans-culottes* during the 1790s.[40]

---

37 J. Markoff, "Peasants and their Grievances," in P. R. Campbell, ed., *The Origins of the French Revolution*, 250.

38 The clearest exposition of this argument has been made by Charles and Louise Tilly. See C. Tilly, "How Protest Modernized in France," in W. O. Aydelotte et al., eds., *Dimensions of Quantitative Research in History* (Oxford, Oxford University Press, 1972), 192–255; L. Tilly, "The Food Riot as a Form of Political Conflict in France," *Journal of Interdisciplinary History* II, no. 1 (1971), 23–57.

39 C. Bouton, *The Flour War: Gender, Class and Community in Late Ancien Régime Society* (University Park, Pennsylvania State University Press, 1993).

40 J. Markoff, "Peasants and their Grievances," 251. See also J. Markoff, *The Abolition of Feudalism: Peasants, Lords, and Legislators in the French Revolution* (University Park, Pennsylvania State University Press, 1996). P. M. Jones, *The Peasantry in the French Revolution*

A spike in rural protest in the 1770s to 1780s, increasing peasant litigiousness over seigneurial obligations at the end of the Old Regime, the demands in rural *cahiers* for the abolition of seigneurial dues – all of this must be seen as evidence of the social origins of the Revolution in the French countryside. This social conflict may not have influenced the political crisis that led to the convocation of the Estates General, but just as one can see the Enlightenment as creating an intellectual context in which revolution might occur, rather than being a direct cause, so we might point to these factors in the countryside as creating a climate that would very definitely shape political developments in the summer of 1789.

There has been less contention among historians about two other social and economic factors that are considered short-term causes of the Revolution. The first is the sequence of two bad harvests in 1788 and 1789 that created grain shortages and drove prices up to their highest point of the century, leading predictably enough to considerable unrest both among peasants and among the working poor of French towns and cities. Thus, at a politically sensitive moment, both crown and delegates to the Estates General at Versailles, meeting for the first time in 175 years, were faced with massive social unrest. This was exacerbated by a second factor, the ill-advised textile treaty signed with Great Britain in 1786, which allowed a flood of cheaper goods into French markets and led to serious unemployment in the French textile industry, dramatically affecting such cities as Lyon, Troyes, and Elbeuf, but also much of the countryside stretching from the northeast west through Normandy, where rural textile production was substantial.

Our focus in these last pages has been principally on the countryside, where the majority of French people lived in the eighteenth century, but as already noted, most of the delegates to the Estates General came from the towns and cities, where the more serious revolutionary upheavals would also occur, especially in Paris. The French population had grown over the eighteenth century, to perhaps 28 million, and by 1789 there were at least thirty towns in France whose population exceeded 20,000 inhabitants, led by Paris with well over 600,000. It was in this urban milieu that the "public sphere" took shape, and in which public opinion might assert its greatest influence. A number of works published in recent years shed light on the social tensions engendered by this urban growth, and on the new patterns of sociability that would foster the increasing demands for political change at century's end. Most noteworthy are the books by Daniel Roche and David Garrioch exploring various aspects of

(Cambridge, Cambridge University Press, 1988), especially 42–59, is another valuable resource in navigating the historical debates about the rural origins of the Revolution.

Parisian urban life, but one should take note as well of a number of major studies by French scholars devoted to provincial cities.[41]

Structural and Institutional Origins

There is broad consensus that the French monarchy was faced with an institutional crisis at the end of the eighteeenth century. The crown was bankrupt, deeply in debt, shackled by an inequitable and inefficient tax system, and stymied in its efforts at reform by a centuries-old system of privilege that would shortly be swept aside by the French Revolution. Within that broad consensus, however, lie several areas of debate and disagreement: over the severity of the crisis itself, and the monarchy's capacity to respond to it successfully; over where chief responsibility lay for the fact that the fiscal crisis became as grave as it did; over the role of the parlements, in particular the Paris parlement, as the monarchy attempted to address the crisis in the 1780s; and over the role played by royal ministers, and ultimately the Assembly of Notables, in those efforts.

The main cause of the French monarchy's financial difficulties was war. France experienced three periods of war in the mid- to late eighteenth century: the War of Austrian Succession (1740–48), the Seven Years' War (1756–63), and the War of American Independence (1778–83). Just over half of the years in this period were years of war, then, during which time expenditures almost always outstripped normal sources of revenue. Foreign war did provide the monarchy with a justification for raising taxes (indeed, by tradition, it had been nearly impossible to impose new taxes during times of peace since the Middle Ages), but increased taxes were never fully adequate to the task. The gap was made up by borrowing from international banks and *financiers*, some of whom were the same men responsible for collecting the vast array of France's indirect taxes.

41 D. Roche, *The People of Paris: An Essay in Popular Culture in the 18th Century* (Berkeley, University of California Press, 1987), and *France in the Enlightenment* (Cambridge, MA, Harvard University Press, 1998); D. Garrioch, *Neighborhood and Community in Paris, 1740–1790* (Cambridge, Cambridge University Press, 1986), *The Formation of the Parisian Bourgeoisie, 1690–1830* (Cambridge, MA, Harvard University Press, 1996), and *The Making of Revolutionary Paris* (Berkeley, University of California Press, 2002); M. Garden, *Lyon et les Lyonnais au XVIIIe siècle* (Paris, Les Belles Lettres, 1970); F. G. Pariset, ed., *Bordeaux au XVIIIe siècle* (Bordeaux, Fédération historique du Sud-Ouest, 1968); J. C. Perrot, *Genèse d'une ville moderne: Caen au XVIIIe siècle* (Paris, La Haye: Mouton, 1975).

The controller general was the minister responsible for overseeing the royal finances. Between 1777 and 1781 Jacques Necker occupied that post.[42] In 1781 Necker issued a public accounting of the royal treasury, the first time in history that the royal budget had been openly published. While Necker reported royal finances to be in good shape, his report also detailed a number of seemingly frivolous expenses incurred by the court and its retinue, an indiscretion that eventually cost him his job. Two years later Charles-Alexandre Calonne assumed the post of controller general, and almost immediately there began a debate that has raged to the present day. Calonne soon disputed Necker's optimistic accounting of royal finances, laying blame at his feet for the looming fiscal crisis. By 1786, with the short-term loans that Necker had taken out to finance French involvement in the American War about to come due, it was clear that the royal deficit was enormous, well over 100 million *livres* in an annual budget of just under 600 million *livres*. Calonne blamed this on Necker, asserting that the reporting of royal surpluses under his watch had been erroneous, and Necker blamed Calonne, in published pamphlets, for having squandered the robust surplus that he claimed to have left behind. Historians have been trying ever since to establish who was more to blame, without complete success.[43]

There is more to sorting out this mess than assigning blame to either Necker or Calonne, however. They were, after all, essentially just the chief accountants, lacking the power to control royal expenditures, or those ordered by other ministers. Some critics, then and since, pointed at extravagant royal expenditures, or in a slightly different vein, the persistent monarchical quest to achieve grandeur, which would embrace the war costs, as the fundamental cause of the crisis. Others have pointed to the inefficient and inequitable tax system, under which a substantial portion of the revenue ended up in the pockets of the tax collectors rather than in the royal treasury, and which also rested most heavily on the backs of those least able to pay, the peasantry, while sparing the nobility and the wealthy clergy from paying their fair share. No one today would deny that

---

42 Technically Necker was known as director-general of finances, his Protestant faith precluding him from holding the title of *Contrôleur-Général*.

43 F. Crouzet, *La Grande Inflation: la monnaie en France de Louis XVI à Napoléon* (Paris, Fayard, 1993); K. Norberg, "The French Fiscal Crisis of 1788 and the Financial Origins of the Revolution of 1789," in P. T. Hoffman and K. Norberg, eds., *Fiscal Crises, Liberty, and Representative Government, 1450–1789* (Stanford, Stanford University Press, 1994); J. F. Bosher, *French Finances, 1770–1795: From Business to Bureaucracy* (Cambridge, Cambridge University Press, 1970); R. D. Harris, *Necker, Reform Statesman of the Ancien Régime* (Berkeley, University of California Press, 1979); J. Félix, "The Financial Origins of the French Revolution," in P. R. Campbell, ed., *The Origins of the French Revolution*, 35–62.

the tax system was flawed, but recent scholarship claims that, by and large, the French taxpayer paid less onerous taxes than his counterpart in Great Britain.[44] Very recent scholarship, moreover, places more emphasis on the size of the national debt and the cumbersome and costly system of public credit on which the French monarchy customarily relied in order to fund its debt.[45] The crown was also hampered by the fact that, unlike Great Britain, France had no central bank in the eighteenth century.

As the gravity of the fiscal crisis became clear in 1786, additional structural contradictions or tensions impeded the monarchy's efforts to find a resolution. First we might mention the monarch himself. Older descriptions of Louis XVI as intellectually lazy, isolated at Versailles, scarcely engaged with matters of state have given way to more flattering biographies that portray the king as devoted to his subjects, committed to reform, more the victim of circumstance than of his own failings.[46] Whatever his abilities, however, it is clear that Louis XVI was not the "absolute" monarch that Louis XIV had claimed to be when he allegedly uttered the famous line, "L'état c'est moi." It was customary to think of the king as the only "public" person of the realm, the only person who embodied the public interest, as opposed to a populace of "private" individuals whose interests were defined by the traditional system of privilege that prevailed in the corporate society of Old Regime France. In this conception, sovereignty resided in the person of the king, but by the 1780s the king's authority in this regard was contested, and it is clear that the king could not act alone to resolve the crisis confronting the nation.

To register new taxes, or introduce any far-reaching reform, the king required the approval of the Paris parlement, or one of the other dozen provincial parlements, which customarily followed the lead of Paris. The king could impose his will in a special royal session, a *lit de justice*, but to do so in 1786, in the face of parlementary intransigence, would have undermined public confidence in the monarchy and driven up the cost of credit. The Paris parlement refused to authorize new taxes, or additional

---

44 P. Mathias and P. O'Brien, "Taxation in Britain and France, 1715–1810: A Comparison of the Social and Economic Incidence of Taxes Collected for the Central Governments," *Economic History* 5, no. 3 (Winter, 1976), 601–50.

45 This is the conclusion reached by Joel Félix, "The Financial Origins of the French Revolution." See also M. Sonenscher, *Before the Deluge: Public Debt, Inequality, and the Intellectual Origins of the French Revolution* (Princeton, Princeton University Press, 2007), whose scope is obviously considerably broader than fiscal policy alone.

46 J. Hardman, *Louis XVI* (New Haven, Yale University Press, 1993); *Louis XVI: The Silent King* (London, Arnold, 2000); M. Price, *The Road from Versailles: Louis XVI, Marie Antoinette, and the Fall of the French Monarchy* (New York, St. Martin's Press, 2003).

loans, and in the face of this opposition Calonne recommended that Louis XVI convene an Assembly of Notables. One hundred forty-four delegates, selected by the king, convened in February 1787 to consider a series of fundamental reforms, drafted by Louis himself in consultation with Calonne. These included the creation of provincial assemblies, liberalization of the grain trade, and the imposition of a new land tax, to be borne equally by all landowners, whether commoner, noble, or clergy. The Notables, aristocrats almost to a man, refused to endorse the proposal, insisting that they lacked the authority, ultimately forcing Louis XVI to call the Estates General.

Historians have long debated the genesis and the implications of this impasse. Calonne's failure to persuade the Assembly of Notables was at least in part due to opposition from Marie-Antoinette and the Polignac clique that surrounded her at Versailles, pointing to the existence of factions at court and the politics of ministerial intrigue.[47] When Calonne stepped aside in April 1787 he was replaced by Etienne-Charles Loménie de Brienne, Archbishop of Toulouse, who had been Calonne's most vocal critic among the Notables. A favorite of the queen, Loménie now adopted a program little different from Calonne's, although with no more success. Some have seen in the Assembly's opposition a principled defense of privilege, both their own and that of the provinces and towns from which they hailed, in the face of monarchical despotism, while others have seen it as an obstinate assertion of vested self-interest.[48]

A key role in all this was played by parlementary judges, a number of whom were delegates to the Assembly of Notables. The Paris parlement, in particular, had opposed the royal will at several pivotal moments in the second half of the eighteenth century – first in the 1750s during the controversy over the denial of sacraments to practicing Jansenists, then in the early 1770s in the face of Chancellor Maupeou's reforms, which would have abolished the parlements, and finally in the 1780s over the issue of new taxes. In those disputes the parlement clearly assumed a political role in addition to its more traditional judicial responsibilities. There has been considerable scholarship on the parlements in recent

47 Thomas Kaiser has produced a substantial body of work in recent years tracing the contours of an Austrian faction around the queen at Versailles and establishing the degree to which this fed suspicions of conspiracy. See in particular T. E. Kaiser, "Who's Afraid of Marie-Antoinette? Diplomacy, Austrophobia, and the Queen," *French History* 14 (2000), 241–71; and "From the Austrian Committee to the Foreign Plot: Marie-Antoinette, Austrophobia, and the Terror," *French Historical Studies* 26 (2003), 579–617.

48 See J. Hardman, "Decision-making," in P. R. Campbell, ed., *The Origins of the French Revolution*, 63–86, who emphasizes the role of factional strife at Versailles in this period.

decades, some of it interpreting the judges, in their judicial opinions and published remonstrances, as advocates of constitutional government, while others view the parlements as defenders of aristocratic privilege. The latter view is supported, in some measure, by the fact that in September 1788 the Paris parlement ruled that the Estates General should convene and deliberate as in 1614, ignoring demands from the Third Estate that their delegation be doubled and that voting be by head rather than order. By this act the parlement alienated the people of Paris, who one year earlier had viewed the judges as champions for opposing the new royal taxes.[49]

To return to the question posed at the outset of this chapter, in the face of these many challenges and problems was the French Revolution inevitable? In his Bicentennial history of the Revolution, *Citizens*, Simon Schama took a very clear position, praising the reforms initiated by Louis XVI and his ministers and arguing that with better luck they might well have succeeded, and that had that occurred France would have been in much better shape at the dawn of the nineteenth century than it was after a decade of revolution.[50] This is not, in my view, a tenable position. Nor is it credible, as François Furet argued, to see the Revolution as the result of a purely political crisis. The economic expansion of the eighteenth century, the growth in population generally and urban population in particular, the emergence of the public sphere, the burgeoning resentment of the seigneurial system among the peasantry – these were all deeply rooted in the social fabric of France, and all must be counted among the origins of the French Revolution. Whether the fiscal crisis of the 1780s was the product of legitimate national policy and commitments, or was rather the product of either royal extravagance or ministerial despotism, by 1786 public opinion viewed it in the latter terms. This, along with the impediment of a system of privilege that was as old as the monarchy itself, made it impossible for the crown to solve its financial

49 J. Egret, *Louis XV et l'opposition parlementaire, 1715–1774* (Paris. A. Colin, 1970); D. Echeverria, *The Maupeou Revolution: A Study in the History of Libertarianism, 1770–1774* (Baton Rouge, Louisiana State University Press, 1985); W. Doyle, "The Parlements of France and the Breakdown of the Old Regime," *French Historical Studies* 6 (1970), 415–58; D. K. Van Kley, "New Wine in Old Wineskins: Continuity and Rupture in the Pamphlet Debate of the French Prerevolution," *French Historical Studies* 17 (1991), 448–65; B. Stone, *The Parlement of Paris, 1774–1789* (Chapel Hill, University of North Carolina Press, 1981); J. Félix, *Les Magistrats du parlement de Paris, 1771–90* (Paris, SEDOPOLS, 1990; P. R. Campbell, "The Paris Parlement in the 1780s," in P. R. Campbell, ed., *The Origins of the French Revolution*, 87–111.

50 S. Schama, *Citizens: A Chronicle of the French Revolution* (New York, Alfred A. Knopf, 1989).

crisis without turning to the nation, by convoking the Estates General. That act ushered in a whole new dynamic, to be explored in a separate chapter, but it is significant that the renunciation of privilege would be among the first decisive legislative actions of that body, rechristened by its members the National Assembly.

2

1789

A great deal happened in 1789. The Estates General met at Versailles for the first time in 175 years. Prior to that, a flood of pamphlets was published on all aspects of the current crisis, ranging from analysis of every conceivable problem afflicting France to proposals for reform and recommendations on the procedures to be followed in the election of delegates and the drafting of grievance lists. All across France people met in local assemblies: great people, common people, aristocrats, merchants, priests, bishops, landowners, peasants, artisans, men, and women. Some were literate, most were not, but once they had chosen their delegates and sent them off with their *cahiers*, they all waited in keen anticipation for news from the august assemblage at Versailles. There was drama at the king's palace, but little progress over the first two months, producing a mood of restiveness throughout the kingdom, but most especially in Paris. On 14 July the Bastille fell, three days later King Louis XVI journeyed to Paris, and three months later the market women of Paris repaid his gesture and journeyed to Versailles. In the interim, the Great Fear swept across the French countryside, self-styled patriots in towns and cities throughout the country overthrew traditional authorities, elected new municipal councils, and created bourgeois militias. By year's end many French people were speaking of the revolution that had occurred in their country, lending to that word an entirely new meaning. Some dared to hope that the Revolution might very nearly be over.

This whirlwind of events will be the focus of this chapter, leaving for the next chapter discussion of two of the most momentous achievements of 1789: the Declaration of the Rights of Man and the Citizen, and the abolition of feudalism. As we explore the upheavals of 1789, however, we should be mindful of two tendencies on the part of those looking back to the eighteenth century from our vantage point here in the twenty-first. First, given our general familiarity with the course of the Revolution, is a tendency to think of it as a train moving in a particular direction, with a destination already in mind. Certainly the Revolution gathered momentum as it moved along, particularly in its first four years, but I would emphasize here that for those meeting in primary assemblies in the first months of the year, or heading off to Versailles as delegates in May, there was no clear sense of what the future might hold, and an exhilarating anticipation (apprehension for some) that they would have an unprecedented opportunity to influence that future. Indeed, among historians working on the origins of the Revolution it has become a commonplace in recent years to observe that whatever constellation of factors may have caused the Revolution, once it began it developed a dynamic of its own. Few could have anticipated in 1787 what would transpire in 1789, let alone on into the 1790s. Second, given the centrality of Paris geographically and its importance in French national life still today, we often have a tendency to view the provinces as the tail on the dog. All eyes were on Paris, in some sense, or more correctly on Versailles, between May and October 1789, and events in the capital did profoundly influence what happened elsewhere. But the reverse was also true at times, and as we will see in this chapter there were occasions on which people in provincial towns, or in the countryside, acted without waiting for a signal from Paris, where their actions sometimes had a powerful resonance. Paris may have been a dominant presence in the cultural and political life of France, but we might better think of the relationship between Paris and the provinces as a dialectical, or symbiotic, one.

Convocation of the Estates General

Lynn Hunt has argued that the convocation of the Estates General unleashed an explosion of politics in France, that most fundamentally 1789 brought a "revolution in political culture."[1] Peter Jones, in his recent study of six villages during the Revolution, writes that "an interactive mode of political expression came to replace the paternalism of Bourbon administrative monarchy."[2] Michel Biard and Pascal Dupuy, in

---

1 L. Hunt, *Politics, Culture, and Class in the French Revolution* (Berkeley, University of California Press, 1984). This phrase is the title of Hunt's concluding chapter, but it is a point made as well in the first two chapters of the book.

2 P. Jones, *Liberty and Locality in Revolutionary France: Six Villages Compared, 1760–1820* (Cambridge, Cambridge University Press, 2003), 86.

a new survey of recent historiography on the Revolution, borrow a phrase from Louis-Sébastien Mercier in characterizing 1789 as "l'année sans pareille," the unparalleled year.[3] Peter McPhee refers to 1789 quite simply as "the revolutionary year."[4] No one alive at the time would have denied that 1789 ushered in a new era. But what exactly did that mean? What changed in their world, and how did that change happen?

It is risky in writing about history to point to what came first, because there is almost always something else that came before. And so it was with the Estates General. 1789 was not the first time they met. But they had not met in 175 years, so no one alive, including the king, could remember how it was done. Thus, there was a huge debate from August 1788 into the first months of 1789 as to how the delegates should be elected, how many there should be for each estate, and how they should deliberate and vote once they reached Versailles. The last two points remained unresolved even as the delegates filed into the great meeting hall at Versailles on 4 May.

The fact that it had been so long since the Estates General had met is indicative of the degree to which the power of the king had grown over the course of two centuries. Not since 1614 had a French king felt a need to consult his estates. Indeed, the theory of royal absolutism held that sovereignty resided in the person of the king, that the king was the only "public person" in the realm. In that sense, the royal will was the national will.[5] But by convening the Estates General, Louis XVI had essentially conceded that the royal will alone was not adequate to meet the crisis confronting the nation in 1788. This opened the door to an array of groups ready to lay claim to a share of political power and national sovereignty: the parlements, the nobility, the princes of the blood, and the Third Estate.

Between August 1788 and May 1789 hundreds of pamphlets were published on the question of how the Estates General should be constituted. Some of these were sponsored by the court, some by royal ministers, some were written by members of the Paris parlement, others by an array of liberal nobles and prominent bourgeois associated with a group based in Paris known as the Society of Thirty. Georges Lefebvre presented this pamphlet debate as essentially pitting the interests of the Third Estate, determined to increase their representation, against the vested interests of the privileged aristocracy, determined to see that the Estates General met

---

3 M. Biard and P. Dupuy, *La Révolution française: dynamiques, influences, débats, 1787–1804* (Paris, A. Colin, 2005).

4 P. McPhee, *Living the French Revolution, 1789–99* (New York, Palgrave Macmillan, 2006).

5 Keith Baker develops this idea at length in "Public Opinion as Political Invention," in K. M. Baker, *Inventing the French Revolution* (Cambridge, Cambridge University Press, 1990), 167–99.

as they last had in 1614.[6] Recent historiography paints a rather more complicated picture.

The key issues in the debate were two in number: how many delegates should each estate send to Versailles, and how should they vote, by order or by head? In 1614 each estate (clergy, nobility, and Third) had sent a roughly equal number of delegates, the estates had deliberated separately, and they had voted by order. Were this system to prevail, progressive members of the Third Estate feared that the clergy or nobility alone might block recommendations for reform. The crown, anxious to see the tax system made more efficient and universal, similarly worried that either of the privileged orders might stand in the way of such change, as the Assembly of Notables and Paris parlement had done to date. In September 1788 the Paris parlement ruled that the Estates General should meet and deliberate as in 1614, thereby alienating the Third Estate and offending the king. By year's end, after a second Assembly of Notables had met and Jacques Necker had worked behind the scenes to pressure judges, the parlement revised its ruling and agreed to a doubling of the Third Estate, but left the issue of voting unresolved. This was the situation, then, as the pamphlet debate continued and as members of all three estates made their way to assemblies in the early months of 1789 to elect their delegates to Versailles.

Most scholarship in recent decades has pointed to Abbé Sieyès, whose famous pamphlet, *What is the Third Estate?*, was first published in February 1789, as the most influential voice in this pamphlet debate. Both François Furet and Keith Baker see this pamphlet as an important expression of Rousseau's political philosophy and a clarion call for the creation of a National Assembly. William Sewell, in his intellectual biography of Sieyès, makes the case quite succinctly and forcefully: "In his pamphlet, Sieyès succeeded in scripting both the triumph of the National Assembly on 17 June and its radical abolition of privileges on 4 August. He did this by joining a rhetoric of political revolution that pointed toward a seizure of power by the delegates of the Third Estate with a rhetoric of social revolution that inflamed bourgeois resentment against the aristocracy."[7] While Sewell shares with Furet and Baker an emphasis on discourse and its emotive power, his analysis meshes easily with that of Lefebvre when he stresses the social resentment that divided the bourgeoisie from the

---

6 G. Lefebvre, *The Coming of the French Revolution* (Princeton, Princeton University Press, 1947), 76–83.

7 W. H. Sewell, Jr., *A Rhetoric of Bourgeois Revolution: The Abbé Sieyès and What is the Third Estate?* (Durham, Duke University Press, 1994), 185. For another perspective on the rhetoric of Sieyès see J. Guilhaumou, *Sieyès et l'ordre de la langue: l'invention de la politique moderne* (Paris, Editions Kimé, 2002).

aristocracy. In Sewell's interpretation of Sieyès and his influence, the drama of 1789 pits the bourgeoisie against the aristocracy.

A script is written to be followed, of course, and the fact that the Third Estate, joined by liberal nobles and clergymen, *did* declare a National Assembly on 17 June and *did* go on to abolish privilege in the days following 4 August may incline us to see in those subsequent events a validation of Sieyès' influence. As academics, most of us are willing to acknowledge the power of the written and spoken word! But this may be to read history backwards, to take the effect as evidence of the cause. Ken Margerison has challenged this reading of Sieyès' influence, arguing that there were other pamphlets more influential than his in the winter and spring of 1789, advocating a quite different political strategy. Margerison points to the Society (or Committee) of Thirty, a group of liberal nobles and bourgeois, probably closer to fifty in number, who met thrice weekly at the Paris home of Adrien Duport. Between October and December 1788 the Society financed the publication of a series of pamphlets, penned by Guy-Jean-Baptiste Target, a barrister in the Paris parlement, which advocated the doubling of the Third Estate, voting by head at the Estates General, and a union of orders that would bring together like-minded delegates from all three estates to rally around a common program of reform. Margerison has examined more than 600 pamphlets published between January and May 1789, and finds much more evidence that their ideas were influenced by the pamphlets of Target than those of Sieyès. While the events of June through August match the "script" of Sieyès very closely in some regards, Margerison also notes that there was a substantial group of deputies at Versailles that worked throughout the summer, and even beyond, toward the achievement of some sort of union of orders. That dynamic runs counter to the strident opposition between liberal bourgeois and reactionary aristocrats that Lefebvre described.[8]

There can be no doubt that these many pamphlets had an influence on political thinking on the eve of the Estates General – they were published in large press runs, and circulated throughout the country. But there were other forces at work in these months as well. As noted in Chapter One, the ministers Calonne and Loménie de Brienne had instituted a set of reforms in 1787, calling for the creation of new municipal councils in the *pays d'élection*, and the revival of provincial estates in the *pays d'état*. During the summer of 1788 Jean-Joseph Mounier led a movement in Dauphiné for

8 K. Margerison, *Pamphlets and Public Opinion: The Campaign for a Union of Orders in the Early French Revolution* (West Lafayette, IN, Purdue University Press, 1998); and "The Pamphlet Debate over the Organization of the Estates General," in P. R. Campbell, ed., *The Origins of the French Revolution* (New York, Palgrave Macmillan, 2006), 219–38.

the revival of a provincial assembly in that province, and in the midst of a somewhat tumultuous series of events he and his supporters succeeded in their cause, both doubling the representation of the third estate and adopting a procedure for voting by head. The Society of Thirty thus had a tangible example of the union of orders in practice, and Mounier and his allies of course added their own pamphlets to the proliferation of publications through the winter months.

Paul Friedland has recently added another provocative argument to the scholarship addressing the convocation of the Estates General. In his words, "to the inhabitants of premodern France, the political body of the Estates General meeting in assembly with the king was synonymous with the entirety of the French mystical body." In this *corpus mysticum*, the king constituted the head and the delegates the body of the French political nation, and when the Estates General convened, at least up into the sixteenth century, Friedland argues, the delegates were understood to be re-presenting to the king the views of the assemblies that had chosen them as delegates. In this traditional conception, there was complete transparency between the delegates and their constituencies, who were expected to deliver a literal message to the king, the very message with which they had been entrusted back home. Thus, it mattered little how many delegates were sent, nor how many delegates each order might send. Sovereignty resided in the person of the king, who convened his subjects to hear their views.[9]

By the eighteenth century, this traditional conception no longer prevailed. Delegates were sent to Versailles to represent their constituents, not to re-present their views (Friedland employs these two spellings to emphasize this point). There was no consensus about how that should work, nor about where sovereignty resided in this changing political order. Not only was there no agreement among the three orders on these questions, there was very little within the orders. Indeed, the primary assemblies of the clergy had been among the most contentious in the realm. Not all delegates embraced this new conception of representation. After Louis XVI acceded to the declaration of a National Assembly in late June, a number of conservative aristocrats quit Versailles and returned home, insisting that their constituents had not mandated them to serve in a National Assembly, but rather in the Estates General. They were not prepared to represent the nation; they had been elected, they insisted, to re-present their estate. Of equal importance in this shift, by declaring a National Assembly the delegates (might we call them revolutionaries now?) were

9 P. Friedland, *Political Actors: Representative Bodies and Theatricality in the Age of the French Revolution* (Ithaca, Cornell University Press), 29–51. See 32–33 for the quotation above.

implicitly asserting that sovereignty henceforth resided not in the person of the king, but in the nation. How this would work in practice is the question that lies at the very heart of the French Revolution.

But we are getting a bit ahead of ourselves here. In the months leading up to the Estates General, the Society of Thirty and other civic-minded groups and individuals were busy not only writing pamphlets but also drafting and circulating model *cahiers*, the notebooks in which local communities compiled their grievances, to assist primary assemblies in their own drafting of grievance lists. The assembly of the Third Estate meeting in Riom, for example, located in the Auvergne, adopted a grievance list essentially identical to the model *cahier* circulated in advance by Pierre-Victor Malouet, who had served as Naval Intendant in Toulon in the 1780s. A native son of Riom, he would be elected its first delegate to the Estates General, the only royal intendant among the Third Estate delegates at Versailles. Malouet had a very traditional view about royal power and politics. The king's authority was absolute, and the people had more need of being governed than to govern themselves. The common people, in particular, should assume only a passive role in political affairs.[10]

The people of Riom may have valued Malouet's leadership, but many others in France, even among the peasantry, were not prepared to accept a passive role in the new political landscape taking shape in 1789. As Peter McPhee puts it, through the summer months of 1789, "members of the former privileged elite were horrified by another manifestation of rebellion, a sudden collapse of deference."[11] This manifested itself most strongly during the weeks in late July and August that have come to be known as the Great Fear, to which we shall turn shortly, but shifting attitudes among the peasantry also became clear at the time of primary assemblies in the winter and spring. The appeal from Louis XVI to his subjects, calling upon them to elect delegates and draft grievance lists, had a deeply politicizing impact across France – it mobilized the nation in unanticipated ways.

"If only the king knew." Peter Jones cites this as a common, prevailing attitude, not only among the peasantry but throughout provincial France on the eve of the Revolution.[12] These few words conveyed a triple meaning: the traditional faith in the absolute power of the monarch, the

---

10 R. Griffiths, *Le Centre Perdu: Malouet et les "monarchiens" dans la Révolution française* (Grenoble, Presses Universitaires de Grenoble, 1988), 39–55.

11 P. McPhee, *Living the French Revolution, 1789–99* (New York, Palgrave Macmillan, 2006), 51.

12 P. Jones, *Liberty and Locality*, 85. The quotation is drawn from the papers of Auget de Montyon, a former intendant and adviser to Louis XVI.

deferential attitude of the peasantry, and the pervasive sense of an enduring, unchanging world. That mentality did not disappear overnight, but it was seriously challenged in the early months of 1789. As many historians have observed, village assemblies were often presided over by seigneurial judges, though there is disagreement over the degree to which this tended to intimidate the peasants, to call into play the patron–client relationships that were so important in eighteenth-century French society, whether rural or urban. We have noted as well the model *cahiers* that circulated throughout the country, but often there was more than one available, which presented those assembled with options. Evidence suggests that peasants and others were selective about what they drew from these model *cahiers*, and the grievance lists that were ultimately drafted express some of the tensions in rural society. These varied across France. In some regions seigneurial dues and duties weighed heavily on the peasants, and thus became the focus of their grievances. In others the tithes collected by the Catholic Church were onerous, and these became the object of complaint. While the legitimacy of royal taxation was generally recognized, there was widespread sentiment that it should be more equitably levied. Gilbert Shapiro and John Markoff, in their massive study, tend to emphasize the general understatement of the peasant *cahiers*, while Peter Jones argues that there were instances of exaggeration as well. In his words, the "*cahiers de doléances* are best understood as blurred shapshots of a fleeting moment and not as fixed statements, whether endorsing the status quo or looking towards a programme of change."[13]

As this statement suggests, it remains difficult to draw firm conclusions about the content of the *cahiers* and what it tells us about the latent revolutionary potential in French society in 1789. The process itself, however, was galvanizing, particularly in the assemblies of the Third Estate. Those assembled may have tended to listen to, and then elect, their social betters (the vast majority of Third Estate delegates were landowners, lawyers, or other professionals), but in the process of deliberation and debate the traditional sense of timeless immobility gave way to a recognition of the possibility of change. After the spring of 1789, the king could no longer claim not to know. The people had sent him their grievances, had shared with their king their concerns and recommendations. And having done so, they expected the king and the Estates General to act, to respond to this expression of public opinion.

---

13 Ibid., 95. See G. Shapiro and J. Markoff, *Revolutionary Demands: A Content Analysis of the Cahiers de Doléances of 1789* (Stanford, Stanford University Press, 1998), in particular Chapter 9, for a discussion of the composition of local assemblies and the influence of seigneurial judges, and Chapter 18, written by G. Shapiro and P. Dawson, for a discussion of peasant radicalism in the *cahiers*.

The Fall of the Bastille

If there was a moment at which the events of 1789 came definitively to be seen as a revolution, it would have to be 14 July and the fall of the Bastille. As Hans-Jürgen Lüsebrink and Rolf Reichardt put it, "even at the beginning of the Revolution, no event in modern history seemed as suited, in the minds of both politicians and ordinary people, to provide the date for a new national holiday as the anniversary of the storming of the Bastille."[14] The event and the edifice combined to create a potent symbol with multilayered meanings. Indeed, it has long been clear to historians that the Bastille's symbolic power far exceeded its actual importance at the end of the Old Regime. Its 30-meter walls towered menacingly above the artisanal and working-class district of the *faubourg* St.-Antoine at the eastern edge of Paris, but in 1789 there were only seven prisoners held within its walls, all of them rather comfortably housed. Over the previous decade or two, however, one in three of its prisoners had been incarcerated either for writing, printing, or selling forbidden works. Voltaire had spent time within its walls, and although Mirabeau had never been imprisoned in the Bastille, he denounced it so fervently in his writings that everyone believed he had been. It was regularly reviled as a symbol of despotism in the *mémoires judiciaires* of the 1780s, which we noted in Chapter One as an important force in the shaping of public opinion on the eve of the Revolution.

The crowd that marched to the Bastille on 14 July 1789, some 80,000 strong, went not to liberate its prisoners, but rather in search of powder for the guns and cannons they had seized earlier at the Invalides hospital, fearful that the king was preparing a military coup against the National Assembly. As is generally known, the day ended violently, with casualties on both sides and the governor, De Launay, ultimately killed and beheaded by the angry crowd. As Lüsebrink and Reichardt assert, "it was here that the principle of the sovereignty of the people, which the National Assembly had elevated to the fundamental precept of its constitution on 17 June 1789, served to legitimize revolutionary violence for the first time."[15] There was a triple resonance, then, to the symbolism of the Bastille: despotism, popular sovereignty, and revolutionary violence.

14 H.-J. Lüsebrink and R. Reichardt, *The Bastille: A History of a Symbol of Despotism and Freedom* (Durham, Duke University Press, 1997), 147. See also J. Godechot, *The Taking of the Bastille, July 14th, 1789* (New York, Scribner, 1970); and W. H. Sewell, "Historical Events as Transformations of Structures: Inventing Revolution at the Bastille," in Sewell, *Logics of History* (Chicago, University of Chicago Press, 2005), 225–70.

15 Ibid., 45.

Without the popular uprising the tenure of the National Assembly might have been shortlived, and the despotism that the Bastille was seen to embody seemingly justified the people's violence on this occasion. It was not the king, though, whom the people viewed as despotic, but rather his ministers. Three days after the fall Louis XVI traveled from Versailles to Paris and received a tricolor cockade, the new symbol of the unity of Paris and the Bourbon monarchy. As R. M. Andrews has argued, this ceremony introduced another powerful symbolism: the triumph of Paris over the monarchy. Louis XIV had built Versailles following the Fronde (a mid-seventeenth century revolt against royal authority led by prominent noblemen), precisely to secure the crown from the threat of popular upheaval. The assertion of royal absolutism thus came at the expense of Parisian political influence. Now that equation had been reversed, and just three months later the king and his family would move to Paris permanently, where they would spend their final days.[16]

Municipal Revolutions and the Great Fear

Reports of the fall of the Bastille resonated across Europe, and it is clear from memoirs that most people instinctively recognized the implications of the event, but the news had immediate repercussions across France. In nearly all of the major towns and cities of the provinces there were popular upheavals, and in many of them this resulted in the election of new municipal authorities. In some cases it was news of the fall of the Bastille or the dismissal of Jacques Necker that triggered the municipal revolts, but in a handful of towns popular mobilization actually occurred before 14 July. This was also a period of rising grain prices and growing scarcity, so that food riots were a common feature of the popular tumult. In almost every case two major developments followed from these revolts: the creation of revolutionary committees, often put in place by the assemblies that had convened to elect delegates to the Estates General and draft grievance lists; and the creation of bourgeois militias. Each of these new bodies essentially had a dual purpose: to preserve local order in the face of food scarcity and popular unrest, but also to defend the Revolution in the face of growing rumors of aristocratic plots, and in light of the news from Paris. The revolutionary committees were a transitional authority, in charge of local affairs until the election of municipal councils in early 1790. The bourgeois militias became the nucleus of the National Guards,

16 R. M. Andrews, "Paris of the Great Revolution, 1789–1796," in G. Brucker, ed., *Peoples and Communities in the Western World* (Homewood, IL, Dorsey Press, 1979), vol. 2, 56–116.

also formally constituted in 1790. But through the last months of 1789, with the National Assembly fully absorbed by national issues, these new local authorities enjoyed substantial autonomy in the management of municipal affairs, yet another way in which the events of 1789 fostered political mobilization among the populace. If the king and his advisers entertained any further thoughts of turning back the revolutionary tide after 14 July, these municipal revolutions rendered such repression a virtual impossibility.[17]

The final two weeks of July and the first week of August were also marked by a wave of rural protest and unrest, or rather by a number of waves. The classic study of the Great Fear was done many years ago by Georges Lefebvre, and that work, along with his massive work on the peasants of the department of the Nord, laid a solid foundation for much of what we know today about the peasantry in the Revolution.[18] Simply put, the Great Fear was a rural panic, triggered by news of the fall of the Bastille and the dismissal of Jacques Necker, and generated by rumors that brigands, in the pay of the aristocracy, were moving into the fields to cut the grain before it could fully ripen, thereby deepening the economic crisis that was already threatening the peasantry with starvation. There was no truth to the rumor of an aristocratic plot, but this did not prevent the rumors from spreading with astonishing rapidity, touching nearly every region of provincial France. Lefebvre traced the movement of the Great Fear, and identified seven distinct currents of revolt, with an eighth in southwest France more recently uncovered.

In most instances the peasants targeted local seigneurs or tithe owners. Often the entire community mobilized, marched to the nearby château, seized the records of seigneurial dues and duties, generally destroying

---

17 L. Hunt, "Committees and Communes: Local Politics and National Revolution in 1789," *Comparative Studies in Society and History* 18 (1976), 321–46. A great many local studies of the early years of the Revolution in cities and towns throughout France have appeared over the past four decades, with the years just before and after the Bicentennial witnessing a considerable number of works by French scholars. Among the best local studies available in English are J. Kaplow, *Elbeuf during the Revolutionary Period: History and Social Structure* (Baltimore, Johns Hopkins University Press, 1964); L. Hunt, *Revolution and Urban Politics in Provincial France: Troyes and Reims, 1786–1790* (Stanford, Stanford University Press, 1978); W. Scott, *Terror and Repression in Revolutionary Marseille* (London, Macmillan, 1973); A. Forrest, *Society and Politics in Revolutionary Bordeaux* (Oxford, Oxford University Press, 1975), and *Revolution in Provincial France: Acquitaine, 1789–1799* (Oxford, Clarendon Press, 1996); P. R. Hanson, *Provincial Politics in the French Revolution: Caen and Limoges, 1789–1794* (Baton Rouge, Louisiana State University Press, 1989); M. Crook, *Toulon in War and Revolution* (Manchester, Manchester University Press, 1991).

18 G. Lefebvre, *The Great Fear of 1789: Rural Panic in Revolutionary France* (Princeton, Princeton University Press, 1973); and *Les Paysans du Nord pendant la Révolution française* (Lille, O. Marquant, 1924).

them, and then helped themselves to the lord's wine and food. Châteaux were sometimes put to the torch, and significant property was destroyed, but overall very few lives were claimed.

We tend to think of the Great Fear as a distinct and unique event, confined to this three-week period in mid-summer 1789, a moment when the peasantry burst into action. It is important to place the Great Fear in context, however. Lefebvre insisted on distinguishing it from other peasant revolts of 1789, a conclusion that has stood the test of time, but as Peter Jones has observed, "the conclusion that the spirit of revolt developed during the long and miserable winter of 1788–89 seems inescapable."[19] Not only did the hardships of that winter tend to have a radicalizing effect, the process of drafting local grievance lists also served to focus peasants on the abuses of the seigneurial system and to build community solidarity. Peter McPhee cites a report by the steward on the estate of the Duc de Montmorency that illustrates this resentment and also shows that the peasantry was being influenced by the new political rhetoric emanating from Versailles: "Just as I was going to finish my letter, I learnt ... that approximately three hundred brigands from all the lands associated with the vassals of Mme the Marquise de Longaunay have stolen the titles of rents and allowances of the seigneurie, and demolished her dovecotes: they then gave her a receipt for the theft signed *The Nation*."[20]

Lefebvre emphasized the degree to which the Great Fear united the peasantry against seigneurial dues and church tithes, but Peter Jones cautions that even here in 1789 landless peasants, tenant farmers, and more substantial landowners – the *coqs du village* – may not always have found common cause in these uprisings. Contrary to contemporary claims that the revolts were caused by outside agitators, the infamous brigands fingered in the passage above, the troubles were almost always the work of locals, focused on local issues. Clay Ramsey has studied in detail the Great Fear in the Soissonnais, a region of north central France, concentrating on elements of ideology in the language of the protesters. In Ramsey's view, "the roots of the brief and puzzling solidarity across classes and between town and country that was manifested on the occasion of the Great Fear began in the community system of cultivation and the perceptions of shared interests which it engendered."[21] The Great Fear, he argues, was a defense

---

19 P. Jones, *The Peasantry in the French Revolution* (Cambridge, Cambridge University Press, 1988), 74.

20 P. McPhee, *Living the French Revolution, 1789–99*, 45.

21 C. Ramsey, *The Ideology of the Great Fear: The Soissonnais in 1789* (Baltimore, Johns Hopkins University Press, 1992), 3.

of the local, moral economy against outsiders. It articulated traditional, conservative values in the face of an agrarian economy that was moving in the direction of large-scale, individualistic cultivation. At least in the Soissonnais, moreover, the panics tended to originate in areas where arable land bordered forest preserves, which were both a symbol of royal or seigneurial privilege, and an area where bandits or other outsiders might gather in seclusion to attack the local community. Ramsey, like Lefebvre, sees the Great Fear as an expression of the peasantry's antipathy toward the vestiges of feudalism, and unlike Peter Jones sees it as a movement that at least sometimes revealed divisions, rather than solidarity, between town and country. Provincial towns created their bourgeois militias at least in part in response to the roaming bands of protesting peasants, while the peasants sometimes viewed the towns, or townspeople, as the agents of economic change, change which at times threatened the autonomy and viability of local communities.[22] As we will see, the solidarity in the countryside that this panic seems to have engendered would not endure through the revolutionary decade, and what Ramsey describes as a conservative impulse to protect the local community against outsiders would have a decidedly revolutionary impact at Versailles in the week that directly followed the Great Fear's final convulsions.

The October Days

The deputies of the National Assembly were quite productive in the weeks following the fall of the Bastille. By August they had completed a draft of the Declaration of the Rights of Man and the Citizen, and in the wake of the Great Fear and the drama at Versailles of the Night of 4 August, they drafted legislation that abolished the remnants of feudalism as well as the system of privilege on which Old Regime society had rested. We will turn to the substance of those reforms in the next chapter. The efforts of the deputies might have gone for naught, however, had the women of Paris not decided to march to Versailles on 5 October.

As with many other events in 1789, this one resulted from a combination of material want and political concern. The harvest of 1789 was a good one, and in a normal year market supply would have usually improved in September and prices would have come down. Neither of these occurred, for reasons that remain unclear, and the first week of October brought a new spike in grain prices, producing consternation

---

22 P. Jones, *The Peasantry in the French Revolution*, in particular 67–81.

among the market women of Paris. The people of Paris were additionally uneasy about the refusal of Louis XVI to sign the Declaration of Rights or the legislation abolishing seigneurial dues. The king's intransigence fed the rumors of an aristocratic plot at court, already stoked by the uprisings in the provinces of late July and early August.

These persistent concerns were aggravated by news of a banquet held at Versailles on 1 October, by the recently transferred Flanders Regiment, in honor of Marie-Antoinette. The soldiers, after abundant drink and many toasts of the queen, reportedly removed the tricolor cockade from their coats, stomped them underfoot, and replaced them with either the white cockade of the Bourbons or the black of Austria. Outraged at this apparent insult to the National Assembly and the city of Paris, several hundred women walked from the central markets to the Hôtel de Ville, where they decided to march to Versailles to meet with the king. Delegates went back to the neighborhoods to recruit more women to the cause, and a National Guardsman by the name of Maillard was enjoined to lead the entourage, perhaps because of his military experience. The women were armed, but their weapons were more symbolic than real. By noon as many as between six and seven thousand marchers, nearly all of them women, were en route to Versailles. Several hours later General Lafayette followed them, at the head of the Paris National Guard.

When the women reached Versailles, wet and disheveled from the constant drizzle, they entered the National Assembly. The king was reportedly off on the hunt, but by early evening a small contingent of women was escorted to the palace to meet with Louis XVI. The others began to prepare a makeshift camp for the night. The king received the delegation politely, listened to their complaints with concern, and promised to do all that he could to address the problem of food supply in Paris. When they carried that news back to the other women, however, they were greeted with derision: how could they be so naïve as to accept such bland assurances without any specific promises or written orders? At this point the group divided into two, with some inclined to take what they had got and return to Paris, and others determined to press for something more. Some historians have suggested that the king contemplated flight at this time, but there is no evidence to support this. Lafayette intervened with the royal family that night, informing the king that he could only guarantee their safety if they returned with him to Paris, but the king declined – hardly surprising, since Marie-Antoinette loathed Lafayette. In the early morning hours, however, a portion of the crowd invaded the palace, killing two Swiss Guards, forcing the queen and her maids to flee the royal bedchamber. Lafayette's offer now appeared more compelling, and with a growing crowd amassing in the courtyard the king and queen soon appeared on the balcony, accompanied by the general, and pledged to return to Paris. By mid-afternoon they were en route back to the capital, the women on foot, some of the guardsmen on horseback, the king, his family, and their attendants in carriages, all preceded by the heads of the two Swiss Guards on pikes.

A number of questions continue to surround this incident. It is clear that the march was not spontaneous – the women who set off to the Hôtel de Ville on the morning of 5 October were determined to take action, though Versailles may not have been their original goal. Were their intentions violent? Almost certainly not, although witnesses reported numerous epithets directed against the "Austrian whore," and royalists insisted that the entire affair was contrived and paid for by either Mirabeau or the king's cousin, the Duc d'Orléans. What were Lafayette's intentions? Some have suggested that he headed off with the National Guard in order to turn back the women, although he made no effort to do so once he reached Versailles. The predominance of women in this protest was initially denied by nineteenth-century historians, while others characterized them as vagrants and prostitutes rather than the market women, shopkeepers, and artisans' wives that they were.

While the significance of the October Days as a women's protest has now long been recognized, the event still calls out for further investigation and analysis. The participation of women at other times and places in the Revolution seems to have drawn the attention of historians more over the past decade. Olwen Hufton has raised a number of issues that might profitably be pursued in further writing and research.[23] The significance of the event in the context of 1789 is multifaceted. First, it contributed to the continuing desacralization of the king, in a much more personal way than the assault on the Bastille had done. Secondly, it finished the work begun in July: the king now left Versailles for Paris, soon to be followed by the National Assembly. This suggests a third point: the Assembly henceforth would be much more influenced by the Parisian populace than by pressure from the king and his ministers. The dynamic of the Revolution had now decisively shifted. That shift would not be immediately obvious, however, for the outcry against the violence committed at Versailles (though it was not as serious as that of 14 July) and the investigation subsequently carried out by the Châtelet court brought on a period of calm and political reaction that endured well into the following year.[24]

---

23 O. Hufton, *Women and the Limits of Citizenship in the French Revolution* (Toronto, University of Toronto Press, 1992), 6–18.

24 J.-P. Jessenne, *Révolution et Empire, 1783–1815* (Paris, Hachette, 1993), 80–82.

Conclusion

As we suggested at the head of this chapter, some dared to think that the Revolution might be nearing its end in the last months of 1789. The Estates General had become the National Assembly, and along with the king and his family had shifted its seat from Versailles to Paris. The king had now signed the Declaration of Rights of Man and the Citizen, as well as legislation abolishing the seigneurial system. The people of Paris had mobilized in defense of the Revolution on two occasions, as had towns and cities across France, along with thousands of peasants in the countryside. One might argue with some justification that a common sense of purpose motivated the people in the heady atmosphere of "the unparalleled year," but there were tensions as well that emerged in those days, some of them obvious and some yet barely perceptible, and it was these that would sustain the political ferment over at least the next five years.

Historians have long debated, sometimes directly and sometimes only across the decades, what was most significant about this tumultuous year. Was it largely a juridical revolution, the replacement of one political regime by another, a movement carried forward by the rhetoric and discourse of a remarkable group of delegates who transformed themselves from an Estates General into a National Assembly, who snatched from Louis XVI a sovereignty that his forebears had claimed for the king himself, alone, and proclaimed it the birthright of the nation? Or was it a social revolution, the product of urban insurrection, without which the valiant words uttered at Versailles might have proven as futile as the words of the Frankfurt assembly would prove half a century later? And would the uprising in Paris have been enough, without the accompanying salvos of the municipal revolutions across France? While we think of the Revolution as a predominantly urban affair, the work of a newly literate populace, would the very foundation of the edifice of the Old Regime, the system of privilege, have been toppled without the upheaval in the countryside? These events, these ideas, these social forces were all interlocking and interdependent. We have seen them differently over the centuries, have asked different questions and found different answers, in accordance with the shifting political and social currents of our own times. This is why historians have found so much to debate about the French Revolution, and why those debates will continue to invigorate the study of the Revolution for decades to come.

3

The Declaration of Rights and the Abolition of Feudalism

In the previous chapter we examined 1789 from the perspective of events and forces for change, concentrating on five major moments of upheaval that rendered the momentum of the Revolution virtually unstoppable. In this chapter our focus will be on the two most significant achievements of the Revolution in its first year: the Declaration of the Rights of Man and Citizen, initiated in the first weeks of July and presented to the full National Assembly for vote on 26 August; and the abolition of feudalism, first broached during the dramatic late night session of 4 August, and drafted into legislation over the following week. Neither was definitively accomplished in 1789. The Declaration of the Rights of Man and Citizen would be revised in subsequent years in significant ways, although fundamentally the document remained consistent, and the complete elimination of seigneurial dues, the heart of what deputies referred to at the time as the feudal system, would not come until 1793. But the essential work was accomplished in those first two months of the Revolution.

Both achievements had far-reaching consequences that extended well beyond the borders of France at the time, and beyond the eighteenth century to the present day as well. Along with the American Declaration of Independence, the French Declaration of the Rights of Man and Citizen represents the first assertion of universal human rights. Every subsequent claim of such rights has looked to these two documents for inspiration. The French Declaration was derided by Edmund Burke at the time for claiming too much, therefore dooming its ambitious project to failure, and has been critiqued by others in the years since for claiming too little – as we shall see, important segments of the population were initially left out of this "universal" declaration. Karl Marx viewed the 1789 Declaration as fundamentally flawed because, by enshrining private property as an inalienable right, it had rendered impossible the universal enjoyment of the other rights proclaimed. Controversial at the time, the declaration of human rights continues to be debated around the globe today.

Similarly, the abolition of feudalism, an obviously progressive and beneficial legislative act viewed from our perspective today, was enormously contentious in 1789. Louis XVI initially refused to sign the legislation (just as he refused to put his hand to the Declaration of Rights), asserting that he would not see his nobility and his clergy despoiled. They stood to lose an array of dues and duties, for the Church as well as noble lords owned substantial seigneurial domains. Indeed, for a significant number of aristocrats seigneurial dues were an essential source of income, and for this reason they were not abolished outright in 1789, but were to be eliminated over time only after the receipt of redemption payments. This sowed confusion, and resentment, in the countryside. By the end of the decade, however, the seigneurial system had been thoroughly dismantled in France, and in the first decade of the nineteenth century Napoleon's armies and administrators would carry the assault on feudalism to much of the rest of western Europe.

The concepts of privilege and private property were integral to both of these revolutionary acts. The very first article of the Declaration of the Rights of Man and Citizen proclaimed that "Men are born and remain free and equal in rights. Social distinctions may be based only on common utility." By definition this rendered privilege, the very linchpin of Old Regime society, obsolete. Logically, it called into question the legitimacy of noble status, and although at the time this may have escaped the attention of the deputies, within one year noble titles would themselves be abolished. A society of privilege, of "private law" (in which a variety of individuals enjoyed special prerogatives or tax exemptions by virtue of belonging to particular groups, such as the nobility, the clergy, or other corporate bodies), gave way to a society of equal rights and laws applicable to all citizens. Among the most valuable of the privileges of the old aristocracy, at least in economic terms, were the seigneurial dues abolished following the night of 4 August. But in its last article the Declaration of Rights proclaimed that "Property being an inviolable and sacred right, no one may be deprived of it except when public necessity, certified by law, obviously requires it, and on the condition of a just compensation in advance." Accordingly, seigneurial dues were to be seen as a form of property, and as such would be eliminated only after just compensation had been paid.

There were limits, then, to the rights being asserted and tensions inherent in both proclamations. Those tensions and limitations have led to considerable historical debate over the years. Rights that were declared to be universal were initially denied to Jews, blacks, and women. Why was this so? And how did it come to be that Jews and black slaves would both be granted their rights as citizens during the revolutionary decade, while women would not? If those rights were considered to be "natural and inalienable," or "self-evident" in the language of the American revolutionaries, why were they being declared only here at the end of the eighteenth century? Why had they not been "self-evident" before? Such questions have prompted historians to search for origins, and finding those origins in the political, philosophical, and literary culture of the Old Regime has prompted some to ask just how revolutionary the Declaration of Rights really was.

The claim, by the deputies themselves, that feudalism was being abolished on the Night of 4 August lies at the heart of the debate about whether the French Revolution was a bourgeois revolution or not. Those critical of that interpretation have long pointed out that very few peasants could legitimately be called serfs in 1789. Peasants were no longer tied to the land, and had not been for centuries. Many, indeed, were landowners themselves. What was abolished in 1789 were the vestiges of feudalism, the hated seigneurial dues, resented by the peasantry precisely because the reciprocity that had justified them, in some measure, back in medieval times, had long since fallen by the wayside. Seigneurs no longer provided essential services to their peasants, which made the claim that these dues were a form of property all the more galling.

These two major achievements of 1789 – the Declaration of Rights and the Abolition of Feudalism – were both more complicated and more limited than they are often presented in celebratory histories of the French Revolution. And yet it is not an exaggeration to say that each changed the world in a fundamental way. We will explore that apparent paradox in the pages ahead, turning first to the Declaration of the Rights of Man and Citizen and then to the Night of 4 August and the abolition of feudalism.

The Declaration of the Rights of Man and Citizen

Already in the spring of 1789 there was widespread talk of the need for a declaration of rights. The Marquis de Lafayette, who had fought alongside George Washington in the American colonies and maintained regular correspondence with him, had already drafted a version, as had the Marquis de Condorcet, who was perhaps the staunchest advocate of human rights in France at the time.[1] Thomas Jefferson, the principal

1 See A. de Baecque, ed., *L'An I des droits de l'homme* (Paris, Presses du CNRS, 1988) for texts of the various early drafts of a declaration of rights.

author of the American Declaration of Independence, was in Paris in 1789 and in contact with a number of the deputies to the Estates General. It is clear that the American experience had a profound influence on the thinking of the French revolutionaries.

The French project, however, was more ambitious than the American, as Lynn Hunt has recently observed. While the American Declaration of Independence made universalistic claims regarding human rights, it contained no list of rights. The American Constitution and Bill of Rights, drafted later, were more particularistic, establishing limits to the power of the newly established government of the United States, both vis-à-vis its citizens and the individual states of the union. The French Declaration of the Rights of Man and Citizen adopted universalistic language throughout, claiming rights not just on behalf of French citizens but on behalf of all humanity, "in part because it undercut the particularistic and historical claims of the monarchy."[2]

Where did this new impulse to declare human rights come from? Hunt argues that two fundamental shifts in outlook occurred in the second half of the eighteenth century. First, as Diderot had observed, human rights "required a certain widely shared 'interior feeling.'" Hunt characterizes this new "interior feeling" as the capacity to feel "empathy" for others, although the word itself would not come into common usage until early in the twentieth century. Second, "everyone would have rights only if everyone could be seen as in some fundamental way alike."[3] This, of course, ran counter to the traditional "great chain of being" conception of the world, in which each person occupied a different place in a rigidly constituted hierarchical society, the very basis for the Old Regime system of privilege.

Why did this new sense of empathy and ability to see others as similar to oneself emerge in the late eighteenth century? Hunt points to the growing popularity of epistolary novels in this period, especially *Pamela* and *Clarissa* by Samuel Richardson, and *Julie, or the New Héloïse*, by Jean-Jacques Rousseau. These "epistolary novels taught their readers nothing less than a new psychology and in the process laid the foundation for a new social and political order." Not everyone welcomed the widespread influence of this fictional literature – some condemned it as encouraging

---

2 L. Hunt, *Inventing Human Rights: A History* (New York, W. W. Norton, 2007), 117. See also L. Hunt, ed., *The French Revolution and Human Rights: A Brief Documentary History* (Boston, Bedford Books, 1996); D. Van Kley, ed., *The French Idea of Freedom: The Old Regime and the Declaration of Rights of 1789* (Stanford, Stanford University Press, 1994); S. Rials, *La Déclaration des droits de l'homme et du citoyen* (Paris, Hachette, 1988); and M. Gauchet, *La Révolution des droits de l'homme* (Paris, Gallimard, 1989).

3 L. Hunt, *Inventing Human Rights*, 27.

frivolous or sinful behavior – but "ultimately at stake in the conflict of views about the novel was nothing less than the valorization of ordinary secular life as the foundation for morality."[4]

The Declaration of the Rights of Man and Citizen was immediately condemned by Edmund Burke, who pointed to historical tradition and the Christian faith as sources of human morality and the hierarchical order of society. Jeremy Bentham, too, rejected the Declaration and the concept of natural law: "Natural rights is simple nonsense: natural and imprescriptible rights, rhetorical nonsense, nonsense upon stilts."[5] The publication of Thomas Paine's *Rights of Man*, in response to Burke's book, ensured that dialogue about human rights spread across Europe, and the debate between Jeffersonians and Federalists did the same across the Atlantic. Within France, of course, the two decades of the Revolutionary and Napoleonic era would amount to a sustained debate between human rights and the forces of tradition.

We should also make note here of the philosophical and legal traditions out of which the Declaration of Rights of Man and Citizen emerged. Hunt does not ignore these, acknowledging the influence of Grotius, Burlamaqui, and Locke on the evolution of rights thinking in France, as well as Enlightenment figures such as Diderot and Kant, in addition to Montesquieu and Rousseau. The contributors to the volume edited by Dale Van Kley emphasize the French tradition of jurisprudence, however, and Van Kley himself has, of course, explored the influence of Jansenism on French constitutional thought.[6] What Hunt's argument addresses, more than past scholarship, is the shift in sensibility by which human rights came to resonate broadly among the French populace, thereby contributing to the popular mobilization that became the essence of revolutionary politics. Still, as Hunt admits, very few peasants were reading epistolary novels on the eve of the Revolution, whereas many of them remained devoted to their Catholic faith, a factor that may explain, at least in part, one of the persistent tensions in French society through the revolutionary decade.

Nearly seventy years ago, Georges Lefebvre suggested that the seventeen points of the Declaration of the Rights of Man and Citizen could be read as a pointed critique of the abuses of the Old Regime, rather than as

4 Ibid., 38 and 57.

5 Ibid., 125.

6 See in particular D. Van Kley, "From the Lessons of French History to Truths for All Times and All People: The Historical Origins of an Anti-Historical Declaration," K. M. Baker, "The Idea of a Declaration of Rights," D. A. Bell, "Safeguarding the Rights of the Accused: Lawyers and Political Trials in France, 1716–1789," and T. A. Kaiser, "Property, Sovereignty, the Declaration of the Rights of Man, and the Tradition of French Jurisprudence," in D. Van Kley, *The French Idea of Freedom*.

an abstract expression of universal principles.[7] It is easy to support such a reading: Point 9, "Every man being presumed innocent until judged guilty ..." can be seen as an indictment of the *lettres de cachet*, by which the king, or despotic parents, might have someone locked away without formal charge or trial. Point 11, "The free communication of thoughts and opinions is one of the most precious of the rights of man" is a clear attack upon royal and church censorship. Point 13, "For maintenance of public authority and for expenses of administration, common taxation is indispensable" is clearly directed against the inequitable and inefficient tax system of the Old Regime. And Point 15, "Society has the right to hold accountable every public agent of the administration" can be read as an effort to rein in ministerial despotism.

The Declaration of Rights is also commonly seen as an assertion of civil liberties, comparable in that regard to the American Bill of Rights and the English Magna Carta, meant to protect individual freedoms from the intrusions of national government.[8] Those rights are generally summarized in Point 2 of the Declaration: "The purpose of all political association is the preservation of the natural and imprescriptible rights of man. These rights are liberty, property, security and resistance to oppression." Freedom of expression, of association, of religion are all asserted as inalienable rights. Freedom of religion, however, was expressed ambiguously in Point 10: "No one should be disturbed for his opinions, even in religion, provided that their manifestation does not trouble public order as established by law." The qualified language can be attributed to the presence in the National Assembly of a large number of Catholic priests and bishops, many of whom pushed for a declaration of Catholicism as the official religion of France. The final clause, regarding the disruption of public order, would serve as justification for the prohibition of public masses conducted by non-juring priests following passage of the Civil Constitution of the Clergy in 1790. Notably absent in the Declaration is any language assuring a right to subsistence, a right that the medieval church had strongly defended, and one that is often asserted today in international debates about human rights.[9] One might see

---

7 G. Lefebvre, *The Coming of the French Revolution*, trans. R. R. Palmer (Princeton, Princeton University Press, 1947), 209–20.

8 D. Van Kley, *The French Idea of Freedom*. The very title of this collection points to the emphasis on civil liberties by most of the essays in the volume.

9 S. G. Swanson, "The Medieval Foundations of John Locke's Theory of Natural Rights: Rights of Subsistence and the Principle of Extreme Necessity," *History of Political Thought* (Fall, 1997), 1–66. It is worth noting that three of the eight preliminary drafts of the Declaration included statements of the right to subsistence. See A. de Baecque, *L'An I des droits de l'homme*, for texts. In recent years, the Chinese government has regularly asserted this right in exchanges with European and American rights activists.

the Declaration of Rights, in its assertion of civil liberties, as an expression of what some have characterized as the modern definition of freedom, that is, a "freedom from" government intrusion on individual liberty, as opposed to the classical definition of "freedom to" participate in government, exemplified by fifth-century BCE Athens, where the essential freedom, and duty, of the citizen was to participate in the polis.[10]

The Declaration of the Rights of Man and Citizen can also be seen, however, as a claim to sovereignty. As Hunt observes, "unlike 'petition,' 'bill,' or even 'charter,' 'declaration' could signify the intent to seize sovereignty." The deputies of the National Assembly, she argues, "were not yet ready to explicitly repudiate the sovereignty of their king," but it is striking that the king is not mentioned either in the Preamble to the Declaration, nor in any of its points. Indeed, Point 3 explicitly asserted that "The principle of all sovereignty rests essentially in the nation." Thus, Hunt concludes, the deputies "effected a revolution in sovereignty and created an entirely new basis for government."[11] Marcel Gauchet goes one step further in his interpretation of the Declaration of Rights, seeing it as an act more than a text, an act that justified the seizure of royal power and impelled the revolutionaries onto a course of action in which the exercise of power superseded a more idealistic pursuit of political principle. Michael Fitzsimmons, by contrast, is more cautious than Hunt, seeing the Declaration of Rights as "a means to an end rather than an end in itself," a tactical effort by liberal deputies to resolve the stalemate in the National Assembly, and not in and of itself a revolutionary break with the past.[12]

In early debates, a number of deputies advocated the inclusion of a declaration of duties along with rights, but in the first week of August that idea was abandoned. The constitution committee presented a draft of the Declaration to the National Assembly on 26 August, and after further debate and some amendments it was adopted the following day and presented to the king. Louis XVI initially refused to sign it, doing so only after the women's march to Versailles on 5–6 October. The Declaration was revised in 1793, when the right of resistance to oppression was given prominent expression, and again in 1795, when that right was essentially removed and the ideal of liberty was given fuller expression than the

10 See A. Walicki, "Marx and Freedom," *New York Review of Books*, 24 November 1983, for a provocative discussion of these issues.

11 L. Hunt, *Inventing Human Rights*, 115–16.

12 M. Gauchet, *La Revolution des droits de l'homme*, 19–28, 107–10; M. Fitzsimmons, *The Night the Old Regime Ended: August 4, 1789, and the French Revolution* (University Park, Pennsylvania State University Press, 2003), 4–7.

ideal of equality. Unlike the several constitutions produced during the Revolution, however, the Declaration of the Rights of Man and Citizen endured, as it has through five separate French republics over the past two centuries.

As noted above, despite its language of universality, the Declaration of Rights did not initially embrace all French people. In regard to political rights, the deputies of the National Assembly went on to mark a distinction between *active* and *passive* citizens. The former, defined as males above the age of 25 who paid taxes equal to at least three days' wages, were granted the vote, while passive citizens were not. This property qualification, adopted on 22 December 1789 and enshrined in the constitution of 1791, was hotly debated at the time, with Maximilien Robespierre arguing that it contradicted the Declaration of the Rights of Man. The distinction between *active* and *passive* citizens would be dropped after 10 August 1792, when universal manhood suffrage was adopted and the voting age lowered to 21.

The National Assembly also initially excluded Jews, black African slaves, and women from the Declaration of Rights, and these omissions have generated impassioned debate over the years. At the time of the Revolution there were approximately 40,000 Jews in France, as well as some 100,000 Protestants. Protestants, who had been granted civil toleration by the edict of 1787, were granted full citizenship by the 24 December 1789 decree according equal political rights to non-Catholics and all professions (actors and domestic servants having been initially excluded as well). The issue of rights for Jews was tabled at this time, some deputies arguing that they represented more than a religious minority and were a separate group within France.

There were in fact two groups of Jews in France in 1789. The majority were Ashkenazim, in Alsace, who lived in separate communities (in part due to discrimination), spoke Yiddish, and followed traditional cultural practices. A smaller number of Sephardic Jews, perhaps as many as 3,000, lived in the southwest of France. These were the descendants of Spanish and Portuguese Jews who had fled persecution after 1492. They had more fully assimilated into French society, and some were prominent merchants in Bordeaux. Even as the National Assembly voted its decree of 24 December, granting political rights to religious minorities, the Jews of the southwest petitioned on their own behalf, and in January 1790 the Assembly accorded them full rights, but refused to extend those rights to the Ashkenazim or to the smaller groups of Jews in Paris and Marseille. Those groups continued to petition the Assembly, supported in their cause by deputies such as Abbé Grégoire and Adrien Duport, and in September 1791 all Jews were granted full civil and political rights.

Lynn Hunt sees this gradual extension of rights to French Jews in a positive light, arguing that the "implacable logic of rights" was the key to this process, as it would be to the eventual granting of rights to free blacks, followed by the abolition of slavery. Having asserted freedom of religion in the Declaration of Rights, and then explicitly recognized the rights of Protestants, it proved impossible to deny the rights of Jews indefinitely. The assertion of general principles, and the avoidance of specific language, was the genius of the document and what made it a living, expansive declaration. Ronald Schechter takes a more critical view, arguing that the decree of September 1791 placed conditions on Jews before they could exercise political rights – the legislation was explicit, it is true, that they were granted rights as individuals, not as a group – and that the Ashkenazim in particular continued to face active discrimination.[13]

Free coloreds and black slaves were similarly excluded from the Declaration of Rights in 1789. Both Abbé Raynal and the Comte de Buffon had drawn attention to the abuses of the slave trade in the decades leading up to the Revolution, and in 1788 a Society of the Friends of Blacks had formed in Paris, counting among its members Jacques-Pierre Brissot, Marie-Jean Condorcet, Lafayette, and Mirabeau. But the French economy depended heavily on the sugar trade from the Caribbean, and among French colonies none was more important than Saint-Domingue, where 30,000 white colonists controlled nearly 500,000 black slaves. Anticipating the implications of the Declaration of the Rights of Man and Citizen, a group of plantation owners and colonial traders formed the Massiac Club in 1789 to defend the institution of slavery, which obviously depended on the denial of human rights to black slaves.

In one important sense, the issue of human rights for blacks was fundamentally different than for Protestants or Jews. The total population of Jews and Protestants in France was very small, and each was a tiny minority in every community or region that they inhabited. While there were also very few blacks in France itself, the nearly half-million blacks in Saint-Domingue represented an overwhelming majority of the population, one whose slave labor was essential to the profits that made their way back from the Caribbean colonies to the Atlantic ports of Bordeaux and Nantes, and from there percolated throughout the French economy. Not all blacks on Saint-Domingue were enslaved – there was a population of

13 L. Hunt, *Inventing Human Rights*, 150–60; R. Schechter, *Obstinate Hebrews: Representations of Jews in France, 1715–1815* (Berkeley, University of California Press, 2003); and G. Kates, "Jews into Frenchmen: Nationality and Representation in Revolutionary France," in F. Fehér, ed., *The French Revolution and the Birth of Modernity* (Berkeley, University of California Press, 1990), 103–16.

free coloreds roughly equal to the white population (30,000), and a number of mulattoes as well. Under the terms of the *Code Noir*, which had governed the French slave trade since 1685, many of these free coloreds and mulattoes oversaw slave laborers on the plantations, some were property owners, and some even slave owners.

The situation was a complicated one, then, but almost immediately in 1789 the free coloreds and mulattoes of Saint-Domingue saw the implications for themselves of the debate about rights that was underway at Versailles. A delegation, led by Vincent Ogé, traveled to France in 1789 to petition the National Assembly for equal rights for free men of color. Ogé and those who supported his cause, such as Abbé Grégoire, argued that their status as property owners gave them a shared stake with white colonists in overseeing the slave economy, while planters and their supporters in the Massiac Club argued that to grant full rights to free coloreds and mulattoes would set a dangerous precedent and fan the flames for abolition of the slave trade and ultimately slavery. At the time, many abolitionists supported the moderate position of Ogé, and with the ranks of those supporting human rights for blacks being divided, in the end their cause failed. On 8 March 1790 the National Assembly voted to exclude the colonies from both the Declaration of Rights and the constitution, then being drafted.

Vincent Ogé, now fearing for his life in Paris, made his way undetected to London and from there returned incognito to Saint-Domingue. In the fall of 1790 he led a campaign among free coloreds in anticipation of the impending elections. Facing repression from white colonists, those efforts evolved into rebellion, which failed. Ogé was eventually captured, tried before a kangaroo court, and executed by being broken on the wheel. News of these events infuriated liberals in the National Assembly, who now sought a repeal of the legislation of March. They succeeded in securing full rights only for a minority of mulattoes, those born of both a free mother and father. Not until after the outbreak of a slave rebellion in 1791 would the Assembly grant rights to free coloreds, a gesture which did nothing to quell unrest in Saint-Domingue. By 1793 the island was in total upheaval, and only in February 1794 did the National Convention definitively abolish slavery throughout the French colonies and grant human rights to blacks, legislation that Napoleon would later reverse.[14]

Clearly, the deputies of the National Assembly did not act out of altruism in reaching their eventual decision to extend human rights to blacks, nor

---

14 S. M. Singham, "Betwixt Cattle and Men: Jews, Blacks, and Women, and the Declaration of the Rights of Man," in D. Van Kley, *The French Idea of Freedom*, 114–53; L. Hunt, *Inventing Human Rights*, 160–67; L. Dubois, *Avengers of the New World* (Cambridge, MA, Harvard University Press, 2004).

would that gesture prove to be enduring. Their initial reluctance to include free coloreds in the Declaration of Rights was guided by economic self-interest, and only when full-scale rebellion threatened to destroy completely the sugar plantations of Saint-Domingue did a new assembly of deputies see their way clear to abolishing slavery temporarily. Not until after the 1848 revolution would a French government do so definitively. The "implacable logic of rights," then, worked slowly and circuitously for blacks. It would take even longer for women to be accorded full rights in France.

It is striking that Condorcet, the most ardent advocate of full citizenship rights for women, published a pamphlet calling for the abolition of slavery as early as 1781 but did not speak publicly on the issue of women's rights until 1790. As Lynn Hunt puts it, "Women simply did not constitute a clearly separate and distinguishable *political* category before the Revolution."[15] That changed quickly after 1789, however. In 1790 Condorcet published *On the Admission of Women to the Rights of Citizenship*, and in September 1791 Olympe de Gouges published her *Déclaration des droits de la femme et de la citoyenne*, which she addressed to Queen Marie-Antoinette. While women's rights became a subject of public debate, relatively little progress was made during the Revolution. Divorce was legalized in 1792 (and women outnumbered men in initiating divorce during its brief period of legalization), and under the National Convention laws were passed that allowed women to inherit property. These gains were rolled back under the Directory and then Napoleon, who had little sympathy for the idea of women's rights. It was not until after World War II that French women would gain full citizenship rights.

Shanti Singham has offered an interesting analysis of the different rhetorical strategies employed by de Gouges and Condorcet in arguing on behalf of women's rights during the Revolution. At the heart of de Gouges' pamphlet was a Declaration of the Rights of Woman that exactly paralleled the Declaration of the Rights of Man, asserting women's claim to all of the rights enjoyed by men. But whereas Condorcet had claimed those rights, and specifically women's right to vote, by arguing that women's intellects were the same as those of men, de Gouges "stressed the differences between women and men and argued that it was precisely the superior feminine attributes that entitled women to political and social consideration."[16] Condorcet addressed male fears about female

---

15 L. Hunt, *Inventing Human Rights*, 169.

16 S. M. Singham, "Betwixt Cattle and Men," 141. See also J. W. Scott, "The Uses of Imagination: Olympe de Gouges in the French Revolution," in J. W. Scott, *Only Paradoxes to Offer: French Feminists and the Rights of Man* (Cambridge, MA, Harvard University Press, 1996), 19–56.

aspirations for political dominance while de Gouges, it might be argued, fed those fears by decrying male tyranny over women in the domestic sphere. Neither argument, of course, persuaded many readers – there was no serious discussion of granting women the vote in any revolutionary assembly.

This is not to say that women were not politically active during the Revolution. We have already noted the importance of women in the march to Versailles during the October Days of 1789. In March 1791 Pauline Léon presented a petition before the Constituent Assembly, signed by more than 300 Parisian women, demanding the right to bear arms so that women might join men in the defense of the nation. In support of her appeal she made explicit reference to the Declaration of the Rights of Man. Several months later Etta Palm d'Aelders addressed the same assembly to demand equality both in laws regulating marriage and in education. Manon Roland opposed women's suffrage on the specific grounds that their education was inadequate to the responsible exercise of citizenship. Women did, however, continue regularly to petition the National Assembly, attended and often participated in the meetings of men's political clubs, and formed clubs of their own in many French towns and cities, most notably the Society of Revolutionary Republican Women in Paris, co-founded in 1793 by Pauline Léon and Claire Lacombe. Interestingly, in a pattern that would be repeated in the nineteenth and twentieth centuries, the activism of *sans-culotte* women increased as the French nation went to war.[17]

The issue of women's rights in the French Revolution has generated considerable debate over the past two decades. Lynn Hunt takes a generally positive view, asserting that, given the historical context, "it is more surprising that women's rights were even discussed in the public arena than that women ultimately did not gain them." Joan Landes puts forth a more negative perspective, arguing that the revolutionaries by and large adopted the misogynistic attitudes of Jean-Jacques Rousseau and that the Revolution generally brought a closing off of public space for women. Olwen Hufton might be said to occupy a middle position, stressing the "limits of citizenship" for women during this period. Dominique Godineau, supporting Hunt, observes that while women claimed, or achieved, few rights during the Revolution, "they nonetheless demonstrated citizenship ..." and "invested the political space that was opened." Godineau

---

17 S. M. Singham, "Betwixt Cattle and Men," 139–50. See also D. G. Levy, H. B. Applewhite, and M. D. Johnson, *Women in Revolutionary Paris, 1789–1795* (Urbana, University of Illinois Press, 1979), 72–77, for the full text, in translation, of the Léon and d'Aelders petitions.

also makes clear that the Declaration of the Rights of Man provided a framework within which women, and some men, would continue to advocate for full rights for women throughout the revolutionary decade.[18]

The Abolition of Feudalism

In the midst of their deliberations on human rights, the deputies of the National Assembly took a week's break to abolish feudalism. It was an extraodinary week of debate and legislation, so powerful in its emotion and so symbolically potent that it has come to be known simply as the Night of 4 August, a reference to the late-night session of the Assembly that got things started. The events of that evening are fairly straightforward. Alarmed by the escalation of peasant unrest in the provinces in late July, a group of liberal noblemen and deputies of the commons (the term "Third Estate" having by then been discarded) gathered in the Breton club and made plans for a late-night session, one from which many conservative deputies would most likely be absent. The plan called for the Duc d'Aiguillon, among the largest landowners in France, to begin the session by stepping forward to offer the renunciation of his seigneurial rights in exchange for long-term monetary compensation. In the event, the first to speak was the Viscomte Louis-Marie Noailles, a nearly propertyless nobleman, but the brother-in-law of Lafayette, which presumably counted for something. Aiguillon followed him at the rostrum, and in addition to seigneurial rights called for the abolition of all forms of privilege. Inspired or abashed by these gestures, a parade of nobles and clergy made their way to the dais to add their own pledges of self-sacrifice: seigneurial dues, venal offices, seigneurial courts, the tithe, all came up for renunciation in a welter of sometimes vague and confusing pronouncements. When the session finally adjourned at two in the morning, the remnants of the feudal regime lay in shambles.

Or so it seemed. To be accurate, feudalism properly speaking survived only in the Franche-Comté and parts of Burgundy, and even there mainly in the institution of *mainmorte*, according to which if a peasant died

---

18 J. B. Landes, *Women and the Public Sphere in the Age of the French Revolution* (Ithaca, Cornell University Press, 1988); O. H. Hufton, *Women and the Limits of Citizenship in the French Revolution* (Toronto, University of Toronto Press, 1992); D. Godineau, *the Women of Paris and their French Revolution* (Berkeley, University of California Press, 1998), especially 268–91 (the passages quoted are from her Conclusion, 368); and see L. Hunt, "Male Virtue and Republican Motherhood," in K. M. Baker, ed., *The Terror* (Oxford, Pergamon Press, 1994), 195–208, for a brief discussion of the historiographical debates and an extension of her discussion of the issue of universal rights and women up into the period of the Terror.

without a male heir in residence, the land held by the peasant would revert to the feudal lord. A number of seigneurial dues and duties did survive, however (the requirement that peasants bake their bread in the seigneur's ovens, for example, or that they press their grapes in his winepress, giving a portion of each to him), and these were greatly resented by the peasantry. But it was difficult to convert the pronouncements of the Night of 4 August into legislative decrees. Some deputies regretted their rash statements in the light of day, and some members of the clergy, in particular, would argue that the tithes could not be abolished without approval of a church assembly. It took a full week to sort out exactly what had transpired on the Night of 4 August, to arrive at some semblance of consensus once the full Assembly had reconvened, and to move from principled declarations of self-sacrifice to tangible legislation. Not until 13 August was a decree finally presented to Louis XVI, who for some months refused to sign it, averring that he would not countenance the despoiling of his clergy and his nobility.

Historical debate about the abolition of feudalism has revolved around two issues: the session of 4 August itself – that is, exactly what happened that night and what were the motivations of those who stepped forward to renounce various forms of privilege – and the significance (or otherwise) of the sacrifice of seigneurial rights, given the insistence on redemption payments for some of those rights. Nearly twenty years ago Colin Jones bemoaned in these terms the shifting treatment of the Night of 4 August in the context of the challenge to the traditional social interpretation of the Revolution: "One of the key moments in the social transformation of France, the zenith of peasant influence on the course of events, thus merely becomes a vacuous chapter in group psychology, with the assembly acting as if hermetically sealed from outside social influences."[19]

Two important works have appeared since Jones' stirring broadside against the emerging revisionist interpretation of the French Revolution, the first by John Markoff and the second by Michael Fitzsimmons.[20]

19 C. Jones, "Bourgeois Revolution Revivified: 1789 and Social Change," in C. Lucas, ed., *Rewriting the French Revolution* (Oxford, Clarendon Press, 1991). Jones' references are to S. Schama, *Citizens: A Chronicle of the French Revolution* (New York, Viking, 1989), 439; and M. Fitzsimmons, *The Parisian Order of Barristers and the French Revolution* (Cambridge, MA, Harvard University Press, 1987), 41–42.

20 J. Markoff, *The Abolition of Feudalism: Peasants, Lords, and Legislators in the French Revolution* (University Park, PA, Pennsylvania State University Press, 1996); M. P. Fitzsimmons, *The Night the Old Regime Ended: August 4, 1789 and the French Revolution* (University Park, PA, Pennsylvania State University Press, 2003). See also P. Kessel, *La Nuit du 4 août 1789* (Paris, Arthaud, 1969), for a more detailed account of the actual session of that night than either Fitzsimmons or Markoff provides.

Fitzsimmons does not entirely neglect the peasant unrest of late July – he notes, for example, that the deputies met "in an atmosphere of fear and tension," adding later that the deliberations took place "against a backdrop of reports of disorder and chateau burnings . . . ."[21] He emphasizes, however, the extraordinary mood of generosity and disinterestedness that swept over the deputies present that night, and as the title of his book suggests, he sees the Night of 4 August as having been singularly important: "The meeting of the night of August 4, with its destruction of privilege, offered a new ideal of the polity based on freedom, equality and fraternity under the benevolent auspices of the nation." In Fitzsimmons' view, "the degree to which the meeting of the night of August 4 enabled the National Assembly to forge a sense of identity and purpose has generally been overlooked." Out of that evening emerged a "pact of association" or a "functional consensus" that endured, although not without stress, throughout the tenure of the Constituent Assembly.[22]

Both Fitzsimmons and Markoff draw heavily on the deputies' own recollections of the Night of 4 August, but Markoff arrives at a strikingly different interpretation: "the common element in these tales in letters, journals, and memoirs of those who sat in the National Assembly is the sense of menace that hung over them in personal ways – as property holders, as residents of particular locales, as holders of particular positions on public issues. The great work of the Constituent Assembly and their personal fortune, their political future, and their physical security were, for the moment, inseparable and what made them inseparable was the mobilization of ordinary people." Far more than a "backdrop" of reports of château burnings, Markoff argues, what the deputies were hearing in the daily reports of news from back home was "mounting evidence of a country in chaos."[23]

The evidence presented by Markoff also calls into question the remarkable consensus, or "purity of agreement," within the National Assembly that Fitzsimmons insists upon. We learn from Markoff, for example, of the Duc du Châtelet, who, after hearing the Bishop of Chartres propose the abolition of noble hunting rights, responded by countering with a proposal for an end to ecclesiastical payments: " 'So, he takes away our hunting; I'm going to take away his tithes,' the duke is said to have commented . . . ."[24] As to motivation, Markoff suggests that "conservatives could vote for such a plan with the rationale that it could be rendered

21 M. Fitzsimmons, *The Night the Old Regime Ended*, 14, 63.
22 Ibid., 14–23.
23 J. Markoff, *The Abolition of Feudalism*, 435, 438.
24 Ibid., 429, footnote 5.

meaningless once rural insurrection died down." Or from a slightly less cynical perspective, "by terminating the event with the pledge of a memorial to a king who had nothing to do with it, the deputies themselves turned the event into a myth whose interpretation could be contested even before the final decree of August 11 was accomplished."[25]

Fitzsimmons sees the Night of 4 August as momentous because the sacrifices pledged that night effectively undermined the entire edifice of privilege that underpinned the structure of the Old Regime monarchy and the church, and provided a "functional consensus," in his view, for the important work on the constitution that occupied the Constituent Assembly for the final two years of its existence. Within a year, indeed, noble privilege and noble status would be entirely abolished, and the organization of the Catholic Church would be altered by the Civil Constitution of the Clergy, approved by the National Assembly on 12 July 1790, and signed into law by Louis XVI in December. These were enormously significant developments, to be further discussed in the next chapter. But the peasants of France were much less concerned with honorific privilege or abstract constitutional issues than they were with the fiscal burdens that they bore in the form of seigneurial dues and church tithes, and these did not immediately disappear with the much celebrated "abolition of feudalism" on the Night of 4 August.

It was to be nearly four years until the National Convention definitively abolished all aspects of the seigneurial system and church tithes. As Markoff observes, waves of rural insurrection preceded each period of legislative progress on the matter – in March 1790 and August 1792 – and deputies in Paris were even more likely to act if that rural unrest was accompanied by urban insurrection, particularly in Paris. In the summer of 1793 the *sans-culottes* of Paris forced the proscription of the Girondin leaders from the National Convention, and the country faced near civil war due to the Vendée rebellion in the west and the federalist revolt of four major provincial cities. To ensure that other rural areas did not join those revolts, the National Convention abandoned the idea of indemnity payments, finally encoding in law what the peasantry had by and large imposed in practice since 1789 by simply refusing to make those payments.[26]

---

25 Ibid., 432, 459.

26 Ibid. See pages 452–54 and 510–11 for tables and discussion summarizing the chronology of anti-seigneurial legislation and the pattern of rural unrest and its relation to that legislation.

Conclusion

One might be tempted to conclude this discussion on a somewhat sour note. The National Assembly appears to have adopted in August 1789 a Declaration of the Rights of Man and Citizen that the deputies claimed to be universal, but which did not initially apply to Jews, people of color, or women. Similarly, they pronounced with much fanfare the abolition of a feudal system, the most onerous features of which had long since ceased to exist in most of the country, and only on condition that the peasants would indemnify their seigneurial lords for the dues and rights that they had so generously sacrificed. Must we conclude that the actions of the deputies to the National Assembly simply did not match their rhetoric? Or might it be more reasonable to say that the principles of the deputies were molded, and constrained, by the social context in which they lived, by the culture of the Old Regime, and by their own self-interest?

Michael Fitzsimmons is certainly right to emphasize the generosity of spirit that animated the deputies on the memorable Night of 4 August. The central commitment to the abolition of privilege – even if its implications were not fully understood by all present (and would be resisted by some in the weeks and months ahead) – had far-reaching and enduring consequences. While it is clear that the feudal regime had been in the process of gradual dismantlement for some time – Louis XVI had abolished serfdom on royal lands in 1779 – it is also the case that some aspects of it were easier to let go than others. In parts of the country, at least, seigneurial lords and their agents were more rigorously enforcing the collection of seigneurial dues in the final decades of the Old Regime, and only one month before the deputies declared the "abolition of the feudal regime," three poachers were hanged for hunting in the king's game preserve near Versailles.[27] For peasants living on the edge of subsistence, constitutional principles and the right to private property were of far less consequence than was the source of their next decent meal.

The significance of the Night of 4 August appears greater, perhaps, if we cast our gaze beyond France. Serfdom would survive in Russia until 1861, as it would in much of eastern Europe and in Germany east of the Elbe until the early twentieth century. Privilege played a significant role in the politics of the German, Austrian, and Russian empires until after World War I. Napoleonic regimes weakened those institutions in much of Europe

27 Ibid., 439; P. Jones, *Liberty and Locality in Revolutionary France: Six Villages Compared, 1760–1820* (Cambridge, Cambridge University Press, 2003), 87.

between 1799 and 1815, but they disappeared only after the ravages of war and civil war. That it took peasant resistance, even uprisings, to force French deputies to match their idealistic rhetoric with meaningful legislation is hardly surprising, then. We should perhaps be more surprised that that peasant resistance was not simply met by repression.

Similarly, while we have remarked upon the limitations to the supposedly "universal" human rights asserted by the National Assembly in August 1789, one cannot deny that the Declaration of the Rights of Man and Citizen has continued to resonate around the world up to the present day. No other document more succinctly captures the principles of the French revolutionaries, and along with the slogan "Liberty, Equality, Fraternity," they have inspired revolutionaries throughout the nineteenth and twentieth centuries. As Lynn Hunt has observed, the ideals proclaimed in 1789 served as the foundation for the Universal Declaration of Human Rights proclaimed by the United Nations in 1948.[28]

To declare human rights is not to achieve them, however, and we need not look far to find evidence of that in today's world. Slavery, long since abolished, continues to operate in the underground economy, even in the world's most "advanced" or "civilized" nations, because it serves the economic interests of some, who clearly do not regard it as self-evident that all people have been created free or equal. Children are particularly subject to enslavement in the twenty-first century, but while no one would have thought in the eighteenth century to assert their inalienable rights, perhaps we should take heart in regard to the "implacable logic of human rights," that a Declaration of the Rights of the World's Children appeared at the end of the twentieth century.[29]

We are also daily reminded that the rights so momentously declared, and fought for, at the end of the eighteenth century are not always cherished, or well understood, even in the countries of their birth. Readers of the *New York Times* were reminded in the week following the death of hotel magnate Leona Helmsley in August 2007 that she had once famously asserted, at the time of her trial for tax fraud, that "only little people pay taxes." The limits to Helmsley's empathy for others were further illustrated by her last will and testament, in which she left

---

28 L. Hunt, *Inventing Human Rights*, 200–209.

29 http://www.wcci.org/childrens_rights/form.html. This is the website for World Centers of Compassion for Children International, founded in 1997 by Betty Williams, recipient in 1976 of the Nobel Peace Prize for her work on behalf of children, and for peace, in Northern Ireland. It should also be noted that the United Nations asserted in 1948 that its Declaration of Rights would benefit the children of the world.

$12 million to her dog. Just weeks later, former U.S. Senator Fred Thompson made the first public appearance in his campaign for the presidency, at which he informed the voters of Iowa of the need to remember that "we still get our basic rights from God, not government," a sentiment that did not occur either to the deputies of the French National Assembly in writing the Declaration of the Rights of Man and Citizen, nor to Thomas Jefferson and the other drafters of the Declaration of Independence.[30]

30 See the *New York Times*, 24–29 August 2007 for stories on Leona Helmsley, and 7 September 2007 for the story on Fred Thompson's campaign stop in Des Moines, Iowa.

4

Constitutional Monarchy

From October 1789, when Louis XVI agreed to sanction the Declaration of the Rights of Man and Citizen and the decrees emanating from the Night of 4 August, to August 1792 France was effectively a constitutional monarchy, although the Constituent Assembly would not finish its work on the constitution until September 1791. The central question in this period, and in the historiography that has been written about it, is, "Could a constitutional monarchy have survived in France?" Could a king who had once ruled by divine right accept his new status as a king who ruled in the name of the law, a law to which he would now also be subject, just as all other citizens of the realm? Given the king's attempted flight across the border in June 1791, even before the National Assembly had completed the constitution, and the collapse of the monarchy in the face of armed insurrection little more than one year later, the logical answer to those questions would appear to be No. If that is the case, then where does responsibility lie for the failure of the constitutional monarchy? Did the king and queen, and their closest allies at court, simply refuse to work in good faith within the new constitutional structure? Or did the more radical deputies within the National Assembly succeed in creating a constitutional regime so limiting of royal power and prerogative that no king could have willingly accepted its constraints?

We will begin this chapter with a discussion of that central question, which can also be understood in terms of the struggle between executive and legislative power – an enduring struggle, some might argue, in any parliamentary form of government. There has been a spirited historical debate about this issue in the context of the French Revolution. But we will also explore in this chapter a set of debates or tensions *within* this period of the Revolution, some of which have generated debate among historians, but not all. In addition to the constitution, which can hardly be said to have been an enduring legacy of the Constituent Assembly, since it was rendered invalid within a year of its adjournment, there were two legislative initiatives completed in 1790 that would have a longstanding impact on the history of France. The first of these was, quite literally, the redrawing of the map. On the eve of the Revolution, the administrative and judicial boundaries of the kingdom were confusing and overlapping, very much reflective of the system of privilege that had now been swept away. The deputies quickly set about the business of creating a new administrative map for the nation, one that would be rational in its design and serve the goals of efficient administration and political mobilization: in sum, a quintessential Enlightenment project. The map that they drew remains the map of France today, with only slight modifications reflecting geographic expansion and population growth, and as such stands as one of the most enduring achievements of the Constituent Assembly. But the process of creating new boundaries also revealed local tensions and rivalries, both old and new, some of which flared into open conflict during the early years of the Revolution and contributed to the fragility of the new regime.

A second major legislative initiative undertaken by the Constituent Assembly was the Civil Constitution of the Clergy, presented to the king in July 1790. The logic of this was dictated by both the abolition of privilege and the decision in November 1789 to convert church property into *biens nationaux*, to be sold at auction in order to pay off the national debt. Given the confiscation of church lands, both bishops and priests were to be salaried employees of the state, and an accompanying administrative reorganization of the church seemed to the deputies a self-evidently good idea. Few anticipated the deep divisions that this reform, and the subsequently mandated Civil Oath of the Clergy, would sow not only within the clergy but throughout the social fabric of the entire country. No other single issue generated as much resentment toward the revolutionary government as did this reform of the Catholic Church of France.

Many historians have characterized 1790 as a peaceful, even harmonious, year – there were no insurrections in Paris, no major political crises. As discussed in Chapter Three, Michael Fitzsimmons suggests that a kind of sublime unity prevailed in the National Assembly in the weeks and months following the Night of 4 August. If such was the case, our attention is then drawn to the following years for an explanation of why the king fled to Varennes in June 1791 and the Parisian crowd rose up to topple the monarchy a year later. Other historians, however, point to underlying divisions and tensions already evident in 1790: clashes between Protestants and Catholics in some towns and regions; opposition between the emerging network of Jacobin clubs and a smaller number of Monarchist clubs and other popular societies; tensions within the military, and between the old royal regiments and new National Guards; and organized factions within the National Assembly that contributed to the political polarization of 1791–92. Was 1790 a year of harmony and consensus, exemplified by the Festival of Federation on 14 July, or simply the calm before the storm?

Historians of the Revolution routinely identify a few key dates that carry special significance or symbolic power. We have already discussed 14 July 1789 and 4 August 1789. 10 August 1792, 9 Thermidor II (27 July 1794), and 18 Brumaire VIII (9 November 1799) are also nearly universally recognized as turning points or dates of symbolic importance. Were there key turning points in the short history of the constitutional monarchy? Those who interpret the Revolution principally in terms of political ideology, or who emphasize the primacy of discourse, would say no, that the fate of the king was clear as early as 1789. Others, more inclined to acknowledge historical contingency as a causal variable, would argue that it is worth looking for those moments in these years when the political winds may have shifted decisively. Some have argued that 5 October was such a moment, when the king and his family were forced to leave the safe haven of Versailles and move themselves, and the government, to Paris. Others might point to July or November 1790, when the Civil Constitution of the Clergy was first presented and then finally signed by Louis XVI, as the crucial dates that marked the sowing of an irreconcilable division within French society. Quite recently, Timothy Tackett has argued that 21 June 1791 – the flight of the king to Varennes – was a crucial turning point, unleashing fears, suspicions, and divisions that ultimately led the revolutionaries to the Terror. A case can be made for the fundamental importance of each of these dates, or for none of them, and we will explore that debate before turning, in conclusion, to consider the fall of the monarchy in August 1792.

The Debate over Royal Power

On 27 August 1789, one day after completing the Declaration of the Rights of Man and Citizen, the National Assembly turned to the matter of the constitution. Two issues immediately commanded their attention: the royal veto and the structure of the legislative branch. Lally-Tollendal, reporting for the Committee of the Constitution, advocated an absolute veto and a bicameral legislature. Both proposals were greeted by substantial opposition. Opponents of a royal veto pointed out that to grant the king such power would raise the possibility that he would veto the Declaration of Rights and the decrees of 11 August, thereby undoing all their work of the previous weeks and once again creating a political stalemate. Those who advocated an absolute royal veto argued that only in this way would the authority of the monarch be preserved in the new constitutional system. Debate over a unicameral versus bicameral legislature was similarly divided. Advocates of the latter argued that the creation of an upper house would provide an opportunity for reflection on legislation initiated by a lower house. Opponents feared that such an upper house, rather than providing judicious restraint, would instead revive the system of privilege so recently abolished and give the aristocracy a new institutional base of power. Some saw this as a reversion to the organizational principle of the Estates General, while others pointed to the British House of Lords as an example of what they were determined to avoid. Those in favor of a unicameral legislature argued that only in this form could the Rousseauean "general will" be achieved, that a two-chamber legislature would by definition fragment the will of the people. For supporters of the monarchy (whether absolute or constitutional), the central question was where did the king figure into that formulation and/or expression of the national will.

After two weeks of debate, the Constituent Assembly opted for a unicameral legislature and compromised on the issue of the royal veto, granting the king a "suspensive veto" by which he could suspend legislation for a period of two elected legislatures, what eventually turned out to be a maximum of six years. Those on the left felt that this granted excessive power to the king (and under the Legislative Assembly Louis XVI would indeed be criticized for exercising his veto too frequently), while those on the right (and Louis himself) felt that the king had been effectively stripped of executive power.

François Furet has argued that "the constitutional framework conceived by the Constitutent Assembly laid the foundations for what one might call a 'parliamentary absolutism' that was unlikely to allow for divergent opinions or conflicting interests." He points to the Assembly's assertion, in the Declaration of the Rights of Man and Citizen, that sovereignty was indivisible and resided in the nation (the Declaration made no mention of the king, in fact), being careful to observe that this "does not mean that the Constituent Assembly deliberately paved the way for the Terror, only that it failed to perceive that its conceptions might some day be used as means to establish a democratic despotism."[1] Keith

---

1 F. Furet, "A Commentary," *French Historical Studies* 16 (Fall 1990), 795. Furet has developed this position in many different venues, but this essay has the double virtue of being a succinct expression of his argument, and of being accompanied by commentaries by

Baker, sharing Furet's emphasis on ideology and discourse as the driving force of the Revolution, goes one step further: "In the most general terms, [the Constituent Assembly] was opting for the language of political will, rather than of social reason; of unity, rather than of difference; of civic virtue, rather than of commerce; of absolute sovereignty, rather than of government limited by the rights of man – which is to say that, in the long run, it was opting for the Terror."[2]

There is obviously a larger issue here than simply the nature of royal power in the new constitutional regime, an issue to be discussed at some length in Chapters Six and Nine. Many historians, myself included, have challenged the notion that the Terror was implicit, whether intentionally or not, in the decisions to adopt only a suspensive veto and a unicameral legislative body. There is disagreement, too, however, on the narrower question of the nature of the constitutional monarchy as defined by the constitution of 1791. Michael Fitzsimmons, for example, offers a much more positive assessment in regard to these two key elements, and lays more blame on Louis XVI for the eventual demise of the monarchy. He argues that "the propelling force of the Revolution, in its critical formative stage from 1789 to 1791, was the National Assembly. It gave the Revolution definition as it imparted new ideals through the creation of institutions that completely reshaped the nation." Fitzsimmons views that process as a collaborative one, between the Assembly and the nation, stressing that the National Assembly sought to establish the rule of law by making the constitution independent of the person of the king. If anything, he concludes, the suspensive veto gave Louis *too much* power rather than too little. As for the failure of the constitution of 1791, Fitzsimmons points to the self-denying ordinance, by which the deputies prohibited their own re-election to the Legislative Assembly, and the declaration of war in 1792, which we will consider in the next chapter.[3]

Claude Langlois, David Bien, and Donald Sutherland, in an exchange that took place at the December 1989 annual meeting of the American Historical Association.

2 K. M. Baker, *Inventing the French Revolution* (Cambridge, Cambridge University Press, 1990), 305.

3 M. P. Fitzsimmons, *The Remaking of France: The National Assembly and the Constitution of 1791* (Cambridge, Cambridge University Press, 1994), 253–56. As in his *The Night the Old Regime Ended: August 4, 1789, and the French Revolution* (University Park, Pennsylvania State University Press, 2003), Fitzsimmons stresses the good will among the deputies and the "pact of association" that emerged out of the Night of 4 August and guided the Constituent Assembly in its work. With regard to the "self-denying ordinance," as it was called, see B. Shapiro, "Self-Sacrifice, Self-Interest, or Self-Defense?: The Constituent Assembly and the 'Self-Denying Ordinance' of May 1791," *French Historical Studies* 25 (Fall 2002), 625–56.

The Redrawing of the Map of France

While the constitution of 1791 proved to be an ephemeral document, the new map of France created by the deputies of the Constituent Assembly has been much more enduring. Its creation may be the best example of the collaborative process between nation and Assembly that Fitzsimmons identifies as the hallmark of this period, for once it became known that the deputies had embarked on this project they were flooded by petitions and deputations from their constituents back home. As with so much else undertaken by the Constituent Assembly, the drawing of a new map represented an assault on privilege, for the old provincial boundaries were laden with tradition. The *pays d'état*, for example, more recently annexed to the kingdom in most cases, enjoyed tax exemptions and a measure of political autonomy that the older *pays d'élection* were denied. The new map was to be a logically conceived construction, with new administrative and judicial boundaries to be drawn up on a consistent and rational basis.

The drawing of a map would seem, at first glance, to be a mundane task, but as Ted Margadant has clearly shown, it was a process that generated a number of spirited local rivalries and one that proved integral to the revolutionary project in surprising ways.[4] The same committee that drafted the constitution took responsibility for this task, and among the deputies most actively engaged in the work we find some who had also figured prominently in more purely political debates, men such as Sieyès, Duport, Bergasse, and Mounier. The ideal of equality, central to the drafting of the Declaration of the Rights of Man, was also an ideal to be incorporated into the map, but it was not immediately obvious what this should mean: should the new *départements*, as they came to be called, be equal in size or equal in population? If the former, as was ultimately decided, how large should they be? And if the departments were to vary in population, how would their representation in national assemblies be determined?

Among the goals of the deputies was to create departments that would be effective and efficient administrative units, play a constructive role in the political mobilization of the nation, and also contribute to economic development. Most agreed that they should not be too large, so that the

4 T. Margadant, *Urban Rivalries in the French Revolution* (Princeton, Princeton University Press, 1992). My discussion in this section is drawn principally from this work, but see also the work of French geographer M.-V. Ozouf-Marignier, *La Formation des départements* (Paris, Editions EHESS, 1989).

services provided by local administrative and judicial bodies would be as accessible as possible to the people. Just as with the advent of the railroad a half-century later, local elites quickly realized that the designation of departmental and district *chefs-lieux*, where administrative and judicial offices would be located, would also have economic implications for those towns. Delegations traveled to Versailles to plead their case before the deputies, and petitioners denounced the "aristocratic despotism" of provincial capitals in the competition that ensued. Some argued that small towns should be favored in the distribution of district seats and judicial tribunals.

The rivalries that emerged in this process sometimes proved to be quite bitter, as between Aix-en-Provence, which was named *chef-lieu* of the Bouches-du-Rhône, and Marseille, unjustly denied in the view of its ardent revolutionaries. The Marseillais would eventually wrest that honor away from Aix, a bastion of aristocratic privilege and reactionary politics. In the north, Rouen and Le Havre were persistent rivals in the Seine-Inférieure, although in that instance the old provincial capital of Rouen managed to preserve its status as *chef-lieu* despite its reputation for royalist sympathies.

The desire of the deputies to stimulate political engagement through the drawing of departmental boundaries had unanticipated consequences in other regards as well. The inhabitants of each department elected a departmental council, charged with overseeing the administration of the department, preserving public order, collecting taxes, etc. But in the tumult of the Revolution, departmental councils often came together to express themselves on political issues, culminating in the summer of 1793 in the federalist revolt, during which a number of departments declared themselves in opposition to the purge of Girondin deputies and refused to recognize the decrees of the National Convention. In the wake of that rebellion, the national government made it very clear that departmental administrations exercised only an administrative function and had no legitimate political role to play.

Despite the commitment to equality that the deputies pledged in drawing the map, it proved impossible to avert all inequities. On 20 October 1789 the Constituent Assembly voted to create two classes of citizens, active and passive. Active citizens, those who paid taxes equivalent to three days' wages, were eligible to vote in primary assemblies (to be eligible to be elected the tax requirement was roughly ten times more). All women were classified as passive citizens, as were domestic servants and actors. This distinction was the focus of heated debate, with Maximilien Robespierre taking a leading role among those who opposed it, but it stood as law until August 1792. Its application varied somewhat across the country, however, since departmental administrations set the standard for the tax requirement: three days' wages ranged from as low as 15 *sous* to as high as 3 *livres* (a *livre* equalling 20 *sous*). The percentage of citizens classified as active thus varied from department to department, and from city to city. Generally speaking, roughly 30 percent of the citizenry in cities tended to be eligible to vote, whereas in the countryside the rate sometimes approached 100 percent.[5] While we tend to think of the Revolution as principally an urban affair, this is one area in which we might argue that rural people were favored.

The new tax system was similarly uneven. The inequality of taxation under the Old Regime, rooted as it was in the system of privilege, had of course been one of the most common complaints in the *cahiers de doléances*. As early as September 1789 the Constituent Assembly decreed that all future taxes would be equally applied, with no distinction for either person or place. The Assembly created two new taxes in late 1790 and early 1791, and to soften the fiscal blow (at least psychologically) they labeled them *contributions* rather than *impôts*, one to be levied on land and the other on moveable property. In practice, however, it was difficult to achieve equality in these new taxes. The Assembly assigned quotas to each department, based roughly on the taxes collected in the Old Regime provinces of which those departments had been a part, leaving it to departmental administrations to levy individual taxes. Within departments, then, there might be rough equality in tax rates, but two individuals in different departments who owned comparable parcels of land might well pay substantially different taxes. In this instance, as in may others, the ideals of the revolutionaries ran up against the necessity of collecting adequate revenues to cover government expenses, a necessity that was rarely met through the early years of the Revolution.

In his book studying the creation of departments, Margadant is sensitive to the importance of rhetoric, observing that "the abolition of the old regime confronted townspeople with a unique moment, when discourse seemed more powerful than institutions."[6] He parts company with Furet and Baker, however, in insisting that discourse was not an independent agent, that rhetoric must be firmly situated both in its social context and amidst the parochial interests out of which it flowed. The new map of France was not crafted only in the halls of the Constituent Assembly – provincial Frenchmen had their say as well. Margadant also engages Alexis de Tocqueville's famous argument that the Revolution continued the centralizing tendencies of the Old Regime monarchy, which had stifled

---

5 M. Biard and P. Dupuy, *La Révolution française: dynamiques, influences, débats, 1787–1804* (Paris, Armand Colin, 2005), 63.

6 T. Margadant, *Urban Rivalries*, 143.

political liberty in France. In the process of debating new boundaries, Margadant insists, "political liberty fostered a veritable explosion of civic initiative in provincial towns," building upon, and to some degree institutionalizing, the political mobilization unleashed by the convocation of the Estates General and the drafting of grievance lists.[7]

The Civil Constitution of the Clergy

The Declaration of the Rights of Man and Citizen asserted, in Point 10, that "No one should be disturbed for his opinions, even in religion, provided that their manifestation does not trouble public order as established by law." This guarantee of religious freedom was much debated in the Constituent Assembly, as many of the clergy (who constituted, it will be remembered, roughly 25 percent of the deputies) felt that Catholicism should retain its status as the official church of France. In early November 1789 the deputies further complicated the position of the Catholic Church by voting to confiscate church property, estimated to be as much as 10 percent of total landholdings in France, and place it at the disposal of the nation. Those properties, the *biens nationaux*, would then be sold at auction in exchange for the *assignats* (paper currency) that the government had issued to creditors of the state, thereby liquidating the national debt.

This solution to the problem of the national debt, so compelling in its simple logic, proved problematical on several counts. The *assignats*, although never intended to circulate, soon did, and speculation led within a year to a 25 percent depreciation in their face value. Inflation thus replaced national bankruptcy as a pressing economic problem. Deprived of its income-generating lands, the church was confronted with the problem of supporting the clergy and other clerical officials. The Constituent Assembly addressed that problem in the Civil Constitution of the Clergy, adopted on 12 July 1790 and presented to the king for his signature. By this legislation, both bishops and priests were made salaried employees of the state – the poorest of the parish priests would now be relatively better off, and no bishop would live as lavishly as some had under the Old Regime. The number of bishops was reduced from 136 to 83, one per department, and in some towns and cities the number of parishes was reduced as well.

The Civil Oath of the Clergy was the most controversial element of the Civil Constitution of the Clergy, and the most divisive. It seemed logical to the deputies that the clergy, who like themselves would now be salaried

---

7 Ibid., 442.

officials of the state, should swear the same oath as other public officials, pledging "fidelity to the nation, the law, the king and the constitution." For many clergy, however, this oath posed a crisis of conscience, for it presented the possibility that their first loyalty to God might come into conflict with a sworn loyalty to a temporal authority. It posed a crisis of conscience for Louis XVI as well, who for months refused to sign the legislation, hoping for some guidance from Rome. None was forthcoming, however, and so on 26 December 1790 the king reluctantly signed the legislation. Three months later Pope Pius VI denounced the Civil Constitution of the Clergy and threatened those who swore the oath with excommunication.

The requirement of the Civil Oath immediately accentuated the split between the upper and lower clergy that had become apparent during elections to the Estates General. During the first months of 1791 approximately 60 percent of parish priests swore the oath, whereas only seven of eighty-three bishops did so. After Pius VI denounced the Civil Constitution in March 1791, a number of parish priests retracted their oath, so that in the end just over 50 percent of the parish clergy swore the oath. Those who refused to swear it came to be known as refractory clergy. They were removed from their parishes, but for a time were allowed to say mass and perform sacraments for those parishioners devoted to them. These unofficial masses, however, tended to draw protests, sometimes leading to violence, and eventually, citing the clause of Article 10 that read "provided that their manifestation does not trouble public order," the refractory clergy were forbidden to perform public services. By 1792 they would be threatened with deportation.

The Civil Constitution of the Clergy proved, then, to be quite divisive. Some refractory clergy effectively went underground, saying mass at clandestine services, sheltered by sympathetic parishioners, generally country dwellers, often aristocrats. To support the refractory clergy was to oppose the Revolution, and on a map of revolutionary France those departments in which the incidence of refractory clergy was high correlate strongly to those departments in which counterrevolutionary opposition was strongest. Critics of the Revolution, at the time and since, have tended to see this legislation as a veiled atheistic attack on religion, a prelude to the de-Christianization campaign unleashed during the year of the Terror. On the other side, ardent republicans from the 1790s on have seen the Catholic Church as an intransigent foe of popular democracy and a defender of traditional political hierarchy.

It would be a mistake, however, to view this issue purely in terms of an opposition between religion and secularism. The impetus for the Civil Constitution arose in part out of Jansenist currents within the Catholic

Church, as Dale Van Kley has argued.[8] Tension over the Civil Constitution, then, is reflective of divisions within the Catholic Church in France itself. And as the work of Timothy Tackett has shown, one cannot understand patterns of resistance to the Civil Oath purely in terms of religiosity. In the west, for example, where the rate of non-juring clergy was high, Tackett found that resentment of the upper clergy among parish priests was relatively low, that the rate of local recruitment of parish priests was higher than in other regions of France (especially in rural areas), and that there was a particularly high gap in literacy rates between town and country. All of these factors tended to make local clergy in the west loyal to the church hierarchy, and to make parishioners strongly loyal to their non-juring priests. Thus, a socioeconomic clash between town and country in the west was paralleled by a cultural clash, in part religious.[9]

That the Civil Oath of the Clergy confronted many priests with a crisis of conscience is undeniable. As Claude Langlois has observed, to ask that priests swear an oath of loyalty to a nation that had just chosen, through its elected representatives, *not* to recognize Catholicism as the official church of France was asking a lot, particularly of men who had been trained to take oaths, or vows, very seriously. For some, the swearing of the Civil Oath meant making a choice between the Revolution and their faith, while for others it did not. For historians, Langlois argues, the study of the Civil Oath is particularly revealing of the fundamental contradictions and ambivalences that lie at the heart of the French Revolution.[10]

The antagonisms engendered by the Civil Constitution of the Clergy were initially subdued, but grew more intense as the Revolution progressed, culminating with the de-Christianization campaign during the Terror. As priests and local churches came increasingly under attack, it was often women who came together to shelter them and eventually to organize campaigns demanding the reopening of closed churches. Olwen Hufton and Suzanne Desan have each examined the activism of women in

8 D. K. Van Kley, *The Religious Origins of the French Revolution* (New Haven, Yale University Press, 1996), 351–67. For an opposing view, see E. Préclin, *Les Jansénistes du dix-huitième siècle et la Constitution civile du clergé* (Paris, Imprimerie les presses modernes, 1929).

9 T. Tackett, "The West in France in 1789: The Religious Factor in the Origins of the Counterrevolution," *Journal of Modern History* 54 (December 1982), 715–45; and *Religion, Revolution, and Regional Culture in Eighteenth-Century France: The Ecclesiastical Oath of 1791* (Princeton, Princeton University Press, 1986). Tackett's statistics on the swearing of the oath – he estimates that slightly more than half of parish priests across France swore the oath – are accepted as definitive by most historians. But for a dissenting view see J. de Viguerie, *Christianisme et Révolution* (Paris, Nouvelles éditions latines, 1988), who argues that slightly more than half refused the oath.

10 C. Langlois, "Le serment révolutionnaire: archaisme et modernité," in J.-C. Martin, ed., *Religion et Révolution* (Paris, Anthropos, 1994), 25–39.

this regard, making it clear that to defend local priests and their churches was not necessarily to adopt a counterrevolutionary posture.[11] Indeed, while the church became a target in 1793–94, it is also the case that clerics and ex-clerics were among the most ardent of revolutionary activists.

Points of Tension or Conflict

Many historians have observed that compared to the "unparalleled year" of 1789, full of upheaval and violence, 1790 was a calm year, one that François Furet has even characterized as the "happy year" of the French Revolution. Michel Biard and Pascal Dupuy, to whom we owe the appelation "unparalleled" for 1789, have recently suggested that one can think of 1790 as happy only if one's focus is principally on Paris and the National Assembly. There was plenty of conflict and strife to be found, they argue, if one turns one's gaze to the provinces.[12]

Points of tension often emerged out of efforts to apply at the local level the abstract ideals expressed in the Declaration of the Rights of Man and Citizen, or the decrees that followed the Night of 4 August, but in some instances they reflected age-old divisions and animosities. Such was the case, for example, in the violence that erupted in Nîmes and Montauban, where significant Protestant communities had endured Catholic domination for the previous two centuries. Protestants in both towns greeted the Revolution with enthusiasm, seeing in it not only the promise of religious freedom but also an opportunity for increased participation in public life. In Nîmes, the creation of National Guard companies and the election of local administrations revived Protestant–Catholic rivalries, and in June 1790 that contestation erupted into violence as electors gathered to choose the first departmental administration. The *bagarre de Nîmes*, as the upheaval came to be known, claimed the lives of between 200 and 300 Catholics, and ended with Protestants in control of departmental politics. The first *camp de Jalès* followed close on the heels of that violence in Nîmes, bringing as many as 25,000 nobles, clergy, and Catholic peasants together on an isolated plain on the northern edge of the Gard, the first of a series of such counterrevolutionary assemblages in that

11 O. H. Hufton, *Women and the Limits of Citizenship in the French Revolution* (Toronto, University of Toronto Press, 1992), especially chapter two; S. Desan, *Reclaiming the Sacred: Lay Religion and Popular Politics in Revolutionary France* (Ithaca, Cornell University Press, 1990).

12 F. Furet and R. Halévi, *La Monarchie républicaine: La Constitution de 1791* (Paris, Fayard, 1996); M. Biard and P. Dupuy, *La Révolution française*, 62.

region. In Montauban, it was the initial efforts by local authorities to enact the nationalization of church lands that provoked violence between Protestants and Catholics in the spring of 1790. Alerted to the conflict, authorities in Bordeaux dispatched a force of 1,500 National Guardsmen, who succeeded in restoring order without additional bloodshed, earning for their city a reputation for revolutionary patriotism.[13]

Protestant–Catholic conflict was not common across France, since in most towns and cities the Protestant population was a tiny minority. A more common source of tension, and sometimes violence, was the appearance of political clubs, or popular societies, in towns and cities across the country. The best known of these, of course, was the Jacobin Club, which by 1793 would come to exercise a dominant influence on revolutionary politics, not only in Paris but in the provinces as well. The first Jacobin club emerged out of the Breton Club, formed at Versailles in April 1789. By early 1790 there were 1,000 members of the Paris Jacobin Club, including many deputies who sat on the left in the Constituent Assembly. Throughout that year a network of clubs began to grow, many of them formally affiliated with the "mother society" in Paris. By late 1790 there were more than 250 Jacobin clubs across France, over 400 by March 1791, and more than 900 by the summer of 1791.[14]

The growth of Jacobin influence was contested in 1790–91 by the appearance of monarchist clubs, the first of them organized in Paris in late 1790 under the leadership of Stanislas Clermont-Tonnerre and Pierre-Victor Malouet, both prominent deputies on the right in the Constituent Assembly. Their stated goal was to work for the preservation of the monarchy, and to that end its members were urged to support the creation of similar clubs in the provinces. At least thirty-five such clubs did form over the coming year, many of them taking the name *Amis de la Paix*. Some of them formed in order to sponsor slates of candidates in local elections; some had ties to *émigrés* in Turin and Coblenz and were accused of fostering counterrevolutionary activities; some stated their objective to be the elimination of all political clubs. In all cases their appearance provoked controversy, sometimes violence, as in Aix-en-Provence and Perpignan. Local Jacobins denounced them, and eventually local officials

---

13 J. Hood, "Protestant–Catholic Relations and the Roots of the First Popular Counterrevolutionary Movement in France," *Journal of Modern History* 43 (June 1971), 245–75; G. Lewis, *The Second Vendée: The Constituency of Counterrevolution in the Department of the Gard* (Oxford, Clarendon Press, 1978); D. Ligou, *Montauban à la fin de l'Ancien Régime et aux débuts de la Révolution, 1787–1794* (Paris, M. Rivière, 1958); and A. Forrest, *Society and Politics in Revolutionary Bordeaux* (Oxford, Oxford University Press, 1975), 44–46.

14 M. L. Kennedy, *The Jacobin Clubs in the French Revolution: The First Years* (Princeton, Princeton University Press, 1982).

ordered the monarchist clubs to close their doors. By the end of 1791 they had virtually all disappeared.[15]

Seldom did these local tensions and conflicts generate violence spectacular enough to attract national attention, but clearly the "sublime unity" that some have claimed prevailed in the National Assembly did not hold true in very many places beyond Paris. There were no national elections between 1789 and September 1791, but Frenchmen gathered in electoral assemblies to choose municipal councils, district and departmental administrators, justices of the peace, officers of the National Guard, parish priests and bishops – more than a half-dozen opportunities, all told, to exercise political citizenship. These assemblies were generally orderly, but often contentious. The process of drawing up jury lists for the new departmental criminal tribunals in early 1791 also proved to be an occasion for competing interests, vying perspectives on the new order (one might say), to come into conflict. Tensions also erupted on occasion between new National Guard companies and the old royal regiments garrisoned in provincial towns. We might also note that the fall of 1790 marked the first harvest following which many peasants refused to make payments on seigneurial dues, claiming in practice an outright abolition that the Constituent Assembly had granted only with indemnity.

All of these are examples of ways in which ordinary Frenchmen, and women, began to negotiate and contest the new rights, responsibilities, and reforms that they had been promised. At the level of the local community, the practical problem of defining both sovereignty and public opinion became more viscerally apparent earlier than in Paris. Deputies might speak eloquently about the sovereignty of the nation, but it was not at all clear yet just who that meant, or how that sovereignty should be exercised. What did become clear quite quickly was that traditional elites would do all they could to protect their own interests. How could the poor, or even those of middling means, compete with the wealthy in the political arena? Or put differently, from the perspective of those with property, how could a poor peasant or urban worker be expected to exercise political citizenship responsibly and intelligently? These might seem abstract questions to deputies in the National Assembly, but as National Guard units, popular societies, and jury lists came into being at the local level in 1790 and 1791 they generated tension and conflict.

15 R. Griffiths, *Le Centre perdu: Malouet et les "monarchiens" dans la Révolution française* (Grenoble, Presses Universitaires de Grenoble, 1988); P. R. Hanson, "Monarchist Clubs and the Pamphlet Debate over Political Legitimacy in the Early Years of the French Revolution," *French Historical Studies* 21 (Spring 1998), 299–324.

Turning Points

Let us turn, in conclusion, to the final question posed in the introduction to this chapter: were there any events or developments in the nearly three years of the constitutional monarchy that might be identified as key turning points? Or was the Revolution, from 1789 forward, on a fixed course, driven either by Rousseauean ideology on the one hand, or by the inability of the Bourbon monarchy and privileged aristocracy to accept the new order of things on the other, with the Terror as its inevitable destination?

If one sees violence as the very essence of the Revolution, then one might point to the October Days in 1789 as a critical date. These days marked a second major entry of the Paris crowd onto the historical stage – more purposive, perhaps, than 14 July had been – and initiating an activism among Parisian women that would not abate until at least 1794. The march and demonstration forced the transfer of the royal family and the Constituent Assembly from Versailles to Paris, a dramatic reversal of the relocation of royal power to Versailles that Louis XIV had engineered in the seventeenth century. The king, and the deputies, would henceforth be subject to the constant vigilance, and potential violence, of the Parisian populace. And yet, the violence of the October Days, more vocally decried by the deputies than that of Bastille Day had been, did not persist. The next year and a half were remarkably peaceful in Paris, and the reputation of Louis XVI as the devoted father of his people seemed to emerge intact from the jostling that the royal party had endured on their carriage ride back to the Tuileries palace.

Given the divisiveness engendered by the Civil Constitution of the Clergy and the Civil Oath, some might point to November 1790 and the months that followed as a crucial turning point for revolutionary France. Certainly resentment over this legislation gave impetus to the counterrevolutionary movements that would plague France, particularly in the Vendée, for the rest of the decade. On the other hand, it seems likely that many devout Catholics would have come to oppose the Revolution as it grew more radical even had their priests not been required to swear an oath of loyalty. And as noted above, reaction to the Civil Constitution, as to many other aspects of revolutionary legislation, varied across France, suggesting that we might add geographical contingency to historical contingency as we strive to explain the course of the Revolution – which was not, after all, a purely Parisian affair.

Two books by Timothy Tackett, exploring different aspects of the Constituent Assembly, are relevant to our discussion here. The first of them, *Becoming a Revolutionary*, offers a kind of collective biography of the members of the Constituent Assembly. Drawing heavily on letters and memoirs by the deputies themselves, Tackett challenges the revisionist argument that there was little social basis to the Revolution. Although not adopting a Marxist perspective, he presents strong evidence of social distinction between deputies of the second and third estates, in their family backgrounds, their wealth, and their education, and argues that those social differences fostered divisions between aristocrats and commoners and affected their political attitudes. Contrary to those who have emphasized the early formation of the Jacobin Club as a radical and divisive element, Tackett insists that it was deputies on the right who first organized voting blocs within the Constituent Assembly. Not only does this call into question the "sublime unity" that Michael Fitzsimmons has argued prevailed in the Assembly after the Night of 4 August, it places responsibility on the right, rather than on the left, for the earliest manifestation of the factionalism that came eventually to characterize revolutionary politics. Finally, as the title suggests, Tackett emphasizes that the deputies were affected and influenced by the events of which they were a part. Becoming a revolutionary was a process, and few of them could have anticipated in 1789 all that they would experience, or the distance they would travel, both literally and figuratively, by 1791.[16]

In a more recent book, Tackett makes a case for the Flight to Varennes, 20–21 June 1791, as a critical turning point in this early phase of the Revolution. On this occasion, Louis XVI and his family fled surreptitiously from the Tuileries palace, in the dead of night, and made their way toward the eastern border, ostensibly to rally the *émigré* forces gathering on foreign territory to restore the king to his former place. The king and his party were recognized and apprehended in Varennes, and returned under escort several days later to a subdued and suspicious capital city. Both the deputies and the populace were stunned, and in the following weeks the first public calls for the creation of a republic and an end to the monarchy were heard in Paris.[17]

This event, Tackett argues, fundamentally altered the political landscape in France. The image of the king as the good father may not have

---

16 T. Tackett, *Becoming a Revolutionary: The Deputies of the French National Assembly and the Emergence of a Revolutionary Culture, 1789–1790* (Princeton, Princeton University Press, 1996). See also H. B. Applewhite, *Political Alignment in the French National Assembly, 1789–1791* (Baton Rouge, Louisiana State University Press, 1993), which supports Tackett's position; and E. H. Lemay and A. Patrick, *Revolutionaries at Work: The Constituent Assembly, 1789–1791* (Oxford, Voltaire Foundation, 1996).

17 T. Tackett, *When the King took Flight* (Cambridge, MA, Harvard University Press, 2003).

been permanently shattered, but it was certainly severely tarnished. Because the king's party had traversed northeastern France, and raised fears throughout the countryside of an Austrian or Prussian invasion, tensions were heightened across the country, not just in Paris. For those inclined to see conspiracy behind every political ill wind, this incident provided proof that there were indeed people plotting against the revolutionary government, and raised serious suspicions about Louis XVI's willingness to accept a constitutional monarchy. In the aftermath of Varennes, new waves of *émigrés*, both aristocrats and refractory clergy, fled to foreign havens, and government repression of perceived enemies of the Revolution increased. In Tackett's view, the betrayal of trust that was implicit in the Flight to Varennes, and the increased paranoia that resulted, made the Terror conceivable.

And yet, less than three months after Varennes, the king would accept the new constitution. National elections would be held and a new Legislative Assembly convened. The constitutional monarchy would survive for nearly another year. But as we shall see in the next chapter, the declaration of war against Austria in April 1792 brought new stresses to bear on the nation and raised a new set of suspicions about the king's commitment to the constitutional regime.

5

The Republic

From our perspective today, the declaration of a republic in 1792 may seem to have been almost as inevitable as the Terror. There is a logic to this, given the assertion in the Declaration of the Rights of Man and Citizen that sovereignty resides in the nation, as well as the widely held view among historians today that the French Revolution marked the foundation of modern democracy. But for most Enlightenment thinkers republicanism was not an ideal but was rather a discredited form of government that had been shown historically to lead either to mob rule and anarchy or to tyranny. Even Rousseau, that champion of republican government in the abstract, was skeptical that a republic could function in a country as large as France. Among the revolutionaries themselves, there were still very few committed republicans as late as the summer of 1791. Even in the midst of the crisis triggered by the king's Flight to Varennes, a number of revolutionaries whom we would today consider radicals publicly disavowed the idea of a republic, and when a public demonstration sponsored by the Cordelier Club gathered on the Champ de Mars on 17 July 1791 to sign petitions calling for the king's abdication, the Marquis de Lafayette ordered the National Guard to open fire on the crowd. In the aftermath of this massacre, those who had most actively rallied the people against the king were forced into hiding, and the idea of a republic became once again disreputable.[1]

All that changed in little more than a year. As with the Revolution itself, the first French Republic was born in violence, twice over indeed.

---

1 D. Andress, *Massacre at the Champ de Mars: Popular Dissent and Political Culture in the French Revolution* (Suffolk, The Boydell Press, 2000).

First came a popular insurrection on 10 August 1792, the second of the great *journées* of the Revolution, which toppled the monarchy. That upheaval, hailed by nearly all as a glorious victory for the people, was tainted three weeks later by the prison massacres in Paris during the first week of September. The massacres were a panicked response to reports from the front that the war against Prussia and Austria was going badly, that Paris itself might be threatened within weeks. Instead, the French army scored a great victory at Valmy on 20 September, and one day later, flushed with pride and a newfound confidence at the reports of that victory, the deputies of the newly elected National Convention declared France to be a republic. Thus, the violence of popular insurrection and the violence of war together ushered the republic into existence.

Given the circumstances of its birth, it should not surprise us that the republic was rent by division from the very outset. The origins of this lay, in part, in the declaration of war against Austria in April 1792. Calls for war had increased after the king's Flight to Varennes in June 1791, fueled by the growing wave of aristocratic *émigrés*, many of whom gathered in Coblenz and Turin, ostensibly preparing to return to France at the head of royalist armies. Two-thirds of the officer corps of the French army, nearly all aristocrats, had emigrated since the Revolution began. Some revolutionaries were eager for war with Austria, given Marie-Antoinette's connection to the Austrian royal family (her brother, Leopold II, now sat on the throne). For her part, the queen encouraged Louis XVI to declare war in the hope that this would lead to a defeat of the revolutionary army and bring about the restoration of the absolute monarchy.

Jacques-Pierre Brissot was among the first of the revolutionaries to call for war. Brissot had published a newspaper in Paris since 1789, *Le Patriote français*, was among the founders of the Society of the Friends of Blacks, and by 1791 was both a prominent figure in the Paris Jacobin Club and a leading deputy in the Legislative Assembly, in which a group of his supporters had come to be known as Brissotins. Opposing Brissot on this issue, nearly alone, was Maximilien Robespierre, who feared that the French army was not yet battle-ready and that going to war would play into the hands of those who opposed the Revolution, both abroad and at home. In the short term Robespierre proved to be correct. The war went badly, and Brissot's influence and popularity declined, both at the Jacobin Club and among the Parisian populace more generally. When new elections were called, for the National Convention, Brissot stood as a candidate from the Eure-et-Loir, fearful that he could no longer win election in Paris.

The events of August and September deepened the political divisions in Paris. There were in fact two uprisings against the monarchy that summer, the first of them occurring on 20 June 1792, prompted by the king's veto of legislation calling for the creation of a camp of *fédérés* in or near Paris to protect the National Assembly. An unruly crowd invaded the Tuileries palace, forcing Louis XVI to don a phrygian cap (among the new symbols of the Revolution), but failing in its aim of securing the king's abdication. In the weeks that followed, letters poured into the capital from departmental administrations and other provincial authorities denouncing this insult to royal authority, evidence that the king's Flight to Varennes had not completely soured the French on their monarchy. In Paris, however, the movement calling for a republic steadily gathered strength in the clubs and section assemblies, leading to a city-wide petition campaign demanding the king's removal, and culminating in the far better organized and more massive uprising of 10 August.

The collapse of the monarchy created an awkward political void and opened a new debate about the nature of political sovereignty in France. When the sections of Paris had petitioned the Legislative Assembly in early August, declaring their lack of confidence in the monarchy, the president of the Assembly, Pierre-Victurnien Vergniaud, turned the petition away, asserting that "sovereignty belongs to all the people and not to a section of the people."[2] In the months to come, Vergniaud and Brissot, at the head of a group of deputies who now came to be called the Girondins, would vigorously oppose what they claimed to be the excessive influence of Paris – especially its militant clubs and sections – on national politics.

By contrast, Robespierre and his supporters in the Jacobin Club became the champions of Paris. Excluded from the Legislative Assembly by the legislation he himself had proposed, Robespierre spent 1791 publishing a newspaper in Paris and sitting as a delegate on the general council of the Paris Commune. In his newspaper, *Le Défenseur de la Constitution*, Robespierre celebrated the 10 August uprising, characterizing it as "the triumph of the 'passive' citizens who have now avenged their exclusion from the politics of the Revolution."[3] Perhaps chastened by those words, as one of their final acts the deputies of the Legislative Assembly expanded the suffrage, eliminating the property requirement and lowering the voting age to 21. Elections that fall, of deputies to the National Convention and all local administrations, were thus conducted under universal manhood suffrage, the most democratic elections of the Revolution.

The September Massacres, coming as they did in the midst of the fall elections, rendered that triumph of the people problematical. The violence

---

2 See P. R. Hanson, *The Jacobin Republic under Fire: The Federalist Revolt in the French Revolution* (University Park, Pennsylvania State University Press, 2003), Chapter Two, for a more extensive discussion of this period.

3 D. Jordan, *The Revolutionary Career of Maximilien Robespierre* (Chicago, University of Chicago Press, 1985), 113.

did not immediately become a contested issue. Deputies on all sides initially characterized the killing as regrettable, but necessary. On 16 September, however, Vergniaud publicly condemned the massacres and demanded that those responsible be brought to justice. The following month, Jean-Baptiste Louvet directly accused Robespierre of orchestrating the killing, supported by Danton and Marat in an alleged conspiracy to install themselves in power as a dictatorial triumvirate. Robespierre easily parried that blow, supported as he was by the Commune, the Paris sections, and the Jacobin Club, but for the Girondins and their supporters in the provinces the September Massacres remained emblematic of Parisian anarchy for months to come.

Such was the polarization that confronted the young republic as the deputies of the National Convention met to embark on two momentous tasks: the drafting of a new constitution and the trial of Louis XVI. Much of the historiography for this period has focused, understandably, on the drama in the capital: the opposition between Girondins and Montagnards, the trial of the king, the rise of the Jacobin Club to prominence, and the emergence of the *sans-culotte* movement as a potent political force. To commence this chapter we will survey the debates around those issues. But much as the Girondins insisted in 1792–93, Paris is not France, and in recent decades historians have produced an impressive body of work focusing on an array of issues that extend well beyond the capital, and these will draw our attention as well. The most far-flung is the slave revolt in Saint-Domingue, which began under the constitutional monarchy but had a profound effect on France in the early months of the republic. Long treated as a kind of addendum to the Revolution, the uprising in Saint-Domingue, modern day Haiti, is now coming to be seen as a more integral part of its history. Closer to home, the Revolution in the provinces has increasingly come under the scrutiny of historians in recent years. Traditionally, the emphasis has been on provincial responses to political currents emanating from Paris, whether counterrevolutionary upheavals (as in the Vendée or the Midi) or the federalist revolts of 1793, a response to the proscription of the Girondin deputies. But just as 1792–93 was a period of political ferment in Paris, so was it in much of the rest of the country, not only in major towns and cities, but in the countryside as well. The elections of late 1792 brought a new cohort of revolutionary activists into local politics, as did the expansion of the Jacobin club network, the sale of national lands, and the de-Christianization campaign of late 1793. While we tend to think first of peasants opposing the republic, as in the Vendée, there was peasant activism in this period as well, as rural people sought to benefit from the reforms introduced by the Revolution. Those reforms tended to reinforce the distinctive smallholding pattern that characterized French agriculture up into the twentieth century, but some recent scholarship has also explored the environmental impact of revolutionary change on the countryside.

Two underlying themes run throughout all of these issues: how was sovereignty to be defined, and how would it be exercised, in the new republic; and how was individual liberty to be defined, emerging as it did in a society in which hierarchy and community had long predominated. Particularly in a time of war, to what degree did personal responsibility, to the nation, constrain individual liberty? And in the midst of revolution, at what point did liberty give way to licence, even anarchy? These questions were on the minds of many in 1792–93.

Girondins vs. Montagnards

In the classic interpretation of the French Revolution, the dynamic tension in the National Convention lay in the opposition between two factions of deputies, the Girondins and Montagnards, the first so called because their most prominent leaders (Vergniaud, Gensonné, Guadet, Ducos, Bergeoing) came from Bordeaux and the department of the Gironde. The Montagnards took their name from the fact that these deputies sat on the highest benches in the meeting hall of the National Convention. Their base of support was among the Parisian *sans-culottes* – indeed, twenty-one of the twenty-four deputies elected from Paris sat with the Montagnards. Robespierre, Danton, Marat, St. Just and Billaud-Varenne were among their leaders. In the Marxist historiography, the Montagnards were seen as the champions of the common people, while the Girondins were said to represent the propertied classes, in particular the commercial bourgeoisie.

There has been a longstanding debate among historians about the Girondins and Montagnards. Nearly fifty years ago now, Michael Sydenham published a book, simply titled *The Girondins*, in which he argued that the subjects of his book did not exist as a coherent group. Some of the supposed Girondins were friends, some dined together on a regular basis, some did indeed come from the Gironde, but apart from that coincidence of geography there was nothing to give them definition as a group, either socially or in terms of a recognizable political agenda. They have come down to posterity as a political faction only because they were denounced and proscribed from the National Convention by the Montagnards, who did exist as a political faction in Sydenham's view.[4]

---

4 M. J. Sydenham, *The Girondins* (London, University of London Press, 1961).

Alison Patrick responded to this argument with an extensive study of voting patterns, speeches, participation on committees, and assignment as representatives on mission to the provinces. She concluded that the Girondins were indeed a cohesive group within the National Convention, particularly if one focused on key votes such as those at the trial of Louis XVI or for the impeachment of Jean-Paul Marat. The Girondins' identity as a group, Patrick argued, was principally defined by their opposition to the growing strength of the Montagnards.[5] Some years later another group of researchers joined the debate, and their statistical anlysis of voting patterns supported Patrick's position. Lewis-Beck, Hildreth, and Spitzer emphasized in particular the importance of the vote in January 1793 on the *appel au peuple*, an effort on the part of the Girondin deputies to refer the issue of the king's punishment, after he had already been found guilty of treason, to a national referendum. On this issue, more than any other, they argued, the cohesion of the Girondin deputies as a political group was evident.[6]

The vote on the fate of the king was a telling moment, not only in the struggle between Girondins and Montagnards, but also in the debate over sovereignty. The Girondin deputies advocated the *appel au peuple* by asserting that only in this way would the will of the people be known regarding the fate of Louis XVI. The Montagnards, generally thought of as advocates of popular sovereignty, opposed the referendum, arguing that the people had already expressed themselves twice – once in the streets of Paris on 10 August, in the insurrection that toppled the monarchy, and secondly when they elected their representatives to the National Convention. It was now their duty as deputies, the Montagnards argued, to decide the fate of the king. In the end, the *appel au peuple* was defeated decisively, although this vote, and the one that followed, are good examples of how difficult it can be to resolve these historical debates, even when the "facts" seem quite clear. Patrick, the Lewis-Beck group, and David Jordan have all examined the vote on the *appel au peuple*, and each has arrived at a different vote total: Patrick, 418 to 277, Lewis-Beck et al., 414 to 281, and Jordan, 424 to 283.[7] At least the result of the vote is not in doubt! But while Patrick argues, based on earlier speeches and pamphlets, that the breakdown of the vote was predictable, Jordan insists that there was little correlation between political allegiance (that is, whether one was thought to be aligned with the

5 A. Patrick, *The Men of the First French Republic: Political Alignments in the National Convention of 1792* (Baltimore, Johns Hopkins University Press, 1972).

6 M. S. Lewis-Beck, A. Hildreth, and A. B. Spitzer, "Was There a Girondin Faction Within the National Convention?," *French Historical Studies* 15 (Spring 1988), 519–36. The article is followed by commentary from Michael Sydenham, Alison Patrick, and Gary Kates.

7 D. Jordan, *The King's Trial: Louis XVI vs. the French Revolution* (Berkeley, University of California Press, 1979), 173–77.

Girondins or the Montagnards) and the final vote, with deputies shifting their position between late December and mid-January. On this issue there is evidence to support both views. Clearly there was nothing like party discipline governing the votes of these political factions in the National Convention. Condorcet, for example, who is associated with the Girondins on most issues, voted against the *appel au peuple*.

The final vote on the fate of Louis XVI has been similarly surrounded by controversy. It is not uncommon to read in general histories that the death of the king was decided by a single vote. This makes for great drama, and is a poignant civics lesson for the youth of today's democracies: every vote counts. But it is not quite true. There were 749 deputies in the National Convention, of whom only 721 cast votes on this issue (one deputy was carried into the meeting hall on his sickbed). It was a complicated vote, with amendments offered and several options presented. 361 deputies voted for death without conditions, hence the argument that only one vote decided the king's fate. But there were not 360 votes for any other single option. Two deputies voted to imprison Louis XVI in irons, 46 voted for death with intrinsic conditions attached (e.g. the execution was not to be carried out until after the war was over), 286 voted for imprisonment to be followed by banishment, and 26 voted for the Mailhe amendment, which no one quite understood. Those last-mentioned votes are generally combined with the 361 to give a total of 387 deputies voting for death, a comfortable majority. It should also be observed that on the question of the king's guilt on the charges of treason, the vote was unanimous.[8]

Opposition between Girondins and Montagnards had crystallized, then, by January 1793, and the preponderance of evidence supports the argument that the Girondins did exist as an identifiable faction within the National Convention, though deputies adhered to no party discipline, and contemporaries referred to them as Brissotins perhaps more often than as Girondins, though the latter term was clearly in usage prior to 31 May 1793. What is less clear, however, is that there was any social distinction between the Girondin and Montagnard deputies. Albert Soboul has argued that the Girondins "were passionately attached to the idea of economic freedom, freedom to undertake trading enterprises and to make uncontrolled profits, and they showed their hostitlity to economic regulation, price controls, requisitions, and the forced use of *assignats*, all measures which were, by way of contrast, strongly advocated by the *sans-culottes*."[9]

8 D. Jordan, *The King's Trial*, is the best source for analysis of the votes and proceedings. See also M. Walzer, *Regicide and Revolution: Speeches at the Trial of Louis XVI* (New York, Columbia University Press, 1992), for translated texts of some of the more important speeches.
9 A. Soboul, *The French Revolution, 1787–1799* (New York, Vintage Books, 1975), 276–77.

He stops just short of associating the Girondins with a particular class, but the clear implication is that they represented the interests of the commercial bourgeoisie. Other historians have found, however, that there was no social distinction between the Girondin and Montagnard deputies – they all were drawn predominantly from the professional classes, most of them having trained as lawyers.[10] Jean Jaurès, the celebrated socialist historian of the late nineteenth century, concluded that "the true root of the conflicts between the Gironde and the Mountain lay not in social antagonisms, but in the strength of the most common human passions: ambition, pride, vanity, and the egoism of power."[11] In a similar vein, Marisa Linton has recently argued that personal loyalties and friendship networks played an important role in political alignments.[12] Ladan Boroumand, taking a different approach, has argued that the Girondin vision of the republic grew out of natural law tradition, emphasizing the liberty of each citizen, while the Montagnards leaned more on Rousseau's notion of the "general will," emphasizing the duty of each citizen to the social body. In the end, though, the Girondins' republicanism depended very much on the existence of a king. Once Louis XVI had been executed, their fear of the radicalism of the Parisian *sans-culottes* accentuated their commitment to social order and the rule of law.[13] The roots of that commitment, however, as Alan Forrest has argued, may have lain in the commercial milieu of Bordeaux from which the Girondin leadership emerged.[14]

If the political struggle between Girondins and Montagnards represents one key aspect of the history of the early republic, another is the emergence of the Parisian *sans-culottes* as a potent political force in 1792–93, most crucially in the insurrection of 10 August 1792 that toppled the monarchy, then in late May 1793 in the Paris uprising that forced the proscription of the Girondin leaders from the National Convention, and again in early September 1793 in demonstrations that resulted in an expansion of price controls and the addition of Collot-d'Herbois and Billaud-Varenne to the Committee of Public Safety. On each of these occasions the Parisian *sans-culottes* can be said to have influenced national

---

10 J. Chaumié, "Les Girondins et les Cent Jours," *Annales Historiques de la Révolution française* XLIII (1971), 329–65; and "Les Girondins," in A. Soboul, ed., *Actes du colloque Girondins et Montagnards* (Paris, Société des études robespierristes, 1980), 19–60.

11 Quoted in Pierre Bouretz, "Jaurès et la Gironde," in F. Furet and M. Ozouf, eds., *La Gironde et les Girondins* (Paris, Editions Payot, 1991), 103.

12 M. Linton, "Fatal Friendships: The Politics of Jacobin Friendship," *French Historical Studies* 31 (Winter 2008), 51–76.

13 L. Boroumand, "Les Girondins et l'idée de République," in Furet and Ozouf, op. cit., 233–64.

14 A. Forrest, "Bordeaux au temps de la Gironde," in F. Furet and M. Ozouf, *La Gironde et les Girondins*, 25–43.

politics in a decisive way. Here, too, there has been considerable debate among historians in regard to the social composition of this popular political movement.

For one position in this debate we might look again to Albert Soboul, whose seminal work on the *sans-culottes* characterized them as a sort of proto-proletariat, more concerned about the cost of living than about wages, as the Marxist proletariat of the nineteenth century would be, and drawn largely from the social milieu of artisans, wage laborers, and small shopkeepers.[15] Soboul, along with George Rudé, was reacting in part to the unflattering nineteenth-century depiction of the revolutionary crowd as the mob, or the rabble (in French, *la canaille*), as in the work of Adolphe Thiers or Hippolyte Taine. Soboul's *sans-culottes* were respectable workers and artisans of modest means, not vagrants, beggars, and common criminals. This view of the *sans-culottes* as a social group came under scrutiny with the revisionist critique of the Marxist interpretation, most notably by historians such as Richard Andrews and Michael Sonenscher, who argued that the *sans-culottes* were not a social class at all and that their world was a complex one in which clientage (e.g. between journeymen and master craftsmen, or between wholesalers and small shopkeepers), kinship, and neighborhood networks were more important in forming political sensibilities than class consciousness.[16]

More recently, Haim Burstin has followed up a magisterial study of the *faubourg* Saint-Marcel, one of the strongholds of the Parisian *sans-culottes*, with a shorter work provocatively entitled *The Invention of the Sans-culotte*.[17] Burstin does not go quite as far as his title might imply, to suggest that the *sans-culottes* were some kind of fictional creation, but he does observe, tellingly, that the Revolution is the only period in French history in which we speak of the *sans-culottes*. They have no place, for example, at least as an identifiable group, in the revolution of 1848.

15 A. Soboul, *The Sans-culottes* (Princeton, Princeton University Press, 1980). A very similar position is taken by G. Rudé, *The Crowd in the French Revolution* (Oxford, Oxford University Press, 1959).

16 R. M. Andrews, "Social Structures, Political Elites and Ideology in Revolutionary Paris, 1792–94: A Critical Evaluation of Albert Soboul's *Les Sans-Culottes Parisiens en l'an II*," *Journal of Social History* 19 (1985), 71–112; M. Sonenscher, "The Sans-culottes of the Year II: Rethinking the Language of Labour in Revolutionary France," *Social History* 9 (1984), 301–28; "Artisans, *sans-culottes* and the French Revolution," in A. Forrest and P. Jones, eds., *Reshaping France: Town, Country and Region during the French Revolution* (Manchester, Manchester University Press, 1991), 105–21; and *Work and Wages: Natural Law, Politics, and the Eighteenth-Century French Trades* (Cambridge, Cambridge University Press, 1989).

17 H. Burstin, *L'Invention du sans-culotte: regard sur le Paris révolutionnaire* (Paris, Odile Jacob, 2005); and *Une révolution à l'oeuvre: le faubourg Saint-Marcel, 1789–1794* (Seyssel, Champ Vallon, 2005).

Burstin is in sympathy, then, with Andrews' argument (and that of Andrews' mentor, Richard Cobb), that the *sans-culottes* were essentially a political grouping, or in Cobb's view, a political accident. But he does not abandon entirely the idea of a social meaning to the term. Just as the term *aristocrate*, which clearly had a social content under the Old Regime (even if somewhat malleable), came to have a broader political resonance during the Revolution (any counterrevolutionary might be denounced as an *aristocrate* by 1793–94), so did the term *sans-culotte* have a multivalent meaning. Burstin has no easy answer to the question, "What was a *sans-culotte*?," but offers what might be called a sociology of political attitudes, situating the *sans-culottes* in a social milieu that was complex and in transition at the end of the eighteenth century, even perhaps under threat, as both Daniel Roche and David Garrioch have suggested.[18] George Rudé long ago observed that it was most often food – either its shortage or its cost – that galvanized the *sans-culottes* into action. One might amend that slightly to suggest that their political activism was motivated by a desire to protect their livelihood, or even to defend their way of life, and in that endeavor women were often as committed, and active, as men. One of the notable features of popular politics in Paris from 1792 through 1794 was the active participation of women in sectional assemblies, political clubs (women's clubs as well as men's clubs such as the Cordeliers), and on the insurrectionary committee that prepared the uprising of 31 May 1793.[19]

Popular Politics in the Provinces

The advent of the republic brought with it as well a broadening of political activity in the provinces. Two developments in particular were responsible for this: the declaration of universal manhood suffrage by the Legislative Assembly in August 1792, and the expansion of the Jacobin club network across France in the year that followed. By the fall of 1793, the Jacobins had reached the zenith of their political influence during the Revolution.

After the election of deputies to the National Convention, towns and cities throughout the country elected new municipal councils. These may

---

18 D. Roche, *The People of Paris: An Essay in Popular Culture in the 18th Century* (Berkeley, University of California Press, 1987); D. Garrioch, *Neighbourhood and Community in Paris, 1740–1790* (Cambridge, Cambridge University Press, 1986); and *The Making of Revolutionary Paris* (Berkeley, University of California Press, 2002).

19 D. Godineau, *The Women of Paris and their French Revolution* (Berkeley, University of California Press, 1998); R. Monnier, *L'Espace public démocratique: essai sur l'opinion à Paris de la Révolution au Directoire* (Paris, Editions Kimé, 1994).

have been the most democratic elections held during the Revolution in two senses: they were conducted under a system of universal manhood suffrage; and unlike the national elections or the elections of departmental and district councils, which were indirect (eligible voters selected an electoral assembly, which chose deputies and administrators), in municipal elections citizens voted directly for the candidates who took office. The result was often the radicalization of local politics and the election of new people to municipal office. As Lynn Hunt has observed, "the Revolution opened political access to groups that previously had been excluded for social reasons, and the more left local government became (in 1793–94 everywhere, and in Jacobin strongholds more than elsewhere), the more likely it was to include modest merchants, artisans and shopkeepers, and minor professionals."[20] In most provincial cities, the first municipal councils elected in 1790 were dominated by Old Regime elites, including aristocrats and prominent clerics. Gradually those old elites disappeared from office, indeed some disappeared from the country as *émigrés*, to be replaced by merchants, lawyers, and other professionals. The 1792 elections brought a yet more modest occupational milieu to municipal councils, reflected not only by the appearance of artisans and shopkeepers, but also men of more modest means, as shown by the average taxes they paid. In some cities, notably Lyon and Marseille, the municipal elections of 1792 (and early 1793 – the election in Marseille dragged on for weeks) were quite contentious. Local Jacobins prepared organized slates of candidates, which the propertied elites tried to counter, and when those slates of candidates were indeed elected charges of voter fraud and electoral manipulation were hurled about. As in Paris, this resulted in a highly charged political atmosphere, and in the late spring moderates regained control of the municipal council in both cities, quite violently in Lyon.[21]

Throughout the fall and winter of 1792–93, then, the nature and definition of sovereignty was being contested, first in the electoral arena with the adoption of universal manhood suffrage, but also in the increasingly active clubs and section assemblies, which in big cities such as Paris, Lyon, and Marseille were now meeting virtually every evening.

---

20 L. Hunt, *Politics, Culture, and Class in the French Revolution* (Berkeley, University of California Press, 1984), 170. Chapter Five is entitled "The New Political Class," and analyzes electoral patterns over the revolutionary decade in four provincial cities: Amiens, Bordeaux, Nancy, and Toulouse.

21 W. Scott, *Terror and Repression in Revolutionary Marseilles* (London, Macmillan Press, 1973); W. D. Edmonds, *Jacobinism and the Revolt of Lyon, 1789–1793* (Oxford, Clarendon Press, 1990). See also A. Forrest, *Society and Politics in Revolutionary Bordeaux* (Oxford, Oxford University Press, 1975); and P. R. Hanson, *Provincial Politics in the French Revolution: Caen and Limoges, 1789–1794* (Baton Rouge, Louisiana State University Press, 1989).

Most revolutionaries might agree that sovereignty resided in the people, but there was less consensus regarding *which* people, or the manner in which they might legitimately exercise their sovereignty. Among the deputies of the National Convention, differences on these issues were both philosophical and tactical. For the Montagnards, it was the *sans-culottes* of Paris who most clearly and forcefully represented the people, in the clubs, in the sections, and on the streets. These were the people whom Robespierre credited with having established the guilt of Louis XVI on 10 August 1792. But the Montagnards were also happy to accept as part of the people those *fédérés*, volunteers from the provinces, who had joined in the assault on the Tuileries palace. The Girondins, leery of the people in arms (unless they were off at war on the frontier), had a more restrictive notion of popular sovereignty. Once the people had voted, they had exercised their sovereignty, and had transferred it, in effect, to the deputies of the National Convention, which became the repository of national sovereignty and unity. The militant activism of the *sans-culottes* bordered on anarchy in their view. And yet, in the midst of the king's trial, the Girondins were willing to invoke the sovereignty of the people by the proposed referendum on the king's sentence, a process by which they hoped to counter the influence of the Paris crowd with the votes of their provincial constituents.

Once Louis XVI had been executed, the drafting of a new constitution was the principal task before the National Convention, but the deputies could make little progress, given the political acrimony and recrimination that prevailed throughout the winter and spring. Their work was made more difficult by the fact that Great Britain, Holland, and Spain joined in the war against France following the execution of the king. Wartime is not conducive to the drafting of a liberal constitution. A virtual stalemate developed within the National Convention, and the citizens of France grew weary of the factionalism and delay. The Parisian *sans-culottes*, encouraged by the Jacobin and Cordelier clubs, focused their complaints on the most prominent Girondin leaders. Countering this was a constant stream of letters from departmental administrations and provincial clubs, critical of Robespierre and Marat, the perceived leaders of the Montagnards, and the threat of anarchy posed by the Paris crowd. The Jacobin club network now approached one thousand clubs, with virtually every town and village included, but it is important to note that not all provincial Jacobin clubs supported the Montagnards or remained affiliated with the mother society.[22] In the end, however, the popular support for the Montagnards

22 M. L. Kennedy, *The Jacobin Clubs in the French Revolution: The Middle Years* (Princeton, Princeton University Press, 1988). See Appendix F for a breakdown of the political alignments of provincial clubs in January 1793, and Appendix G for alignments later in the spring.

was close at hand, while that for the Girondins was quite distant. A satchel full of letters from the provinces, no matter how eloquent or forceful, was no match for 80,000 *sans-culottes* massed in the courtyard of the Tuileries palace. Although the Girondin leaders had alleged throughout the winter that they were the targets of violent plots, the three days of insurrection that began on 31 May 1793 were remarkably peaceful. But the threat of violence was undeniable, and on 2 June the National Convention succumbed to the pressure of the crowd and voted the proscription of twenty-nine Girondin deputies and two ministers.[23]

Initially, the response from the provinces was resoundingly negative. Roughly fifty of the eighty-three departmental administrations protested the proscription of the Girondin deputies by letter, denouncing this violation of the National Convention as an assault on the unity and indivisibility of the nation, and demanding that the proscribed deputies be returned to their seats. Four provincial cities – Bordeaux, Caen, Lyon, and Marseille – became the centers of prolonged resistance in what came to be known as the federalist revolt.

How should this uprising in the provinces be understood? General histories of the Revolution have tended to present it as a vaguely royalist reaction against a central government now dominated by the Montagnards, an essentially counterrevolutionary upheaval. Michael Sydenham challenged that view in an article in which he proposed that the term "federalist" be dropped and that the movement could more properly be termed the "republican revolt."[24] The rebels were, by and large, committed republicans, but while the rebellion did not have a truly federalist agenda, it *was* a revolt against the dominance of Paris in national politics, so in that sense the label fits. And to term the rebellion "republican" would seem to suggest, by implication, that the Jacobins and Montagnards were *not* republicans, which would be misleading in its own way. Antonio de Francesco has characterized the departmental revolt as an exercise in popular sovereignty, an assertion of local power against a strong central government. In this he is thinking both of the tradition of the Bourbon monarchy, and also of the centralizing tendencies of the Jacobin government of the Year II. But as the summer wore on, one of the striking features of the federalist revolt was the absence of popular support for

23 M. Slavin, *The Making of an Insurrection: Parisian Sections and the Gironde* (Cambridge, MA, Harvard University Press, 1986).

24 M. J. Sydenham, "The Republican Revolt of 1793: A Plea for Less Localized Local Studies," *French Historical Studies* 11 (1981), 120–38.

active resistance to the National Convention, which in my view makes it difficult to see this as any kind of popular uprising.[25]

The National Convention responded to the revolt in three ways. First, it promised amnesty to any local official who admitted his error and retracted his support for a declaration of revolt, which most did. Representatives on mission were dispatched to the rebel cities, supported by troops, and in Caen and Marseille the revolt collasped before summer's end. Bordeaux and Lyon sustained their resistance into the fall, with the rebels in Lyon capitulating only after an extended siege.[26] Secondly, the Montagnard leadership made public the case against the proscribed Girondin deputies, a task made somewhat easier by the fact that more than a dozen of them fled Paris for Caen, where they expressed their support for the brewing rebellion. Finally, by the third week of June the constitution committee completed a draft of the new constitution, which the Convention approved and submitted to the nation for ratification by referendum in July.

The 1793 constitution was the most democratic constitution of the Revolution. The language of the constitution made clear that the people, rather than the nation, were the source of sovereignty, thereby reversing the formula first uttered by Sieyès in the Estates General when he asserted that wherever the National Assembly might meet, there the nation would be found. The constitution was accompanied by a revised text of the Declaration of the Rights of Man and Citizen, which asserted the people's right to insurrection. It also asserted the right to subsistence, which the 1789 Declaration had neglected. Yet, this commitment to democracy and popular sovereignty had been the subject of contestation throughout the previous year, leaving some unsure as to how the people would vote in primary assemblies.

Voter turnout in the referendum on the 1793 constitution was relatively low – just over a third of eligible voters cast a ballot, although this was higher than any turnout since 1790, and may have been the highest of the Revolution – but an overwhelming majority, virtually 99 percent,

---

25 A. de Francesco, "Popular Sovereignty and Executive Power in the Federalist Revolt of 1793," *French History* 5 (1991), 74–101; P. R. Hanson, "The Federalist Revolt: An Affirmation or Denial of Popular Sovereignty?," *French History* 6 (1992), 335–55.

26 By the end of the summer, the revolt in Lyon had shifted in character from federalist resistance to royalist counterrevolution. The port city of Toulon, to the east of Marseille, also rebelled in the summer of 1793, with the rebels ultimately turning the port over to the British. I have viewed the Toulon uprising as essentially royalist, while Malcolm Crook has argued eloquently that the city should be included among the federalist cities, insisting that like Lyon, it turned toward royalism only in the last desperate days. For Lyon, see W. D. Edmonds, *Jacobinism and the Revolt of Lyon*; for Toulon, see M. Crook, *Toulon in War and Revolution: From the Ancien Régime to the Restoration, 1750–1820* (Manchester, Manchester University Press, 1991).

voted in favor of the proposed constitution. As Malcolm Crook has observed, the fact that ballots were taken by voice vote and in public assemblies tended to discourage both dissenting votes and attendance by those in a minority, but the minutes from many assemblies also make clear that discussion was free and spirited. Indeed, some who opposed the Montagnards voted in favor of the constitution, hoping that this would usher in new elections that would allow them to vote the Montagnards out of office. Crook also points out that continued resistance to the republic – in the Vendée and the federalist cities of Bordeaux and Lyon – plus the number of young men away at the front, renders the overall turnout rather remarkable. Finally, as Peter McPhee reminds us, these assemblies, like the 1789 assemblies to draw up *cahiers*, drew considerable participation from women, especially in rural areas. They were very much community gatherings and by all accounts succeeded, as the Montagnards hoped they would, in rallying the populace to the republic.[27]

As liberal and democratic as the constitution of 1793 was, however, the people would never enjoy the liberties or democracy it promised. Due to the war, and continuing threat of civil war, the National Convention suspended its implementation until peace should be restored. Before that could happen, Robespierre and the Montagnards would fall from power on 9 Thermidor (27 July 1794), the Terror would come to an end, and the more conservative majority that emerged would draft a new constitution in 1795 that once again restricted the electorate and reined in political liberties.

Slave Revolt in Saint-Domingue

The slave revolt in Saint-Domingue was more integral and important to the French Revolution than most general histories would suggest.[28] We have already discussed, in Chapter Three, the failure of the revolutionaries to extend the Declaration of the Rights of Man and Citizen to blacks in the colonies, whether free or enslaved, and the subsequent agitation among

---

27 M. Crook, *Elections in the French Revolution: An Apprenticeship in Democracy, 1789–1799* (Cambridge, Cambridge University Press, 1996), especially Chapter Five; P. McPhee, *Living the French Revolution, 1789–99* (New York, Palgrave Macmillan, 2006), 129–31.

28 Few general histories, whether long or short, devote more than a page or two to events in Saint-Domingue. Among recent works, that by Jack Censer and Lynn Hunt is an exception, although here, too, the fuller treatment is not fully integrated, coming at the end of the chapters on the Revolution and just before a chapter on Napoleon. See J. R. Censer and L. Hunt, *Liberty, Equality, Fraternity: Exploring the French Revolution* (University Park, Pennsylvania State University Press, 2001), 115–38.

freed coloreds in Saint-Domingue and resultant repression. Following the execution of Vincent Ogé in February 1791, his martyrdom was commemorated on the stage in Paris, and under renewed pressure the Constituent Assembly extended political rights to all freed coloreds and mulattoes born to free parents, still a minuscule number. By September 1791 the slaves of Saint-Domingue were in open rebellion and most of the sugar cane plantations burned to the ground. The magnitude of the revolt in Saint-Domingue prompted French colonists on Martinique and Guadeloupe to grant reforms, made easier in those colonies by the fact that white settlers outnumbered freed coloreds and mulattoes. In France, a number of the Girondins elected to the Legislative Assembly became members of the Society of Friends of Blacks, despite the colonial interests of a number of their constituents in Bordeaux, and in April 1792 the deputies extended full civil liberties to all freed coloreds. They left both slavery and the slave trade intact, however, and even in the midst of the devastation in Saint-Domingue some 10,000 new slaves would be brought from Africa in 1792.

The declaration of a republic would change the situation in Saint-Domingue, however, particularly following the trial and execution of Louis XVI. Spain and Great Britain now entered the war against France, and this altered the dynamics in the Caribbean every bit as much as it changed them on the European continent. Great Britain, hoping to expand its foothold in the West Indies, made overtures to white planters in Saint-Domingue, while the Spanish, who occupied the larger portion of the island of Hispaniola, promised freedom to those slave insurgents who joined their army. Many did, including the man who would eventually emerge as the leader of a free Haiti, François-Dominique Toussaint-Louverture.

Just as the republic was being declared in Paris, two new commissioners had arrived in Saint-Domingue, Léger Félicité Sonthonax and Etienne Polverel. Both were lawyers, inexperienced in colonial affairs, who had become acquaintances and allies of Jacques-Pierre Brissot, an avid abolitionist and leader in the Legislative Assembly. It was Brissot who secured their appointment as commissioners to Saint-Domingue, empowered to replace or suspend all colonial authorities and to see that the April decree granting civil rights to freed coloreds would be enacted. Not surprisingly, they were greeted by considerable resistance from the white planters in the colony. In February 1793, as royalist sympathies spread among the planters and as the Spanish prepared to invade Saint-Domingue across their shared border, Sonthonax wrote to a friend back home that the "slaves of the New World are fighting for the same cause as the French armies."[29]

---

29 Laurent Dubois, *Avengers of the New World* (Cambridge, MA, Harvard University Press, 2004), 154.

Although Sonthonax had not sailed to Saint-Domingue with either a mandate or intention to free the slaves, his sentiments were clearly taking him in that direction. The continued recalcitrance of the white planters, who soon found an ally in the new military governor for the colony, led by late spring to open hostilities and renewed insurrection among the slave population. As with the Jacobins in France, then, Sonthonax found himself facing both internal opposition and a foreign enemy. In June 1793, as the Girondins were being proscribed from the National Convention, the main town of Le Cap (called by some the Paris of Saint-Domingue) was in flames, and the two commissioners issued a decree promising that any black slave who took up arms in support of the republic would gain both freedom and all the rights enjoyed by French citizens.[30]

The deteriorating situation in Saint-Domingue had an impact on the Revolution in France in at least two ways in this period. First, the disruption of sugar production on the island drove prices up in Paris by late 1792, which soon drove women to protest in the markets. One often sees cited Robespierre's dismissive comments at the time of the February 1793 food riots: "I don't say that the people are guilty . . . but when they rise in revolt, should they not have a worthy objective? Should they be concerned with paltry merchandise?. . . The people must rise, not to collect sugar but to lay low the brigands."[31] But one seldom sees the connection made to the slave revolt in Saint-Domingue and its impact on the French economy, not only for consumers but for the traders of Bordeaux as well.

The rise in the cost of sugar fed popular discontent in Paris and aided the Montagnards in their struggle with the Girondins, which ultimately benefitted the slaves of Saint-Domingue. It would be another year, however, in February 1794 – after the proscription of the Girondin deputies and the repression of the federalist revolt – until the National Convention would formally abolish slavery and grant full civil rights to all black men in the colonies. The "implacable logic of rights" may have pointed toward

---

30 Ibid., 143–59. See also, L. Dubois, *A Colony of Citizens: Revolution and Slave Emancipation in the French Caribbean, 1787–1804* (Chapel Hill, University of North Carolina Press, 2004); D. Geggus, *Slavery, War and Revolution: The British Occupation of Saint-Domingue, 1793–1798* (Oxford, Oxford University Press, 1982); D. Geggus, *Haitian Revolutionary Studies* (Bloomington, Indiana University Press, 2002); C. Fick, *The Making of Haiti: The Saint-Domingue Revolution from Below* (Knoxville, University of Tennessee Press, 1990); and J. D. Garrigus, *Before Haiti: Race and Citizenship in French Saint-Domingue* (New York, Palgrave Macmillan, 2006).

31 N. Hampson, *The Life and Opinions of Maximilien Robespierre* (London, Duckworth, 1974), 139; see also D. Jordan, *The Revolutionary Career of Maximilien Robespierre* (Chicago, University of Chicago Press, 1985), 135.

that goal, but it took the largest slave insurrection in world history, urban protest in Paris, and colonial competition with Great Britain to finally get there. Meanwhile, the island of Saint-Domingue lay in ruins.

The Republic in Rural France

The advent of the republic brought both promise and disappointment to the peasantry of France. As with the black slaves of Saint-Domingue, for whom the republic would at least make possible the realization of liberty and equality, so for the peasants of rural France did the declaration of the republic, and even more the triumph of the Montagnards, bring hope that the abolition of seigneurialism would now become a reality. Just days after the fall of the monarchy, on 14 August 1792, the Legislative Assembly had issued a decree making all non-wooded common lands liable to partition. Peasants had been clamoring for such partition since 1789, and the relatively poor harvest of 1792, along with the increasing demand for food brought on by the war, raised the volume of the clamoring. The August decree was completely unworkable, however, and was essentially revoked two months later, with no official action taken for the next ten months.

Another dramatic political shift, the proscription of the Girondin deputies on 2 June 1793, brought new legislation, no doubt prompted in part by the desire in the National Convention to avert potential resistance in the countryside, and as a response to continuing peasant revolts against the persistence of the seigneurial regime. The decree of 10 June, however, was much better crafted than that of the previous August and had clearly been under consideration for some weeks. Simply put, it decreed that common lands should be divided equally among members of the community provided that one-third of those members voted for partition. As Peter Jones has written, "On the face of it, the decree of 10 June 1793 should have been the answer to every poor peasant's prayer."[32] In practice, however, division of the common lands created dissension in some rural communities, may not have been as extensive as some historians have claimed, and had deleterious ecological consequences in some areas where it did take place on a substantial scale.

Early in the twentieth century, Georges Lefebvre argued that peasants, at least those with little or no land, were opposed to division of the commons because they depended on those lands to graze their animals;

32 P. M. Jones, *The Peasantry in the French Revolution* (Cambridge, Cambridge University Press, 1988), 147.

they were, moreover, opposed to the capitalist spirit embraced by rich peasants and large-scale farmers. Proposals to divide the common lands, as well as wooded lands formerly controlled by seigneurs, thus tended to polarize rural communities. More recent research, inspired in part by the work of the Soviet historian Anatoli Ado, has challenged Lefebvre's interpretation, suggesting that the land hunger of small peasants did indeed lead to a particular form of rural capitalism in France that resulted in the pattern of smallholding that would prevail until late in the twentieth century, in contrast to the tendency toward large landholdings that the enclosure movement initiated across the Channel in England. It is difficult to offer generalizations on this matter, because landholding patterns and cultivation practices varied substantially throughout France. More local studies will need to be done before anything resembling a definitive verdict can resolve this debate. But for the moment, Peter Jones is skeptical that the decree of 10 June led to any extensive partition of common lands. For one thing, peasants tended to have a more customary conception of property than the predominantly bourgeois deputies of the national assemblies, and this favored the continuation of traditional usage. Secondly, in some areas pastoralists resisted the division of common lands, which would have interfered with the unfettered grazing of their flocks. Thirdly, those larger farmers, whether absentee or resident, who employed day laborers, may have resisted such division of the land for fear that this would shrink the available supply of labor. Still and all, it is clear that in some parts of France division of the commons did occur, sometimes made mandatory by local officials. The sale of *biens nationaux*, to be discussed in the next chapter, also contributed to the consolidation of a characteristically French pattern of smallholdings.[33]

While the extent to which the common lands were divided remains under investigation, in much of France there was a strong drive on the part of the peasantry to clear as much land as possible for cultivation, whether common lands or the woodlands controlled by former seigneurs, and in some areas this had serious environmental consequences. As we saw in Chapter Three, although the abolition of seigneurial dues and obligations that followed the Night of 4 August was not as definitive as most peasants would have hoped, or expected, peasants in many parts of

33 Ibid., 137–54. Ado's work, which first appeared in 1971, has never been translated from the Russian. Jones offers this English title: A. Ado, *The Peasant Movement in France during the Great Bourgeois Revolution of the End of the Eighteenth Century* (Moscow, 1971). See also G. Lefebvre, *Les Paysans du Nord pendant la Révolution française*, 2 vols. (Lille, O. Marquant, 1924); F. Gauthier, *La Voie paysanne dans la Révolution française: l'exemple de la Picardie* (Paris, F. Maspero, 1977); and J. Markoff, *The Abolition of Feudalism: Peasants, Lords, and Legislators in the French Revolution* (University Park, Pennsylvania State University Press, 1996), 485–515.

France simply chose to ignore the dues that remained legally in place until their final elimination by decree of the National Convention on 17 July 1793. Peter McPhee has studied in depth one region in southern France, the Corbières, which suffered serious environmental degradation over the decade of the 1790s. Particularly hard hit were the *garrigues*, hillsides covered with scrub oak, some under seigneurial control and some held in common. These lands were valuable as a source of firewood, building timber, grazing for herds of small sheep and goats, acorns and chestnuts that helped sustain poor peasants through difficult winters when grain was in short supply. Prior to 1789, either the seigneurs or the community had managed these lands, had protected them in some measure against misuse. In the 1790s, however, liberty soon gave way to license and many of the *garrigues* were cleared, either to allow cultivation or because the trees were felled for building timbers, firewood, or charcoal. The bark of the green oaks was also prized for tanning. Not only poor peasants but also the former seigneurs themselves joined in the exploitation of those resources. McPhee concludes that by 1795, "the consequences of clearances and woodcutting had become of national importance" and quotes one despondent observer: "Even in living memory, people believe that the climate has changed; vines and olives suffer from frosts now, they perish in places where they used to flourish, and people give the reason: the hillsides and peaks were formerly covered with clumps of woods, bushes, greenery … the greedy fury of clearances arrived; everything has been cut down without consideration; people have destroyed the physical conditions which conserved the temperature of the region."[34] Global warming, it would seem, has not been confined to the late twentieth century, nor has the industrial world enjoyed a monopoly on environmental abuse.

Conclusion

On 24 October 1793, barely one week after the execution of Marie-Antoinette, the deputy Fabre d'Eglantine reported to the National Convention on the introduction of a new revolutionary calendar, to commence retroactively with the declaration of the Republic just over one year before. A new age had dawned for France. Much had been achieved in this tumultuous year. The French people had shaken off their shackles by toppling the monarchy, and universal manhood suffrage had been

34 P. McPhee, *Revolution and Environment in Southern France: Peasants, Lords, and Murder in the Corbières, 1780–1830* (Oxford, Oxford University Press, 1999), 132.

decreed. Black slaves in Saint-Domingue had risen up to claim their freedom, which the National Convention would soon formally sanction. Elections across France had brought new people into local government, and in much of the country, particularly in the towns and cities, an unprecendented level of political engagement prevailed, not just in the electoral process but in clubs and sectional assemblies as well. The nation had mobilized to defend *la patrie* against the armies of France's enemies, the monarchies of Europe. A new, democratic constitution had been adopted, and the final vestiges of feudalism had been abolished.

As dramatic and promising as those achievements were, however, they also created new tensions and divisions. Patriotic zeal may have carried the citizen armies of France to impressive victories on the battlefield, but military recruitment also generated resistance, particularly in the west where, in combination with resentment over the Civil Constitution of the Clergy, resistance broke out into open rebellion. While Robespierre and the Montagnards may have welcomed "the people," the *sans-culottes*, as political allies, the Girondins and the propertied elites who supported them viewed those same people with alarm and warned that the country was headed toward anarchy and unbridled violence. The proscription of the Girondin leaders expanded the areas of resistance to the national government, and while the federalist cities had all been subdued by October 1793, the leaders of the revolt were still to be punished. Thousands of people had fled France since the beginning of the Revolution, most of them former aristocrats, and many of them now stood eager to support the monarchist forces arrayed against the republican armies of France. We turn in the next chapter to consider the Montagnards' response to those challenges: the regeneration of the nation on the one hand, and terror on the other.

6

Regeneration and Terror

In his classic study of the Terror, R. R. Palmer compared France in 1793 to an old house undergoing renovation. An array of workmen come and go, but they do not always work together:

> Foremen stand by giving directions from blueprints, but the blueprints do not correspond. A few eccentrics will labor only at little corners of their own. A great many struggle to keep standing what others would tear down. Some are doing nothing constructive; workmen who have turned against their work, or inhabitants who dislike the way the alterations are turning out .... Meanwhile, in the distance coming closer may be seen a band of armed attackers, whether gangsters or policemen is not clear, but obviously bent on stopping the whole proceeding.
>
> The house so beset is France in the fifth summer of the Revolution. The approaching band is the armed force of monarchical Europe. The distracted throng is a babel of revolutionists, royalists and republicans, constitutionalists and insurrectionists, civilly sworn clergy, refractory clergy, renegade clergy, aristocrats and plebeians, Jacobins, Girondists, Mountaineers, Vendéans, Muscadins, federalists, moderatists and Enragés.[1]

Palmer offers three important points in this analogy. First, there was something under construction in France in 1793–94. In our popular depictions of the Terror, and even in our histories, we tend to emphasize a situation of civil chaos, of violence aimed at the elimination of political enemies, of the unrelenting rise and fall of the guillotine. But there was

---

1 R. R. Palmer, *Twelve Who Ruled: The Year of the Terror in the French Revolution* (Princeton, Princeton University Press, 1941), 22.

also renovation going on in the midst of war and civil war. The revolutionaries used the word "regeneration" to characterize that project, and it will be one of the themes of this chapter. Second, Palmer's "band of armed attackers," the monarchies of Europe, points out that the threat to the French republic was a real one, that the Terror was not born purely of ideology or fanaticism, though he would not deny that both played a role in the bitter politics of that year. Finally, Palmer's long list of actors in the final sentence – political, social, and professional – is a salutory reminder of the complexities of the French Revolution, and of the fact that there were enemies within the country in addition to the armies beyond its borders. We all tend, at times, to reify the Revolution, if only for the sake of dramatic effect or literary shorthand. But "the Revolution" did not exist as an entity, it did not "do" anything, it did not eliminate its enemies, even if Pierre Vergniaud did famously say that "the Revolution, like Saturn, devours its children."

Yet, as most standard political histories of the Terror make clear, a succession of political groups did go to the guillotine in the Year II: first the Girondins, then the *enragés*, followed by the Hébertistes, the Dantonists (or Indulgents, as they are sometimes called), and finally, in Thermidor, Robespierre and his closest Jacobin supporters. There had been divisions among the revolutionaries from the start, but they had grown more bitter and deadly by 1793. Seldom in the first years of the Revolution did those who were perceived to have abandoned the cause pay for that with their lives. Both François Furet and Lynn Hunt have emphasized the role of conspiracy, or more precisely the fear of conspiracy, in the political dynamic of the French Revolution.[2] Such fears were present almost from the outset, however, and seldom led to widespread bloodletting. Timothy Tackett has argued that the Flight to Varennes was a pivotal moment in this regard, that the king's departure from Paris with his family made the abstract fear of hidden plots suddenly quite tangible, and moreover made it clear that such plotting was occurring at the highest levels of government.[3] One might also argue that the advent of foreign war created a political climate in which toleration of opposing views, much less outright dissent, became increasingly difficult.

In addition to regeneration and the persecution of political enemies we should also note, again following Palmer, that statebuilding was an

2 F. Furet, *Penser la Révolution française* (Paris, Gallimard, 1978), 78–79; L. Hunt, *Politics, Culture, and Class in the French Revolution* (Berkeley, University of California Press, 1984), 38–44.

3 T. Tackett, *When the King Took Flight* (Cambridge, MA, Harvard University Press, 2003), 222–23.

important part of the Terror. In mid-November 1793 the deputy Billaud-Varenne addressed the National Convention on behalf of the Committee of Public Safety, which had been created the previous April to function as the executive branch of the government. Citing the disorder, indeed near-anarchy, that had afflicted the republic throughout the previous summer, Billaud proposed a set of measures aimed at the centralization of power, based on the premise that in a republic of virtue in which justice and reason prevailed, there could be no legitimate political opposition. After two weeks of debate and discussion, the National Convention adopted the Law of 14 Frimaire (4 December 1793), establishing the revolutionary dictatorship that would rule France until 9 Thermidor (27 July 1794).

The Law of 14 Frimaire formalized the authority of the Committee of Public Safety; in reaction to the federalist revolt it curtailed the authority of departmental administations and increased the role of district administrations; it appointed new national agents as liaisons between the central government and local authorities, and empowered them to purge local administrations; it more clearly defined, and restrained, the authority of representatives on mission and made them answerable directly to the Committee of Public Safety; it suspended local elections until the wartime emergency should be declared at an end. "The law of 14 Frimaire," Palmer argued, "had as permanent a significance as the Declaration of the Rights of Man. They were poles apart, for they attacked antithetical extremes, anarchy and despotism."[4] All modern governments, Palmer argued, whether democratic or dictatorial, depend on laws that guarantee public order and facilitate the mobilization of resources, both material and human, in the interests of the state and the common good. On those counts, most would agree, the government of the Year II succeeded. But in democracies, as Palmer acknowledged, there is a constant tension between public order and individual liberty, and few would deny that the latter was sacrificed in the name of the former under the Terror. The argument, at the time and ever since, is whether or not the circumstances justified the sacrifice.

Since historians agree on so little else about the Terror, it is perhaps not surprising that they differ in regard to the chronological definition of the Terror. For those who see the Terror as the very essence of the Revolution, the two become almost coterminous, and terror is equated with revolutionary violence. Hugh Gough, although he does not adopt as broad a conception as some, has suggested that we think in terms of two terrors: a first terror that began with the assault on the Tuileries palace in August 1792 and prevailed through the spring of 1793, and a second terror that extended from the summer of 1793 until the summer of 1794. Thus, the

---

4 R. R. Palmer, *Twelve Who Ruled*, 128.

insurrection that toppled the monarchy and the September Massacres that followed inaugurated this first terror, which Gough characterizes in two ways, as a "transition from political normality to terror" and as a "slide from constitutional politics to terror."[5] It is difficult, it seems to me, to characterize the first three years of the Revolution as a time of "political normality," and the constitution of 1791 was undermined by the king almost as soon as it was formally adopted. More importantly, however, I think it important to distinguish popular violence from state terror, even if, as Gough argues, the violence of August and September 1792 did mark a break from the liberal tolerance for opposing views that largely prevailed in revolutionary politics in 1789–90.

François Furet began his Bicentennial essay on the Terror with a reference to 5 September 1793, on which date a Paris uprising led by the *enragés* ended with a declaration from the National Convention that terror was now "the order of the day." Furet went on to argue that the "circumstances surrounding this celebrated vote indicate that before becoming a set of repressive institutions used by the Republic to liquidate its adversaries and establish its domination on a basis of fear, the Terror was a demand based on political convictions or beliefs, a characteristic feature of the mentality of revolutionary activism."[6] This view is problematical on two counts. First, if Terror was "a characteristic feature of the mentality of revolutionary activism," then we must see it as a natural outgrowth of popular violence, rather than as a break from or an effort to control that popular violence. Second, Jean-Clément Martin has recently insisted that the National Convention did *not* declare terror to be "the order of the day" on 5 September. Bertrand Barére did indeed use the phrase in a speech that day, but both the Convention and the Committee of Public Safety resisted the pressure of the crowd and made no formal declaration.[7]

Many historians would still stress the importance of the insurrection of 5 September because in its wake the National Convention did pass legislation that could be said to have institutionalized the Terror: the creation of the Parisian revolutionary army on 9 September; the decree of the Law

5 H. Gough, *The Terror in the French Revolution* (London, Macmillan Press, 1998), 21, 23. This is the best short history of the Terror currently in print.

6 F. Furet, "Terror," in F. Furet and M. Ozouf, eds., *A Critical Dictionary of the French Revolution* (Cambridge, MA, Harvard University Press, 1989), 137–50.

7 J.-C. Martin, *Violence et Révolution: essai sur la naissance d'un mythe national* (Paris, Seuil, 2006), 188–90. In an H-France forum discussing this book, Martin went so far as to assert that there exists no clear definition of what the Terror was in the historiography on the French Revolution. See Martin's comments at http://h-france.net/forum/forumvol2/Martin1Response.html. On this webpage you will also find links to the reviews of Martin's book by David Andress, Lynn Hunt, Donald Sutherland, and Sophie Wahnich.

of Suspects on 17 September; and passage of the general *maximum* on 29 September, which imposed price controls on many staple goods. Others, adopting this same institutional approach, might point to March 1793 and the creation of the Revolutionary Tribunal, explicitly charged with trying those accused of treason or counterrevolution, or July 1793 when the Committee of Public Safety was consolidated and given expanded executive powers.

The endpoint to the Terror is easier to identify, at least symbolically: 9 Thermidor II (27 July 1794), the day that Robespierre was ousted from power. Executions of political enemies continued for some weeks thereafter – most notably Robespierre and his allies in the immediate aftermath – and the institutions of the Terror, most notably the Revolutionary Tribunal and the Committee of Public Safety, were not immediately dismantled. So powerful is the association of Robespierre with the Terror, however, that there has been general agreement among historians that the two met their demise simultaneously.

Our focus in this chapter will be on Hugh Gough's "second terror," the period stretching from the early summer of 1793 to the late summer of 1794. In regard to judicial repression, the bulk of it came in response to the Vendée rebellion in the west, which began in the spring of 1793, and to the federalist revolts that developed in June. It seems reasonable, then, to speak of the Terror beginning before the autumn legislation that gave it a legal basis. And the representatives on mission, those deputies of the National Convention who carried the Terror to the provinces, began their work in the spring of 1793 among the various armies and in support of military recruitment.

We will devote some attention to the legislation passed in September and October 1793, for despite Gough's observation that the Terror represented a slide from constitutional politics, it was based in law. Some attention must also be paid to the major policy pronouncements by which both Robespierre and St. Just, in particular, attempted to defend and refine the regime of the Terror, as well as to the events and legislative edicts that ushered in what is generally referred to as the Great Terror in the spring of 1794.

As suggested above, however, there was more to the Terror than judicial repression and executions, and we will consider elements of statebuilding undertaken by the Committee of Public Safety, as well as various aspects of the national regeneration that was central to Jacobin politics in this period. This included efforts to reform education, most obviously, but also land distribution (through the sale of *biens nationaux*), aid to the poor, work programs, progressive taxation, and other social programs, including implementation of the divorce law passed in late

1792. The Jacobin clubs were central to this project, and they became virtually an arm of the government during the Year II, but representatives on mission were also crucial actors in conveying the policies of the National Convention to local officials. Sometimes those deputies were received as dictatorial proconsuls, but in other cases they were welcomed as allies by progressive elements of the local population. Finally, we must endeavor in this chapter to consider the impact of the war on France, not only as an impetus to the emergency measures of the Terror, but as an agent of popular mobilization on the one hand, and as a draining influence on the other, depriving local communities of badly needed labor, and often drawing from sectional assemblies and political clubs their most enthusiastic and energetic activists.

Representatives on Mission

> It is not for nothing that most monographs on terror in the provinces start with the arrival of deputies from Paris, since they had virtually limitless powers to organise revolutionary tribunals and order repression as they saw fit.[8]

Representatives on mission have not been neglected by historians, but the ones who most easily come to mind are those who oversaw particularly harsh repression in the provinces: Jean-Baptiste Carrier ordering the drowning of Vendéan rebels in Nantes; Jean-Marie Collot d'Herbois commanding the execution by cannon of federalist rebels in Lyon; Claude Javogues terrorizing the people of the Loire department; or Joseph Fouché aggressively pursuing de-Christianization in the Nièvre.[9] The collective impression is overwhelmingly negative. Consider, for example, this characterization offered by Patrice Higonnet: "Unable to address the true social problems of the age, the Robespierrist Terrorists made up for their powerlessness by the persecution of defenceless people who belonged to social groups whose principles they did not like."[10] There is tension, to be sure, between Higonnet's powerless yet vindictive representatives on mission and the deputies bearing "virtually limitless powers" that Forrest describes, but both were engaged in the business of repression. We gain

8 A. Forrest, "The Local Politics of Repression," in K. M. Baker, ed., *The Terror* (Oxford, Pergamon, 1994), 85.

9 The classic study of a single representative on mission remains C. Lucas, *The Structure of the Terror: The Example of Javogues and the Loire* (Oxford, Clarendon Press, 1973).

10 P. Higonnet, *Sister Republics* (Cambridge, MA, Harvard University Press, 1988), 262.

a strikingly different impression from the work of Jean-Pierre Gross, who has written about five representatives on mission who attempted to put Jacobin egalitarian ideals into practice. Jacques Brival and Gilbert Romme, he tells us, "for their part, practiced what they preached and throughout their terms as members of the Convention donated part of their deputies' salary each month to the poor . . . ."[11] So what were these representatives on mission, we might ask, angels or demons?

As is the case with most historical questions, the truth lies somewhere in between. Gross cites Jacques Godechot's estimation that "some demonstrated revolutionary intolerance and were the artisans of Terror, while the others, and they were the majority, were moderates who endeavoured to establish a reign of justice."[12] Gross puts the ratio at 20:80, while granting that the "artisans of Terror" have gotten more attention from historians than the moderates. Their numbers alone may be one reason why only a minority is widely known. Some 426 deputies in the National Convention served as representatives on mission between March 1793 and October 1795. Their missions did not cease, then, with the end of the Terror. Michel Biard estimates that among those deputies, nearly half sat among the Montagnards in the National Convention, approximately 38 percent sat with the Plain, barely 9 percent were Girondins, while the remaining 5 percent cannot be classified.[13] The small percentage of Girondins is not surprising, since many of them were proscribed from the Convention in June and July 1793. But even in the period prior to that, historians have long recognized the preponderance of Montagnards on mission, which may have been a tactical maneuver on the part of the Girondin leadership, aiming to secure their majority in votes within the Convention.

The representatives on mission generally traveled in pairs, sometimes three to a group. One of those assigned was almost always from the locality to be visited, so that the team would have some familiarity with the region and its politics. The other, it logically follows, was intentionally

11 J.-P. Gross, *Fair Shares for All: Jacobin Egalitarianism in Practice* (Cambridge, Cambridge University Press, 1997), 163.

12 Ibid., 17.

13 M. Biard, *Missionaires de la République* (Paris, Comité des Travaux Historiques et Scientifiques, 2002), 448. This is to date the most comprehensive work on the representatives on mission, offering in its appendix a brief biography of each along with a listing of his various missions. See also H. Wallon, *Les Représentants du peuple en mission et la justice révolutionnaire dans les départements en l'an II (1793–1794)* (Paris, Hachette, 1889–90), 5 vols.; and A. Aulard, *Recueil des actes du Comité de salut public avec la correspondance officielle des représentants en mission et le registre du Conseil exécutif provisoire* (Paris, Imprimerie nationale, 1889–99), 36 vols., which is particularly valuable for the letters and reports written by the representatives on mission.

not a native to the region, in order to assure an element of objectivity. The representatives on mission were appointed by the Committee of Public Safety and reported directly to it. Among the twelve members of the Committee of Public Safety during the Year II, only Maximilien Robespierre and Bertrand Barère did not serve at least once on mission to the provinces. Most performed multiple missions. The dichotomy often presented in the literature, then – between a centralizing Jacobin government based in Paris and dominated by the Committee of Public Safety, and a cadre of representatives on mission out in the provinces acting as independent agents – is somewhat misleading. The members of the Committee often left Paris themselves, and most were originally from the provinces.

This did not mean, however, that they were all comfortable on mission to the provinces, familiar with all parts of France, or sympathetic to the local inhabitants. Lazare Carnot, himself a native of Burgundy, had this to say about the Provençals: "You have no idea of that part of the world: it's like nothing else. Everyone there is a royalist or a terrorist. There's no in between. In Dijon or in Poitiers, people are reasonable; they talk. In Marseille, they start with the knife."[14] Georges Couthon, although he hailed from a town not far to the west of Lyon, clearly had a low opinion of the Lyonnais: "I find myself in a country that is in need of complete regeneration . . .. I believe that the people are stupid here by temperament, that the fogs of the Rhône and the Saône leave in the air a vapor that makes them thick-headed." Louis-Stanislas Fréron, sharing Carnot's negative opinion of the Marseillais, clearly did not have Couthon's faith in the possibilities of regeneration: "I believe that Marseille can never be cured, barring a deportation of all its inhabitants and a transfusion of men from the North."[15]

Nor can the good people of the provinces be said to have been universally hospitable to the representatives on mission, despite their position of authority and extensive powers. Marc-Antoine Baudot and Claude-Alexandre Ysabeau, on mission to Bordeaux in August 1793 to derail the federalist revolt in the city, were chased out of town by an unruly mob of young men.[16] Charles Romme and Claude-Antoine Prieur, on mission to Caen when the federalist revolt broke out there in June, were arrested and held hostage in the Château of Caen for nearly six weeks.[17] Jean-Baptiste

---

14 P. Higonnet, *Goodness beyond Virtue: Jacobins during the French Revolution* (Cambridge, MA, Harvard University Press, 1998), 259.

15 P. R. Hanson, *The Jacobin Republic under Fire: The Federalist Revolt in the French Revolution* (University Park, Pennsylvania State University Press, 2003), 220, 223.

16 A. Forrest, *Society and Politics in Revolutionary Bordeaux* (Oxford, Oxford University Press), 212–14.

17 P. R. Hanson, *Provincial Politics in the French Revolution: Caen and Limoges, 1789–1794* (Baton Rouge, Louisiana State University Press, 1989), 129–32.

Carrier and Claude Javogues would both ultimately be bitterly denounced by residents of the departments of the Loire-Inférieure and Loire respectively, and executed as terrorists. By contrast, the citizens of Calvados sent a delegation to the National Convention in 1796 to intervene on behalf of Robert Lindet, who had overseen the repression of federalism in that department three years before. Lindet eventually married the daughter of one of the departmental administrators whose arrest he had ordered that summer.

Accustomed as we are today to the instant communication of e-mail and text-messaging, it is a challenge to imagine just how isolated the deputies might feel while on mission to the provinces. Not only were they distant from the capital – it took two days, for example, to travel from Paris to Caen, at least five days to travel from Paris to Marseille – but they were distant from each other as well. Those deputies sent to deal with areas of resistance to the National Convention in the summer of 1793 knew that they had colleagues in other regions addressing the same problems, which tended to be exaggerated in public reports, because it was in the interest of both the rebels (in the federalist cities, for example) and the Montagnards in Paris to do so. Faced with a national emergency – war on three fronts – and faced with rebellion in the three largest cities after Paris, plus civil war in the west, the deputies set out on their missions convinced that the future of the republic was at stake. In those circumstances, no one wished to appear less resolute than others, less determined to vanquish the enemies of the republic. Generals had already been executed for failing to secure victory on the battlefield. Knowing this, for the representatives on mission it must have seemed riskier to appear lenient toward those who had declared their opposition to the National Convention than to be overzealous in the application of revolutionary justice.

Some were indeed draconian in their reprisals against counterrevolutionaries, and earned for themselves and their colleagues the pejorative label of proconsuls. The bloody repression they oversaw, most notably in the Vendée and in Lyon, has been well chronicled. Less well known, but drawing increasing attention from historians, are those representatives on mission who acted as mediators rather than proconsuls, who did all they could to work with local officials to pursue a shared agenda.[18] Most of the

18 See, for example, Chapter V in M. Biard, *Missionaires de la République*, entitled "'Agents' du pouvoir central ou médiateurs politiques?" Biard argues that after passage of the law of 14 Frimaire (4 December 1793), the Committee of Public Safety came to see the representatives on mission more as agents of the central government, but that in their role as legislators most of them continued to fulfill their responsibilities more as mediators than as implementers of national policy.

deputies came originally from large towns and cities, so even when they returned to their native departments they were forced to rely on locals to learn the lay of the land in the small towns and villages that were sprinkled across the landscape. Those sent on mission in the late summer and fall of 1793 were charged with "purifying" local administrations, especially the departmental administrations that had flirted with federalism. In those places where the local officials were suspect, the representatives on mission turned to the Jacobin clubs for assistance. Just as the Jacobin Club in Paris had become a sort of shadow parliament, especially in the view of its detractors, so now the clubs in the provinces became virtual arms of local government. Committees of surveillance, first charged with drawing up lists of suspects and later charged with arresting them, were predominantly drawn from the ranks of local Jacobins.[19]

Representatives were assigned to do much more, however, than arrest suspects or purge local administrations. In his study of five "moderate" representatives on mission, Jean-Pierre Gross contrasts the exhortative approach of Gilbert Romme and Jean-Baptiste Bo in the southwest of France to the coercive approach employed by Joseph Fouché in the Nièvre and in Lyon. Whereas Fouché threatened the rich with expropriation of their land, Romme and Bo first assigned local officials to visit neighboring districts in order to catalog both resources and needs, and then advocated a system of collectivized distribution to ensure that the poor would have adequate food and resources to survive. Rather than confiscating outright and selling the lands of *émigrés* and other suspects, they let them in small parcels to sharecroppers, thereby protecting the rights of the accused while seeing to the needs of the community. Like other representatives on mission, they attempted to improve primary education, setting up schools in the empty homes of *émigrés*.

Many of these efforts were hampered by the paucity of available funds, and as we shall see, most were suspended after Thermidor. But Gross emphasizes the progressive thinking of these men: "theirs was a vision of society in which a just distribution of wealth was the precondition of democracy." His analysis, while focused on the periphery, does not neglect the center, and just as many historians have assigned to Robespierre considerable responsibility for the excesses of the Terror, so does Gross credit him for envisioning the agenda of social justice that these representatives on mission were attempting to implement: "Robespierre's main contribution to egalitarian Jacobin discourse was thus to give economic substance to the abstract political concept of the universal 'brotherhood of

19 M. L. Kennedy, *The Jacobin Clubs in the French Revolution, 1793–1795* (New York, Berghahn Books, 2000).

man.'" In this vision, the forerunner (Gross argues) of the twentieth-century social welfare state, fraternity was an essential mediator between liberty and equality. It was a vision that replaced the patriarchal hierarchy of the traditional family with a new communitarian ideal: "if everyone receives a fair share, he and she must in return give their due to the community, for fair distribution within the bosom of the family requires that all should receive according to their needs and all should give according to their abilities." That vision of a regenerated society, so often traced to the thought of Jean-Jacques Rousseau, also had roots, Gross observes, in the writings of Montesquieu: "The love of democracy is the love of equality. The love of democracy is also the love of frugality. Since it promises to each the same happiness and the same benefits, each should find in it the same pleasures and harbour the same aspirations, something which can only be expected from general frugality."[20]

Regeneration

The idea of regeneration was not born of the radical idealism of the Year II, it had been on the minds of the revolutionaries already, and in some of their pamphlets, in the first days of 1789. Even Louis XVI had spoken to the delegates to the Estates General of the regeneration of the kingdom. Initially, the term connoted reform, often with reference to specific aspects of an Old Regime administration that seemed no longer to be working effectively, but soon the term came to have a more all-encompassing meaning. At several points in the first years of the Revolution one finds deputies and activists speaking of a new dawn: 14 July 1789, the Festival of Federation on the first anniversary of Bastille Day, the declaration of the republic on 22 September 1792, the date of Louis XVI's execution, 21 January 1793, which became a national holiday, and 10 August 1793, the first anniversary of the fall of the monarchy, but also the date marking the adoption by referendum of the constitution of 1793. The number of "new dawns" alone suggests the whirlwind of change that had enveloped the French nation.

Mona Ozouf has written that "during the revolutionary decade a thousand institutions and creations converged on the notion of regeneration."[21] Do not despair, we shall not attempt to enumerate all of them

20 J.-P. Gross, *Fair Shares for All*. The quotations are from pages 143, 40, 196, and 200. The passage from Montesquieu comes from *De l'esprit des lois*, R. Derathé, ed. (Paris, Garnier frères, 1973), Volume I, Book V, Chapter 3.

21 M. Ozouf, "Regeneration," in F. Furet and M. Ozouf, eds., *A Critical Dictionary of the French Revolution* (Cambridge, MA, Harvard University Press, 1989), 781–91.

here, but it is worth mentioning some of the more notable innovations and expressions of the new age. We have already noted, in Chapter Two, the creation of departments and a new map of France in 1790. That same year, festivals of various sorts were being held across the country to commemorate important events (Bastille Day) and to foster a new civic spirit. Quite often, liberty trees were planted on these occasions, and new patriotic songs were sung. People adopted modes of dress that reflected their political opinions: tricolored cockades and phrygian caps were donned by supporters of the Revolution, and the term *sans-culotte* denoted those working people who wore long trousers, as opposed to the knee-breeches and stylish silk stockings favored by aristocrats and bourgeois professionals under the Old Regime. In this new age of political transparency, people were expected to display their patriotic convictions publicly, and an array of new symbols emerged to reflect the new order. Modes of speech changed as well, as *monsieur* and *madame* gave way to *citoyen* and *citoyenne*, and the formal and deferential *vous* was replaced in everyday discourse by the informal and egalitarian *tu*. With the fall of the monarchy and the declaration of the republic all this accelerated and became more dramatic. *Place Royale* became *Place de la Liberté* or *Place de la République* in towns and cities all over France. Babies were given names drawn from classical antiquity or nature rather than Christian names. In the fall of 1793 a new revolutionary calendar was introduced, drafted initially by Gilbert Romme while he was a hostage in the Château of Caen during the federalist revolt. 22 September 1792, the day that the republic was officially declared, became retroactively Day 1 of Year I; the months of the calendar, all thirty days long, were given new names reflecting the changing seasons, devised by the poet/deputy Philippe Fabre d'Eglantine. Five days at the end of the calendar were designated *sans-culottides*, and each month was divided into three ten-day *décadis*, replacing the seven-day week, and reducing the days of rest from four to three each month, an aspect of the de-Christianizing agenda of this project that proved to be deeply unpopular with many common people.[22]

---

22 These various aspects of the cultural history of the French Revolution have generated a vast literature over the past quarter century, too voluminous to cite fully here. See in particular, M. Ozouf, *Festivals and the French Revolution* (Cambridge, MA, Harvard University Press, 1988); E. Kennedy, *A Cultural History of the French Revolution* (New Haven, Yale University Press, 1989); M. Agulhon, *Marianne into Battle: Republican Imagery and Symbolism in France, 1789–1880* (Cambridge, Cambridge University Press, 1981); L. Hunt, *Politics, Culture, and Class in the French Revolution* (Berkeley, University of California Press, 1984), and *The Family Romance of the French Revolution* (Berkeley, University of California Press, 1992); L. Mason, *Singing the French Revolution: Popular Culture and Politics, 1787–1799* (Ithaca, Cornell University Press, 1996); T. Crow, *Emulation: Making Artists for Revolutionary France*

In the optimistic, almost euphoric, days of 1789, many seemed to believe that regeneration would occur almost spontaneously, that one need only experience the Revolution to be made a new man, or new woman, and to embrace wholeheartedly the values of the new regime. By 1793 it had become clear that not all were capable of so smooth a transformation, and the deputies began to think more purposively and normatively about how to create virtuous citizens for the republic.

Their efforts focused in large part on two areas, the family and education. In a recent provocative and compelling book, Suzanne Desan has argued that the "Revolution infused politics into the most intimate relationships and wrenched many families away from the partriarchal practices of the old Regime."[23] Having ended the tyranny of the monarchy, the revolutionaries moved under the republic to abolish parental tyranny within the family. They did so by lowering the age of majority, by mandating equal inheritance (including even illegitimate children who could prove their father's paternity), and by abolishing the *lettres de cachet*, which under the Old Regime had allowed fathers to exercise despotic authority over their children. On the very eve of the declaration of the republic, the Legislative Assembly legalized divorce by mutual consent, and the law of 4 floréal II (23 April 1794) made even simpler the process of securing a divorce. Proof of six months de facto separation was all that was required.

Between 75,000 and 100,000 people underwent divorce from 1792 to 1803, when it was once again outlawed by the Napoleonic Civil Code. Not until 1975 would divorce in France again become so easy to obtain. The greatest number of divorces occurred in the years 1793–95, as Thermidor brought a conservative backlash against this legislation. When divorce was by mutual consent, often legally ending a marriage that had long since ceased to function, it is difficult or impossible to say who initiated the split. But in those cases of unilateral divorce that are recorded, between 65 and 75 percent were initiated by women.[24]

Desan concludes that "at every turn, individual family members seized the initiative in remaking their private lives within the cauldron of politics," and her work challenges the argument made by other historians, most notably Joan Landes, that the revolutionaries, especially the Jacobins, effectively set women's rights back a generation or two by excluding

(New Haven, Yale University Press, 1997); J. H. Johnson, *Listening in Paris: A Cultural History* (Berkeley, University of California Press, 1996); and J. Landes, *Visualizing the Nation: Gender, Representation, and Revolution in Eighteenth-Century France* (Ithaca, Cornell University Press, 2001).

23 S. Desan, *The Family on Trial in Revolutionary France* (Berkeley, University of California Press, 2004), 312.

24 Ibid., 96–101.

women from politics and the public sphere. "The Revolution certainly fostered strong rhetoric urging women toward domestic roles," Desan agrees, "but it also enacted laws giving women new civil rights as individuals, granted them new forms of legal and political access to the state, and generated languages and practices for criticizing gender inequities."[25]

If by this legislation the National Convention attempted to inculcate the ideals of liberty and equality within the family and the institution of marriage, through its reform of education it attempted to mold virtuous and patriotic citizens. Under the Old Regime, nearly all education was conducted by religious orders in small, local schools. There was much debate about education early in the Revolution, with Condorcet's vision of education as a liberating force the predominant one, but little was accomplished in the way of institutional reform. Schools were left to the control of departmental administrations, and since ecclesiastical properties devoted to instruction were exempt from confiscation, most teaching remained in the hands of the church.

In July 1793, Robespierre presented to the National Convention the educational plan drawn up by Louis-Michel Le Peletier de Saint-Fargeau, a revolutionary martyr who had died at the hands of a royal bodyguard on the eve of the king's execution. Unlike Condorcet, Le Peletier saw education as a means to regeneration rather than liberation, and his proposed system of instruction was a highly regimented one: "Continually under the eye and in the hand of an active surveillance each hour will be marked for sleep, meals, work, exercise, relaxation; the whole regime of living will be invariably regulated; gradual and repeated tests will be fixed; the genres of physical activity will be designated, gymnastic exercises will be indicated; a salutary and uniform regulation will prescribe all these details and a constant and smooth execution will guarantee every good effort."[26] This decidedly Spartan regimen was never implemented, although elements of it were incorporated into legislation proposed late in 1793 by Gabriel Bouquier for a national system of elementary education. Although individual representatives on mission did undertake educational initiatives in some departments, terror and war combined, as we have seen, to prevent the implementation of national educational reform. The Thermidorian regime would be more successful in this area.

---

25 Ibid., 312–13; J. B. Landes, *Women and the Public Sphere in the Age of the French Revolution* (Ithaca, Cornell University Press, 1988). See also J. N. Heuer, *The Family and the Nation: Gender and Citizenship in Revolutionary France, 1789–1830* (Ithaca, Cornell University Press, 2005), which takes up many of the same issues dealt with by Desan, but focuses more on the late years of the Revolution and the Restoration era.

26 E. Kennedy, *A Cultural History of the French Revolution*, 354.

Our focus in this discussion of regeneration has been largely on reforms and initiatives imposed on French society from above, some with success and some deeply resented and resisted. There is no clearer example of the latter than the de-Christianization campaign of late 1793, advocated by the Hébertistes in Paris and exported to the provinces by the revolutionary armies and Jacobin clubs with considerable enthusiasm, though very little success. Robespierre condemned de-Christianization as aristocratic and immoral as early as November 1793, and by spring 1794 the campaign was effectively abandoned.

It is important to remember, though, that the most effective representatives on mission acted as bridges between Paris and the provinces, and often built their success on local initiatives. Peter McPhee has written of a *sans-culotte* vision of regeneration, one that percolated up from below, "a vision of a France of artisans and smallholders rewarded for the dignity and usefulness of their labour, free from religion, the condescension of the high born, and the competition of merchants and manufacturers."[27] This was a vision consonant with the Jacobin egalitarianism described by Jean-Pierre Gross, but like their ambitious plans for educational reform, it, too, would fall victim to the viscissitudes of terror and war and be abandoned by the Thermidorians and the regime of the Directory.

War

From the spring of 1792 until the Battle of Waterloo in 1815, France was at war almost continuously for more than two decades. The relationship between war and revolution in this period was a complicated and dialectical one. The Girondin deputies, most notably Brissot, had argued that only an expansionist revolution could succeed, and they urged the declaration of war against Austria in 1792. Robespierre, almost alone in opposition at the time, argued that the French army, still essentially the army inherited from the Old Regime, was not prepared for war, and that to embark on that course would place the Revolution in jeopardy. Instead, it was the Girondins who found themselves in jeopardy once France went to war. The general in whose hands they placed their foreign policy, Charles-François Dumouriez, led his troops to defeat at Neerwinden in March 1793 and defected to the Austrians the following month, contributing to the shift in political winds that culminated with the proscription of the Girondin leaders on 2 June. Robespierre, the opponent of war, emerged just one month later as a leading voice on the Committee of Public Safety,

27 P. McPhee, *Living the French Revolution* (New York, Palgrave Macmillan, 2006), 122.

which would oversee the victorious campaigns of the army against the enemies of France over the course of the next year.

How did war affect the Terror? Let us remind ourselves, first, that reports of the defeat by the Prussians at Verdun had led to the panic that resulted in the prison massacres in Paris in September 1792, and that the military recruitment of spring 1793 was an important factor in the Vendée rebellion, the repression of which claimed more lives than any other aspect of the Terror. News that Toulon had fallen to the British similarly aroused the Parisian *sans-culottes* in September 1793, leading to demands for a heightening of Terror and the passage of the Law of Suspects. War, at the very least, contributed to an atmosphere in which people were less inclined to be tolerant of opposing political points of view, and more prone to see plot or conspiracy behind any suspicious or contrarian activity.

War could also be said to have had a galvanizing effect on the country, for while there may have been resistance to recruitment in the Vendée and a few other regions, more often young men volunteered enthusiastically, particularly on the frontiers, and more so in towns and cities than in the countryside. The claim that it was revolutionary élan that produced the triumphs of the French citizens' army may be exaggerated, but the dramatic increase in the army's size (from roughly 100,000 men under the Old Regime to nearly three-quarters of a million by 1794), and its transformation from a professional army commanded by an aristocratic officer corps to a citizens' army in which merit and accomplishment led to promotion, did foster innovation in both strategy and tactics that was crucial to its ultimate success. It was a politicized army, to be sure – the radical Paris newspaper, *Le Père Duchesne*, was distributed to troops at the front; representatives on mission, including St. Just, Carnot, and Prieur de la Marne from the Committee of Public Safety, made frequent trips to the northern and eastern fronts; and recalcitrant, or simply incompetent, generals were sometimes harshly discplined, even guillotined. Peter McPhee has suggested that in some ways the republican army was a microcosm of a regenerated society.[28]

The mobilization for war, however, also placed a strain on French society and revolutionary politics. The departure of young men for the army was a particular hardship in rural communities, where their labor was so important, and desertion was an ongoing, though fluctuating, problem throughout the decade. The need to supply the soldiers at the front with food, clothing, and equipment necessarily brought deprivation to those left at home. A spirit of self-sacrifice, and vigilance, could be said to have sustained the war effort and the Terror throughout the Year II,

---

28 Ibid., 134.

but as the war turned in France's favor in the spring of 1794, that spirit waned. In Paris, the enthusiasm of the *sans-culottes* to fulfill their patriotic duty at the front had weakened the vitality of popular politics (as had some of the policies of the Montagnard government). And yet, the cadence of the Terror continued apace, even accelerated in May and June, which produced a crisis in revolutionary politics and a change in course.[29]

The Great Terror

On 4 Prairial II (23 May 1794), an assassin lurking in a stairway attempted to kill the deputy Collot d'Herbois, a member of the Committee of Public Safety and one of the most ardent advocates of Terror. Just over two weeks later, at the urging of Couthon and Robespierre, the National Convention adopted the Law of 22 Priairial, by which the procedures of the Revolutionary Tribunal were streamlined. From that date to the end of July, the Revolutionary Tribunal sentenced 1,594 people to death, roughly 500 more than in the previous fourteen months of its existence.

Collot d'Herbois was unscathed in that attack, but a simple locksmith by the name of Geffroy was badly wounded in the shoulder. In the month that followed, Geffroy became a cult figure, a symbol of the regenerated man and self-sacrificing patriot. A play was produced in his honor, and his wound became a rhetorical piece in the argument made to justify the intensification of the Terror. In the words of Antoine de Baecque, "Geffroy's wound in fact calls for vengeance, and becomes the occasion for a new outburst of legal violence."[30] In this view, it is a certain revolutionary mentality that led to the Great Terror – a fear of enemies and conspiracy, to be sure, but also a conviction that virtue would triumph over evil, though not without sacrifice and moral fortitude.[31]

---

29 A. Forrest, *Conscripts and Deserters: The Army and French Society during the Revolution and Empire* (Oxford, Oxford University Press, 1989), *Soldiers of the French Revolution* (Durham, Duke University Press, 1990); J. A. Lynn, *The Bayonets of the Republic: Motivation and Tactics in the Army of Revolutionary France, 1791–1794* (Urbana, University of Illinois Press, 1984); J.-P. Bertaud, *The Army of the French Revolution: From Citizen Soldiers to Instruments of Power* (Princeton, Princeton University Press, 1988); and T. C. W. Blanning, *The French Revolutionary Wars: 1787–1802* (New York, Arnold Publishers, 1996).

30 A. de Baecque, *Glory and Terror: Seven Deaths under the French Revolution* (New York, Routledge, 2003), 138.

31 See M. Linton, *The Politics of Virtue in Enlightenment France* (New York, Palgrave, 2001) for a discussion of the origins in Old Regime discourse about virtue in government. Contrary to Furet, Linton argues that the Jacobins did not create the idea of political virtue, but that one of the consequences of the Terror was to discredit this ideal in political practice, at least in England and France.

In perhaps his most famous speech before the National Convention, "On the Principles of Political Morality," delivered on 5 February 1794, Robespierre linked terror and virtue in these words:

> If the mainspring of popular government in peacetime is virtue, the mainspring of popular government in revolution is virtue and terror both: virtue, without which terror is disastrous; terror, without which virtue is powerless. Terror is nothing but prompt, severe, inflexible justice; it is therefore an emanation of virtue; it is not so much a specific principle as a consequence of the general principle of democracy applied to the homeland's most pressing needs.[32]

Virtue alone would not be enough, however, to assure the future of the republic. Energy and commitment would be required as well. As early as October 1793, when the federalist revolts had just been quelled, Saint-Just delivered these words before the National Convention: "You have no longer any reason for restraint against enemies of the new order .... You must punish not only traitors but the apathetic as well; you must punish whoever is passive in the Republic .... We must rule by iron those who cannot be ruled by justice."[33] Back when those words were uttered, and on through the winter months as well, the inflexible justice of the Terror principally targeted enemies and traitors, most often men who had taken up arms against the republic. But after Prairial, it seemed to turn toward the apathetic and the passive, leading many to wonder, even among the deputies of the National Convention, "Who would be next?"

Patrice Gueniffey has characterized the Prairial legislation as murderous, and argues that in those final months of the Terror, it and the Revolution became one. In his view, though, this final stage of the Terror marked a change in its nature.[34] For François Furet, the Great Terror marked a culmination, not a dramatic shift, although he, too, sees the Terror as inseparable from the Revolution. In Furet's view, this final phase refutes definitively those who would explain the Terror in terms of circumstances, because the threat from war and civil war had subsided by

---

32 Robespierre's speeches can be found in numerous documentary collections. Many of them have been published in a new collection, preceded by a provocative essay on the Terror by the political essayist Slavoj Zizek: S. Zizek, *Virtue and Terror: Maximilien Robespierre* (New York, Verso, 2007), 115.

33 H. Gough, *The Terror in the French Revolution* (London, Macmillan Press, 1998), 43.

34 P. Gueniffey, *La Politique de la Terreur: essai sur la violence révolutionnaire, 1789–1794* (Paris, Fayard, 2000), 277–315.

spring 1794. Thus, he argues, we must see the Terror as the product of discourse and ideology.[35] This is an argument that rests in part on chronology. The internal threat to the republic was greatest in the summer of 1793, Furet points out, yet the Revolutionary Tribunal was relatively inactive in that period. The war turned decisively in the republic's favor by the spring of 1794, and then the Terror accelerated. Ideology, rather than circumstance, explains that trend.

But does the chronological evidence point us so decisively toward that conclusion? Clearly we cannot dismiss ideology entirely – the speeches of Saint-Just and Robespierre were meant to be persuasive, to provide a justification for Terror. But in the absence of open revolt and war would those words have been compelling? The inactivity of the Revolutionary Tribunal in the summer of 1793 does not mean that there were no victims of the Terror in that period. Hundreds, if not thousands, of Vendéan rebels died in battle in those months; most historians today count those deaths among the victims of the Terror, even if it is difficult to be precise in calculating the numbers. Nor should we expect the judicial machinery of the Terror to have targeted the federalist rebels *while* the revolt was underway. The Nuremberg trials, after all, did not occur during World War II. One brings one's enemies to justice after they have been defeated, not in the midst of the battle.

One might also think of the impact of war on the Terror in a slightly different way. True, the war had shifted in France's favor by spring 1794. But that shift had come, in part, because the Committee of Public Safety had increasingly insisted on an aggressive prosecution of the war. Attack the enemy, be swift in moving against him, do not adopt a defensive strategy. We see that mentality, so successful on the battlefield, transferred to the domestic front in Prairial. Do not wait for the enemy, hidden in a stairwell, to attack – strike him down before he has the chance, move resolutely, with an iron fist, against the apathetic.

History is replete with evidence, however, that it is easier to score victories on the battlefield than it is to mold virtuous citizens or sow the seeds of democracy. As we will see in the next chapter, those who moved against Robespierre and his allies on 9 Thermidor were not principally motivated by ideology. They were motivated by fear, for themselves as much as for their country. Not all of those who conspired against Robespierre were convinced that the Terror should end. Only in the aftermath of his defeat did they begin to sort out the meaning of their victory.

---

35 F. Furet, "Terror,"146–48.

7
Thermidor and the Directory

The period between 1795 and 1799 has long been seen as a sort of revolutionary wasteland, a desultory interregnum between Robespierre and Napoleon. In part this may have been due to a longheld tendency among historians to focus on great events and great men. There was no figure looming over the political landscape of the Directory comparable to either Robespierre or to Napoleon, no crucial event that could be said to define the period. The first years seemed to be devoted to coming to terms with the Terror, which meant blaming it on Robespierre, and then fashioning a new political structure that would prevent the emergence of another dictatorial leader. Since that effort resulted in four years of political instability and corruption, many argued, and ended with the coup of Brumaire and Napoleon's rise to power, how could one see the Directory as anything other than a forgettable failure?

This is not to say that historians have entirely ignored the period. Both Albert Mathiez and Georges Lefebvre wrote books on the Thermidorians, and each was translated into English.[1] Even the title to Mathiez's book, however – *After Robespierre* – suggested that this period was defined by what had gone before it, and his conclusion established the overwhelmingly negative reputation of the Directory that would endure for the rest of the century:

> Since the 9th Thermidor the men who had overthrown Robespierre had identified themselves and their private interests with the Republic. They had

1 A. Mathiez, *After Robespierre: The Thermidorian Reaction* (New York, Grosset and Dunlap, 1931); G. Lefebvre, *The Thermidorians* (New York, Vintage Books, 1964).

> constantly violated the principles of democracy. They had been even more arbitrary than the government whose place they had taken .... The great majority of Frenchmen despised these men who had made politics a profession and a source of profit.[2]

In recent decades, however, Thermidor and the Directory have drawn attention from historians who have looked upon these years in a more positive light. Isser Woloch has contributed two books to that endeavor: an early work focusing on the Jacobin resurgence of the early Directory, emphasizing that there was at least the possibility that a democratic regime might emerge in this era through the development of a two-party political system; and a more recent work, expansive in scope, detailing the revolutionary transformation of French social and political institutions, many of them initiated during the period of the Directory and early Empire.[3] Martyn Lyons published what remains arguably the best single volume on the Directory, acknowledging the political instability and instances of corruption, but pointing out as well the substantial strides made in the areas of fiscal and financial policy, and educational reform.[4] Somewhat more recently, Bronislaw Baczko issued a revisionist treatment of Thermidor, focusing in particular on the efforts of those who overthrew Robespierre to move beyond the Terror without repudiating the goals of the Revolution. Among his more provocative points is the assertion that our understanding of the Terror ever since has been indelibly colored by what the Thermidorians had to say about it.[5]

Finally, just in the past few years several books have appeared that open new questions about the Directory and its place in the history of the Revolution. The first, by James Livesey, argues that the French Revolution generally, and the period of the Directory in particular, played a crucial role in laying the foundation for European democracy, this despite the fact that the Directory seemed plagued throughout by political instability and ushered in the imperial rule of Napoleon Bonaparte.[6] Jon Cowans, while

---

2 A. Mathiez, *After Robespierre*, 260.

3 I. Woloch, *Jacobin Legacy: The Democratic Movement under the Directory* (Princeton, Princeton University Press, 1970); *The New Regime: Transformations of the French Civic Order, 1789–1820s* (New York, W. W. Norton, 1994).

4 M. Lyons, *France under the Directory* (Cambridge, Cambridge University Press, 1975).

5 B. Baczko, *Ending the Terror: The French Revolution after Robespierre* (Cambridge, Cambridge University Press, 1994). At least in translation, this title, too, as with Mathiez, highlights Robespierre in defining the period. It does seem to me that the original French title, *Comment sortir de la Terreur*, better captures the enigmatic aspect of Thermidor that Baczko tries to evoke in his text.

6 J. Livesey, *Making Democracy in the French Revolution* (Cambridge, MA, Harvard University Press, 2001).

less optimistic than Livesey, perhaps, has also focused on the political culture of the Revolution in a book devoted to the way that public opinion shaped, and was shaped by, representative politics, culminating in the Directory.[7] Howard Brown has recently published an important book that draws our attention to the statebuilding contribution of the Directory (and its shortcomings in this area), focusing not on electoral politics or political culture per se but rather on the challenges faced by the Directory regime in maintaining public order and delivering justice to its citizens. Brown raises new questions about the degree to which the supposedly liberal regime of the Directory was truly different from the Jacobin regime of the Terror, and argues that some of the illiberal elements that we usually associate with the Napoleonic era were actually first put in place under the Directory. Brown has also edited a volume of essays, in conjunction with Judith Miller, which draws attention to the relative neglect of the Directory on the one hand, while also suggesting some new and fruitful approaches to its study.[8]

Thus, both Thermidor and the Directory have become the focus of renewed scholarly attention in recent years, generating some lively debate and controversy. We will explore that scholarship in the pages ahead, paying special attention to the nature of the Thermidorian reaction, the degree to which the Directory regime can be said to have succeeded in laying a foundation for a liberal parliamentary regime, the contributions of this period to the emerging institutions of the modern French state, and the reasons for the ultimate failure and collapse of the Directorial regime.

Historical Overview

Before we embark on that more thematic discussion, it may be useful to review briefly the events of Thermidor and the basic contours of the Directory regime. On 26 July 1794, following two months of the Great Terror, Maximilien Robespierre rose to speak in the National Convention and announced that the Revolution was threatened once again, that conspirators were plotting against the government and must be exposed and punished. Robespierre had been away from the Convention and the Jacobin Club for some weeks, but in early June he had presided over the

7 J. Cowans, *To Speak for the People: Public Opinion and the Problem of Legitimacy in the French Revolution* (New York, Routledge, 2001).

8 H. G. Brown, *Ending the French Revolution: Violence, Justice, and Repression from the Terro to Napoleon* (Charlottesville, University of Virginia Press, 2006); H. G. Brown and J. A. Mil eds., *Taking Liberties: Problems of a New Order from the French Revolution to Nap* (Manchester, Manchester University Press, 2002).

first festival of the Cult of the Supreme Being, which suggested to some that he aspired to dictatorial power, that he was about to claim for himself the role of arbiter of revolutionary virtue. His words on 26 July were not reassuring in that regard. He named no names, but fearful deputies on both left and right came together that evening to plot his denunciation. The next day – 9 Thermidor – Robespierre stood accused before the National Convention, and within twenty-four hours he, Saint-Just, Georges Couthon, and twenty-five others went to their death on the guillotine.[9]

While it is customary to think of Thermidor as marking a turn to the right, the deputies who took a leading role in the plot against Robespierre were for the most part Montagnards – Joseph Fouché, Jean-Lambert Tallien, Jean-Marie Collot-d'Herbois, and Jacques-Nicolas Billaud-Varenne prominent among them. Fouché and Tallien could be described as opportunists, prepared to embrace moderate politics despite their past support of the Terror, but Collot-d'Herbois and Billaud-Varenne, both colleagues of Robespierre on the Committee of Public Safety, were determined to see the Terror continue and saw Robespierre and his supporters as possible impediments to that goal. Denied the right to speak before the Convention, the accused sought refuge in the Hôtel de Ville, but the uprising that they hoped might save them did not materialize. The sections of Paris, so loyal to Robespierre in the past, failed to mobilize, perhaps because so many young militants had joined the army, or perhaps because the *sans-culottes* of Paris, like Robespierre himself, were worn out by five years of revolution.

Despite the mixed pedigree of those who toppled Robespierre from power, it would be conservative republicans who dominated the National Convention over the next fifteen months. First those deputies who had protested the 2 June 1793 proscription of the Girondin deputies were returned to their seats, followed by the surviving Girondins themselves (the latter few in number, their colleagues having been tried and executed in October 1793). The Thermidorians brought a number of the most extreme terrorists to justice, including Billaud-Varenne and Collot-d'Herbois, as well as Jean-Baptiste Carrier; oversaw the closing of the Jacobin clubs; dismantled much of the economic and social legislation of the Montagnards; and created a liberal parliamentary regime that favored the interests of property owners and stifled popular democracy.

The Constitution of 1795 ushered in the regime of the Directory. The new constitution stressed the duties of all citizens more than their rights, and made no mention of the right to insurrection against an oppressive

---

9 See D. P. Jordan, *The Revolutionary Career of Maximilien Robespierre* (Chicago, University of Chicago Press, 1985), 206–20 for a description of these events and insightful analysis of Robespierre's final speech.

government. It vastly reduced the electorate, to approximately 30,000 electors, by reintroducing a property requirement to be eligible to vote, although all adult males were eligible to attend primary assemblies and vote for electors. For the first time in the Revolution, a bicameral legislature was enacted: the Council of Elders, an upper house that would be composed of 250 men aged 40 or older; and the Council of 500, composed of members at least 30 years of age. The Council of 500 was to initiate all legislation, the Council of Elders could only accept or reject proposed laws. Mindful of the power that had been concentrated in the Committee of Public Safety, and concerned about the danger of dictatorship, the deputies created an executive branch composed of five directors. Rather than being chosen in open election, however, the directors were to be selected by the Council of Elders from a list of fifty nominees drawn from both chambers of the legislature and the members of the Council of Five Hundred. One director would retire each year, determined by drawing lots initially, and each would exercise chief executive authority for a period of three months on a rotating basis. In this way, the constitution of 1795 moved France in the direction of a system of checks and balances.

The National Convention submitted this new constitution to the nation for ratification, along with a supplemental decree mandating that two-thirds of the members of the new bicameral legislature must be drawn from the 750 deputies then sitting in the Convention. The deputies considered this a guard against a royalist resurgence, while the people viewed it as self-serving careerism. The rate of abstention was high in the referendum, and while both the constitution and the two-thirds decree were easily ratified, there were many more negative votes cast against the latter.

The aim of the deputies was to bring political stability to the country, to put political power in the hands of what François Guizot would term the *juste milieu* under the July Monarchy of the nineteenth century. Michel Biard and Pascal Dupuy have characterized this period as a "republic without revolution," and in some sense this is exactly what brought about the demise of the Directory regime – it lost the vitality and popular participation that had sustained the Revolution up through 1794.[10] This was to be a regime of property owners, as evidenced by the Thermidorians' decision to abolish the *maximum* in January 1795. The prices of food and grain shot up in the wake of a mediocre harvest and that, in combination with the coldest winter of the century, led to enormous hardship and starvation, long remembered quite simply as the winter of *nonante-cinq*.

10 M. Biard and P. Dupuy, *La Révolution française: dynamiques, influences, débats, 1787–1804* (Paris, Armand Colin, 2005).

When the people of Paris thawed out from that winter they mounted two final revolutionary insurrections, in Germinal and Prairial III (April and May 1795), the second of which culminated with the head of an assassinated deputy, Jean-Bertrand Féraud, being paraded before the speaker's rostrum. Those events clearly influenced the drafting of the new constitution. Revolutionary violence would no longer be tolerated.

When the new constitution was presented, however, it was greeted by a royalist demonstration in Paris, protesting the decree of two-thirds and the constitution, which the voters of Paris had predominantly rejected. The crowd in the streets, numbering some 8,000 people, was composed largely of young men from well-to-do families, the so-called *jeunesse dorée*, or "gilded youth," who had led the public harassment of ex-terrorists and Jacobins over the past year.[11] They were met as they approached the Tuileries palace by 6,000 republican troops under the command of seven generals recruited by Paul-François Barras, soon to be named one of the five directors. Among the generals was Napoleon Bonaparte. The crowd was easily dispersed.

Despite the greatly narrowed electorate, elections proved problematical under the Directory. National elections were held annually, which the deputies hoped would lend political legitimacy to the regime. Instead it presented an annual source of contention and controversy. In 1797 royalist candidates did well at the ballot box and in response three of the directors – Louis-Marie La Révellière-Lépeaux, Paul-François Barras, and Jean-François Reubell – ordered a purge of their two colleagues, Lazare Carnot and François Barthélemy, along with fifty-three newly elected right-wing deputies. To ensure the success of their intervention the three directors sought the support of two key generals, Lazare Hoche and Napoleon Bonaparte. This became known as the Fructidor coup. The following year, La Révellière-Lépeaux and Barras, joined by one of the new directors, Philippe Merlin, attempted to influence electoral assemblies through a combination of propaganda and intimidation. Those efforts failed, and the Directory ended up sponsoring "secessionary" electoral assemblies in twenty-five departments, which allowed the government to choose the slate of candidates it found acceptable. In the end, 106 deputies were floréalized, or excluded from office, and fifty-three seats in the two-chamber legislature were left unfilled. In this instance, however, the Floréal coup removed suspected Jacobins from office as the pendulum swung from right to left. The legislature had its revenge in 1799, when La Révellière-Lépeaux and Merlin were removed as directors in the Prairial

11 F. Gendron, *The Gilded Youth of Thermidor* (Montreal, McGill-Queen's University Press, 1993).

coup. Thus, from year to year the confidence of the nation in the efficacy of electoral politics was steadily eroded.

Thermidor

"The importance of the Thermidorian period," Bronislaw Baczko argues, "lies not in an initial political or ideological programme, but in the problems with which the political protagonists were confronted and which they had to resolve."[12] Those problems, of course, grew out of the early Revolution, but whereas traditional views of Thermidor saw it as a reaction against the ideals of 1789, Baczko shows convincingly that the Thermidorians saw themselves as true revolutionaries determined to get the Revolution back on track by dealing with a series of difficult problems. Foremost among them was the Terror.

Eliminating Robespierre and his closest allies was an essential first step, perhaps, but not a fully adequate one. A host of new difficult questions, or problems, emerged. Who were the collaborators of Robespierre, and how should they be punished? Or, if Robespierre had indeed duped, or tyrannized, the deputies of the National Convention, how had this been possible and why did it take so long for the Convention, that "palladium of liberty" as its members often described themselves, to overthrow the tyrant? After 9 Thermidor a chorus of voices burst forth – seeking to explain, to lay blame, to resolve. Following François Furet, Baczko argues that discourse reigned supreme in this period – in newspapers, pamphlets, letters to the Jacobin Club and the National Convention, rumors in the streets (reported by police informants), but above all the discourse of denunciation. Those voices did not all sing in the same key, however, and one is left wondering why the discourse of Tallien, who saw the Terror as a system of power, should have proved more compelling than the discourse of Robert Lindet, who urged people to distinguish between error and crime and to remember the crisis that confronted the nation during the Year II.

Baczko argues that the paramount goal of the Thermidorians was to shift from "the Terror as the order of the day" to "justice as the order of the day." Yet Robespierre, of course, had seen terror and justice as related, not diametrically opposed, and the Thermidorians seemed unable to separate justice from politics, for as Baczko also observes, "to bring the Terror to an end, it was necessary to resolve the strictly political problem posed by the role of the Jacobins in the structures of power bequeathed by the

---

12 B. Baczko, *Ending the Terror*, ix.

Terror, as well as in public life as a whole."[13] This was a delicate matter, since a number of those who brought down Robespierre were Jacobins themselves, but in November 1794 the National Convention decreed the closing of the Paris Jacobin Club. Clubs soon were closed in the provinces as well, and Jacobin club members, especially those who had held local office during the Terror, now became the targets of a campaign of violence carried out by young men sometimes organized into paramilitary bands, the self-styled *Compagnies de Jésus*, which operated up and down the Rhône valley.[14]

Jon Cowans, in his book on public opinion in the Revolution, offers an interesting gloss on this effort to come to terms with the Terror. From the summer of 1792 forward, Robespierre had identified himself closely with "the people," on whom he based his political legitimacy. Indeed, the Montagnards, much more than the Girondins, embraced the ideal of popular sovereignty. The Thermidorians, in their desire to exonerate themselves for their complicity in the Terror, would assert that "the people" had been duped, just as *they* had. In a sense, after Thermidor it became convenient for both the left and the right (that coalition of odd bedfellows that had brought Robespierre down) to blame the gullibility of the people (i.e. public opinion) for the troubles that France had just endured. But in doing so, they unwittingly undermined the very principle of the sovereignty of the people, which in due time would have grave implications for the future of the republic itself.[15]

Just as the Terror had claimed innocent victims among those genuinely guilty of counterrevolution, thereby creating new enemies of the Jacobin regime, so did Thermidor find it impossible to distinguish between those unjustly suspected under the Terror and ardent opponents of the republic when it delivered its amnesties. Those suspected of federalist sympathies were now released, some of them restored to local political posts; property confiscated from the relatives of *émigrés* was returned; and the laws against emigration were relaxed, which allowed not only lukewarm republicans to return, but ardent royalists as well. The landing of more than 3,000 *émigrés* in an armed expeditionary force on the Quiberon peninsula in southwest Brittany in June 1795 made it clear, indeed, that there were enemies of the Revolution among those who had left France, and that foreign powers, in this case the British, would support their efforts to overthrow the republican regime. Far from healing the wounds

---

13 Ibid., 60, 95.

14 G. Lewis, *The Second Vendée: The Constituency of Counterrevolution in the Department of the Gard, 1789–1815* (Oxford, Clarendon Press, 1978).

15 J. Cowans, *To Speak for the People*, 155–57.

opened by the Terror, the conciliatory politics of Thermidor sowed new divisions and created a climate in which royalists felt safe both to settle old scores and to avow openly their monarchist politics.

The Directory

One could not say, then, that the Directory regime began in auspicious circumstances. The repressive politics of the Terror may have passed, but deep political divisions remained and political violence would prove to be endemic throughout the four years of its existence. Since 1789 prices of staple goods had risen by more than 800 percent, an inflationary spiral fed by political upheaval, the economic strains of war, and the near total collapse of confidence in the *assignats*. Departmental administrations found it difficult to collect taxes, and the national treasury was in little better shape than it had been in 1788, when Louis XVI decided to convene the Estates General.

And yet, despite its lackluster reputation, the Directory made progress in addressing these problems, and the consensus among historians today in evaluating its contribution seems much more positive than it was a generation ago. Some argue that the Directory's reputation for incompetence and corruption began with Napoleon Bonaparte, who had a vested interest in exaggerating the failings of the regime that he had helped to topple through a coup d'état.[16] The Directory's social and economic policies were not progressive or egalitarian – the poor, wage earners, and rural inhabitants could all be said to have suffered economically during these years – but it did manage, with difficulty, to bring some stability to the French economy and finances. Initially this was done through the liberal printing of *assignats*, which continued the inflation of previous years, but starting in 1796 the regime pursued aggressively deflationary fiscal policies, and after experimenting briefly with a new paper currency, the *mandats territoriaux*, eventually returned the nation to hard currency. The minister of finances, Jacques Ramel, repudiated a portion of the national debt, to the dismay of the state's creditors, and introduced new taxes to increase revenue into the treasury, most famously the tax on doors and windows, which weighed more heavily on the rich and also helped to curtail the already apparent national penchant for tax evasion. The foundation was laid under the Directory, as well, for the creation of the Banque de France, which was inaugurated in February 1800. Had a national bank existed prior to the

16 This point is made by Michel Biard and Pascal Dupuy in *La Révolution française*, 118, and by Howard Brown in his introduction to *Taking Liberties*.

Revolution, the monarchy might well have managed the financial crisis of the 1780s more successfully.

The Directory resumed the sale of *biens nationaux*, suspended for a time after Thermidor, though now in large lots. If, during the Year II, some had grumbled that the largest portion of *biens nationaux* had gone to loyal Jacobins, small peasants now complained that their sale chiefly benefited the bourgeois supporters of the Directory. The division of common lands was also formally repealed, although few communities had exercised their option under the Montagnard government to parcel out common grazing lands.

In the field of education, too, the Directory achieved modest gains, putting in place the first *écoles centrales*, mandated by legislation passed in the final days of the National Convention. These central schools, one per department, which replaced the church-run *collèges* of the Old Regime, were replaced by *lycées* under Napoleon. Not until the Third Republic would these first steps toward a national system of state-run secular education achieve fruition.[17] Another innovation under the Directory with long-term implications was the introduction of the metric system, developed by a special commission first created under the Constituent Assembly and replacing the hodgepodge system of weights and measures that had prevailed under the Old Regime.

As we shall see, the implementation of these administrative, economic, and social reforms was hampered by the chronic domestic violence that prevailed in many parts of France throughout this period, but the strains of war were also an important factor in this regard. An armistice was signed with Austria in December 1795, so the regime was given an initial reprieve, but it endured only until the following spring. The Treaty of The Hague, in May 1795, recognized the independence of the Batavian Republic, but by terms of the treaty the Dutch were required to pay an indemnity to France of over 200,000,000 *livres*. Thus began a policy of requiring conquered territories to pay for their own conquest, at the same time as an expansionist strategy was adopted.

Maintaining an army in the field, however, was becoming a real challenge, in part because volunteers enlisted for a single campaign of a year's length, and could then return home. From its high point of 732,000 troops in the summer of 1794 the republican army had dropped to 484,000 in August 1795, and would further dwindle to 381,000 men by August 1797.[18] Soldiers were poorly and irregularly paid, most often

---

17 See M. Lyons, *France under the Directory*, 91–93, for an extensive discussion of the *écoles centrales*.

18 M. Biard and P. Dupuy, *La Révolution française*, 126.

in *assignats*, and the armies were generally badly supplied and fed as well, with the result that troops resorted to plunder of the territories they occupied. Under the Terror, representatives on mission did all they could to curb such lack of discipline among the troops, but after Thermidor officers increasingly tolerated such behavior. As a result the army was shifting from being a citizens' army, an extension of the republic, to being a professional army composed of troops loyal to their commanders.

This trend was exemplified in Italy, where Napoleon Bonaparte was appointed commander in March 1796. He arrived to find a disorganized, undisciplined, and demoralized army, but took immediate measures to restore discipline, dismiss ineffective officers, and restore morale. He made sure that his troops were adequately fed and equipped, and paid them in hard currency. He turned what had been a minor theatre of operations into a major offensive, defeating the Austrians in a series of battles beginning in the fall of 1796. In April 1797 the Austrian commander, Archduke Charles, signalled a truce. By the Treaty of Campo Formio, signed in October 1797, Austria ceded Belgium and the west bank of the Rhine to France.

During the Terror, the Committee of Public Safety had centralized supply of the army and navy under government control, but this system was dismantled after Thermidor and military supply was turned over to private contractors. Private companies drew exclusive contracts to supply the various theatres of operation: Flachat in Italy, Simons in Belgium, Ouvrard for the entire navy. The men at the head of these companies cultivated political connections in Paris and became enormously wealthy, at least some of them, through their contracts. It is in this domain, more than any other, that the Directory's reputation for corruption was earned. Julien Ouvrard began the Revolution keeping accounts for a grocery firm in Nantes. Anticipating the explosion of the newspaper press, he made a fortune in paper manufacturing, and by 1799 was among the richest men in France. Paul-François Barras, one of the directors, was a close friend, and Madame Tallien his mistress. Martyn Lyons is perhaps overly generous when he concludes that "if so many businessmen indulged in speculation, this was because it was hard during this period of war, inflation, and economic stagnation, to make a profit honestly."[19] Some would argue, of course, that this has always been the way of the world.

In a recent provocative and controversial book, already generating a lively debate, James Livesey has turned his attention away from the electoral politics and war profiteering of the Directory to focus on public

19 M. Lyons, *France under the Directory*, 67.

debate and institutional approaches to political, economic, and social problems during this period. He arrives at a startling conclusion: "Between 1795 and 1800 a new democratic republicanism was elaborated. Before 1795 Jacobins and sans-culottes had tried, and failed, to create a polity in which universal rights did not corrode all particular freedoms. After the Terror the republicans at the heart of the Directory laid the basis for such a regime."[20] In making his argument, Livesey focuses on the political thought of men such as Benjamin Constant (a staunch advocate of political liberalism), Pierre-Claude-François Daunou (chief architect of the legislation creating the *écoles centrales*), and Nicolas-Louis François de Neufchâteau (minister of the interior, and later a director). Drawing on the work of political scientist Robert Putnam, however, he also emphasizes changes in this period in social practice, growing in part out of the division of common lands in some areas of the French countryside and contributing to what Livesey characterizes as "commercial republicanism." This concept seems consonant with an argument Colin Jones made some years ago, focusing more on the origins of the Revolution, in defense of the idea of a bourgeois revolution.[21] Ultimately, Livesey argues, "the transformation in the way farmers and peasants talked about their land was of more significance than any constitution: it marked the end of an immemorial world of thought and experience."[22]

This is an argument that would have pleased Napoleon, who once quipped that constitutions should be short and obscure. But there are those who would argue that constitutions and elections are indeed important elements of a democracy, and that it seems odd to credit the Directory with laying the basis for democratic republicanism when its constitution did not endure and its leaders so cavalierly overturned or annulled elections in almost every year of its existence. Some will protest, as many have in the past about the work of François Furet, that we hear more from Livesey about discourse and rhetoric and less about the actual practice among those who were presumably exercising this new commercial republicanism. Surely his book will inspire archival research into exactly that area in the years ahead. Livesey's book also raises questions, though, about how we think about the Revolution as a whole. 9 Thermidor is not to be seen as a fundamental break, it would seem, as a

20 J. Livesey, *Making Democracy in the French Revolution*, 234.

21 R. Putnam, *Making Democracy Work: Civic Traditions in Modern Italy* (Princeton, Princeton University Press, 1993); C. Jones, "The Great Chain of Buying: Medical Advertisement, the Bourgeois Public Sphere, and the Origins of the French Revolution," *American Historical Review* 101 (February 1996), 13–40.

22 J. Livesey, *Making Democracy in the French Revolution*, 247.

repudiation of the radical politics of the Year II. If we look again at the passage quoted above we see that Livesey chooses his words carefully: "a new democratic republicanism was *elaborated,*" he writes, not put in place, which parries, perhaps, the critique of those who would object that the Directory was so shortlived. The Jacobins and *sans-culottes* (both marginalized under the Directory, incidentally) had failed in their attempt, presumably because the polity of the Year II had allowed "universal rights" to corrode "particular freedoms." One might object, however, that the Jacobins also *elaborated* a political vision, and that it is unfair perhaps of Livesey to characterize that effort as a failure, while crediting the Directory for having laid a solid foundation, even though their effort also failed in the short run. One might argue, indeed, and here we anticipate a later discussion of legacy, that the nineteenth and twentieth centuries witnessed an ongoing competition between at least two visions of a democratic polity, the democratic liberalism of the Directory regime versus the democratic egalitarianism of the Jacobins.[23]

Livesey's picture of a society, particularly in provincial France, in which the norms and ideals of democratic culture were being practiced also runs counter to much of the recent work of Donald Sutherland, who emphasizes on the one hand the narrowing of the electorate under the Directory and the tendency in its policies toward the bureaucratization of local political and administrative affairs, and on the other the endemic violence and counterrevolutionary sentiment in the countryside.[24] In regard to the latter, Peter McPhee cautions that while there is ample evidence of popular disaffection in the provinces during this period, most of it comes from particular areas in the west and the south and should not be generalized to the entire country. Moreover, to say that people were disaffected in some measure does not necessarily make them counterrevolutionary. One could be in opposition to the policies of the Directory and to the self-serving actions of its elite and still be a supporter of the republic.[25]

There is little question that the Directory government was hard pressed to maintain public order in much of the west and the southern Massif Central, and this is the focus of Howard Brown's recent book. Quite in

23 Go to http://h-france.net/reviews/alphaauthor.html#gl for David Bell's review of Livesey's book, which raises many of the points I note above, along with a response from James Livesey. This review and response generated a number of other postings and comments from historians, which may also be accessible in the H-France archives.

24 D. Sutherland, *France, 1789–1815: Revolution and Counterrevolution* (Oxford, Oxford University Press, 1986), Chapters 8–9; and *the French Revolution and Empire: The Quest for a Civic Order* (Oxford, Blackwell, 2003), Chapter 9.

25 P. McPhee, *Living the French Revolution, 1789–1799* (New York, Palgrave Macmillan, 2006), 199.

contrast to Livesey, Brown's emphasis is on the ultimate failure of liberal democracy under the Directory, which he attributes to "chronic violence, ambivalent forms of justice, and repeated recourse to heavy-handed repression."[26] Whereas others have emphasized the atrophy of electoral politics in explaining the demise of the Directory, Brown points to the inability of the regime to maintain civic order and its willingness to resort to extrajudicial measures to explain its failure. Since civilian juries could not be counted on to bring convictions of those accused of violent resistance toward local authorities, the Directory created military commissions to try such cases, divided the country into twenty-six military districts, and assigned on average seventy generals to posts in the interior of France in an effort to maintain public order. "Liberal democracy failed and the French Revolution came to an end," Brown concludes, "only after prolonged violence had generated a public sentiment willing to accept exceptional justice and brutal represssion as the price of restoring order."[27]

There are at least two major implications in Brown's work for the way that we customarily think about the French Revolution. First, he suggests that a Hobbesian approach better explains the collapse of the first French republic than a Rousseauean approach, that it was the prevailing state of civil disorder rather than political divisions rooted in ideology or social conflict that spelled the ultimate demise of the Directory. Second, his analysis proposes a different periodization for the revolutionary decade from that found in most histories. Far from instituting the rule of law, the Directory was as arbitrary and repressive, in its way, as the Jacobin republic – 9 Thermidor marks less of a break, then. Brown also argues that the "security state" that most historians associate with the Napoleonic regime was actually put in place under the Directory. 1802, rather than 18 Brumaire (9 November 1799), the date of Napoleon's coup, thus marks the true end of the French Revolution.

Brown's book will surely continue to stimulate lively debate in the years ahead. Some will be uneasy with the devalorization of politics that seems implicit in Brown's analysis. Others, akin to McPhee's demurral from Sutherland's argument noted above, may observe that highway robbery and other acts of brigandage did not constitute political violence in the same way that *chouannerie* did in the west. Not all acts of violence should be interpreted as challenges to the regime. Bernard Gainot, whose own work on this period stresses the Jacobin resurgence of 1799, has taken issue with Brown's downplaying of the Brumaire coup as a turning point

---

26 H. Brown, *Ending the French Revolution*, 1.
27 Ibid., 349.

and suggests that Brown's argument may overreach his evidence.[28] Michel Biard and Pascal Dupuy, although not directly addressing Brown's work, argue that the positive institutional achievements of the Directory regime, rather than the security state that it put in place, are what paved the way for the success of Napoleon after 1802.[29]

One source of public disorder in these years was a resurgence in Catholic observance. In 1795 and 1796 the Thermidorian Convention and Directory relaxed the persecution of the Catholic Church, and priests who had left France voluntarily were allowed to return and reclaim their property. In August 1797, the legislation of 1792–93 regarding refractory priests was formally repealed, opening the way for the return of refractory priests who had emigrated or been deported. But following the Fructidor coup (September 1797), those laws of tolerance for refractory priests were revoked, and by 1798 the persecution of refractory clergy was as severe as it had been under the Terror. Local communities often felt victimized by these shifting currents of official policy, and in some parts of the country, most notably the west, this renewed persecution fed the active resistance to the regime. But in other areas those people who had resumed religious worship and welcomed their old priests back simply ignored the dictums being issued from Paris. One sees in this period the roots of a pattern that would prevail throughout the nineteenth century – women were much more active in this revivification of religious life, and men drifted away from the church. To be active in Catholic devotion in these last years of the republic did not necessarily mean, however, that one's politics were counterrevolutionary. For some, participation in church activities would have been consonant with the emerging sense of civic community that James Livesey sees as laying the foundations for liberal democracy.[30]

While there is certainly no clear consensus about how to interpret the Directory and its relationship both to the regime that preceded it and that which followed, it has emerged from its twilight of relative historical neglect to become the focus of a growing body of serious scholarship and spirited debate. It would not do to conclude this discussion of the period, however,

---

28 B. Gainot, *1799, un nouveau jacobinisme?: la démocratie représentative, une alternative à brumaire* (Paris, Editions du CTHS, 2001). For Gainot's review of Brown's book, and Brown's response, see http://h-france.net/reviews/alphaauathor.html#gl.

29 M. Biard and P. Dupuy, *La Révolution française*, 106.

30 For an excellent brief discussion of these issues see P. McPhee, *Living the French Revolution*, 181–90. For more extensive treatment see S. Desan, *Reclaiming the Sacred: Lay Religion and Popular Politics in Revolutionary France* (Ithaca, Cornell University Press, 1990); "The Rhetoric of Religious Revival during the French Revolution," *Journal of Modern History* 60 (1988), 1–27; and O. Hufton, *Women and the Limits of Citizenship in the French Revolution* (Toronto, University of Toronto Press, 1992), especially Chapters Two and Three.

without mention of the Directory's most celebrated critic, Gracchus Babeuf. Babeuf was a relatively minor figure, a seigneurial clerk on the eve of the Revolution, a local official in the department of the Somme between 1791 and 1793, a publisher of small newspapers, in and out of trouble due to charges of libel throughout the first years of the Revolution. After 9 Thermidor he began publication of his most noteworthy newspaper, *Le Tribun du Peuple*, and his increasingly strident criticism of the Thermidorian regime once again landed him in prison, this time in Arras. There he met Filippo Buonarroti, and when both were released late in 1795 they returned to Paris where Babeuf resumed publication of his paper, and joined the Pantheon club, a political haven for ex-Jacobins.

When police closed down the Pantheon club, in February 1796, Babeuf took his movement underground in what came to be known as the Conspiracy of Equals. Babeuf never attracted a broad popular following in Paris, but the group did have a vague plan to overthrow the Directory, and for this it was denounced in May 1796 by a police spy who had infiltrated the organization. Lazare Carnot chose to prosecute the case aggressively, presenting it to the public as a monstrous conspiracy against the republic. Sixty-five conspirators were brought to trial before the High Court of Vendôme in early 1797. Fifty-six of the accused were acquitted, evidence perhaps that the Directory retained a commitment to justice, but seen by many at the time as an indication that the charges of conspiracy were trumped up. Only Babeuf and Augustin Darthé were sentenced to death. Gracchus Babeuf had his day in court, though, and his defense, with ample reference to the philosophes Diderot, Mably, and Rousseau, was an eloquent indictment of the Directory regime, which he accused of betraying the ideals of 1789. Babeuf's words, too, merit attention as we strive to arrive at our own judgment of the Directory and its place in history.[31]

---

31 For Babeuf's defense at his trial see J. A. Scott, *The Defense of Gracchus Babeuf before the High Court of Vendôme* (Boston, University of Massachusetts Press, 1967). For Babeuf's biography see R. B. Rose, *Gracchus Babeuf: The First Revolutionary Communist* (Stanford, Stanford University Press, 1978). See also L. Mason, "Never Was a Plot so Holy: Gracchus Babeuf and the End of the French Revolution," in P. R. Campbell, T. E. Kaiser, and M. Linton, eds., *Conspiracy in the French Revolution* (Manchester, Manchester University Press, 2007), 172–88, for a preview of her forthcoming book.

8

Napoleon: Heir to the Revolution?

There is no obvious answer to this question, although most people with even a passing familiarity would offer a quick opinion. If one views the Revolution principally through the lens of nationalism, then it is easy to see Napoleon carrying forward the achievements of the revolutionary armies, leading France to the apogee of its glory in modern European history. But if one sees the Revolution as the foundation of modern democracy, a consensus view among historians today and an emphasis in this text, then one can hardly see the man who declared himself emperor as building upon that foundation.

If one considers the question in the context of the motto of the Revolution – Liberty, Equality, Fraternity – one arrives at a similarly ambivalent position. With regard to liberty, the censorship of newspapers and other publications and the political repression practiced under the Napoleonic regime lead one to a decidedly negative conclusion. One might argue that the Napoleonic Civil Code established a system of legal equality that remains the basis of French law today. On the other hand, women and people of color both suffered under Napoleon's rule, as slavery was reintroduced in the French colonies and the patriarchal family was reinforced by the Napoleonic Code. Such considerations, alongside the creation of a new imperial nobility, might lead one to argue that the ideal of fraternity was similarly abandoned, although within the Napoleonic army, among the most important institutions of the regime, a strong bond of fraternity clearly prevailed.

One might also examine this question from the perspective of Napoleon's rise to power. How was it that barely five years after the National Convention adopted a constitution designed, at least in part, to prevent a strong leader from claiming dictatorial power, that Napoleon Bonaparte should be named First Consul? Had the leaders of the Directory so completely abandoned their commitment to the ideals of the Revolution that they were prepared to hand power over to a general? Was the instability of the regime so great that there was simply no other option? Did Napoleon wrest power away from the political elite with the aid of his brother, Lucien, strategically positioned at the time as president of the Council of Five Hundred? Given what we know about the next fifteen years, about Napoleon's charisma and unbridled ambition, about the quick transition from Directory, to Consulate, to Empire, it is tempting to answer "yes" to these three questions, but in each case the more appropriate answer would be "no."

One of the more recent biographers of Napoleon (and there have been many) ended his preface with the hope that someone among his younger colleagues would go on to write the multi-volume study that its subject so richly deserved.[1] Our goals will be, by necessity, much more modest in this chapter. We will start by examining Napoleon's early career, and his was very definitely a career that benefitted from the Revolution, and go on to consider his rise to power and the various interpretations of those events. We will then turn to evaluate, briefly, Napoleon's regime, paying little attention to his military genius and contributions to military strategy, but focusing instead on his political, constitutional, and economic legacy. This will prepare us nicely for our final chapter, on the legacy of the Revolution, for it is difficult to evaluate the one without considering the other, even if one concludes that by and large Napoleon betrayed the ideals of 1789.

The Rise of Napoleon

Napoleon was born in 1769 into a Corsican family of minor nobility, barely a year after Corsica became a French possession. This early good fortune allowed both him and his brother Lucien to study in France, first at Autun, then at the military academy at Brienne, and finally at the Ecole Militaire in Paris. Napoleon was assigned to the artillery in 1785, and were it not for the Revolution his career in the French military likely would have been unexceptional. 1789 opened the officer corps to men of talent, however, and Napoleon made the most of his opportunities. He supported his family's alliance with Pascal Paoli in the cause of Corsican independence, and over the first years of the Revolution Napoleon moved

---

1 A. Schom, *Napoleon Bonaparte* (New York, Harper Collins, 1997), xix.

back and forth between Corsica and France. He was in Paris for the uprising of 10 August 1792, which impressed upon him the capacity of the crowd to bring down a government. He first began to make his mark at Toulon, in October 1793, where he commanded artillery in the siege that recaptured the port from the British. Here he came to the attention of Augustin Robespierre, brother of Maximilien, and Christophe Saliceti, a fellow Corsican, both representatives on mission to the army. Napoleon took an interest in Jacobin club debates in this period, which brought him, along with his Montagnard allies, under suspicion after 9 Thermidor. When he refused to accept a command in the Vendée, commenting that there was no glory in leading troops against one's fellow countrymen, his name was removed from the officers' list and his future appeared cloudy.

Napoleon's fortunes turned in 1795. Paul Barras assigned him to command troops defending the National Convention in the Vendémiaire uprising, and introduced him to Josephine de Beauharnais, whom he would marry and later make his empress. In the spring of 1796 he was assigned to rehabilitate the French army in Italy, which he did with élan, leading the troops in a succession of victories that ended with the treaty of Campo Formio.

When Napoleon returned to Paris at the end of 1797 crowds greeted him as a conquering hero. His political aspirations were already apparent at this time – Barras claimed in his memoirs that Napoleon suggested that he be appointed a director – and it may be that his next endeavor was determined in part by the directors' desire to remove him from Paris.[2] Great Britain was the only enemy of France still active in the field, and General Bonaparte discussed with the government various options to strike against her. A direct invasion of England was broached – there were reports of unrest in the British naval shipyards – but dismissed as logistically infeasible. A second possibility was an invasion through western Ireland, where the United Irishmen reported a growing popular movement prepared to rebel against English rule. Napoleon rejected that option. Earlier expeditions, in 1796 and 1797, the first under the leadership of Lazare Hoche, had been scuttled by inclement weather. A final, small, expedition would indeed be mounted in the summer of 1798, but it would arrive to find the movement in Ireland already largely suppressed. In the end Napoleon took command of an expedition to Egypt, sailing from Toulon in May 1798 with a large fleet and some 35,000 troops.

The Egyptian campaign proved to be a debacle in almost every way. Although Napoleon's fleet eluded Admiral Nelson's navy en route, Nelson

---

2 O. Connelly, *French Revolution/Napoleonic Era* (New York, Holt, Rinehart and Winston, 1979), 201–3.

would later trap the French ships in Aboukir Bay, destroying most of them and leaving Napoleon's army stranded in Egypt. Napoleon's disciplined troops scored easy victories against the Mameluke troops, but France's presence in Egypt alarmed the Ottoman Empire, which claimed Egypt as a possession, and brought it into alliance with Russia and Austria, who now rejoined the British in coalition against the French. Without naval support Napoleon could achieve no grand victory, and in August he turned his command over to General Kléber, eluded the British naval blockade, and returned to France, leaving his troops, already ravaged by plague, to languish in Egypt until autumn 1801. Kléber, who viewed Napoleon's departure as a betrayal, was assassinated in Cairo by an Arab.

The most enduring result of the campaign derived from the scholarly part of the expedition. Several notable scientists accompanied Napoleon, including Gaspard Monge, the mathematician, and Claude Berthollet, a celebrated chemist. Naturalists, geologists, archaeologists, and historians were among the scholars. They established the Institute of Cairo, discovered the Rosetta Stone (which eventually revealed the secret to Egyptian hieroglyphics), and surveyed the isthmus of Suez to explore the feasibility of a canal. Out of their work emerged the field of Egyptology, and their reports upon their return lent an aura of success to the expedition that its military exploits could scarcely have justified.

Napoleon made his decision to return to France based on reports that the situation at home was deteriorating. The return of Austria and Russia to the coalition led to reverses for the French army in Italy and Switzerland, and for the first time in years it was forced to relinquish conquered territory. The Directory's resort to conscription and a forced loan from the rich aroused resistance, and the general unhappiness with the regime led to Jacobin victories at the polls in the elections of 1798.[3] Yet Napoleon was also fleeing a deteriorating situation in Egypt, and most accounts emphasize that when he set foot again on French soil he knew not how he would be received by the people. Unaware of the recent setbacks, however, crowds everywhere greeted him like a conquering hero as he made his way north to Paris from the Mediterranean coast.

In Paris Napoleon found a deeply polarized political situation. Following the electoral successes of the Jacobins the legislature had passed a new Law of Hostages in the summer of 1798, which made *émigrés* and former nobles subject to arrest if there were disturbances in the vicinity of their residence. All civil disorder, in sum, was assumed to be potentially counterrevolutionary, and moderates saw in this legislation a warning sign of a

3 I. Woloch, *Jacobin Legacy: The Democratic Movement under the Directory* (Princeton, Princeton University Press, 1970).

possible return to the politics of the Terror. The Prairial coup (18 June 1799), often seen as the revenge of the legislature on the directors, did force out of office two of the sitting directors, La Révellière-Lépeaux and Merlin, but most importantly strengthened the position of Emmanuel-Joseph Sieyès by adding Pierre-Roger Ducos as one of the directors – a relative nonentity, but a dependable supporter of Sieyès.

For some months Sieyès had been contemplating a turn to the military to shore up the teetering Directory regime, but Bonaparte did not figure in his plans. No one had expected his return from Egypt, and Sieyès had settled on General Joubert as a reliable candidate. Joubert, unfortunately, died on a battlefield in Italy, leaving Sieyès without a general to play the role of figurehead leader. Another revolutionary veteran who had played a prominent role in 1789, Charles-Maurice Talleyrand, brought Sieyès together with Napoleon.

The coup of 18 Brumaire is shrouded in myth. The Napoleonic legend has left us with an image of a dashing and charismatic general who seized political power for himself in a bold stroke that launched him, and France, on the path to glory. Nothing could be further from the truth. Whether 18 Brumaire was principally the product of Napoleon's ambition for power, or Sieyès' determination to see the constitution revised and a stronger executive branch created, it is clear that neither could have succeeded without the other. Alan Schom concedes that Sieyès was the key to the plot that brought Bonaparte to power.[4] It is also clear, though, that the two men could barely stand each other. Talleyrand's diplomatic skills may have been an essential element bringing the two men together, but they had help from others as well. Napoleon's older brother, Joseph, worked behind the scenes; his younger brother, Lucien, occupied a strategic position as president of the Council of Five Hundred; and a group of roughly fifty deputies in the two chambers – united by their anti-Jacobinism and a strong desire for order – was counted upon to smooth the way on the crucial day.

In the event, however, things went anything but smoothly. The Council of Elders convened early on the morning of 18 Brumaire, and deputies in on the plot rose to warn their colleagues of a Jacobin conspiracy to launch insurrection in the capital, aimed at reviving the radicalism of the Year II. They proposed, for safety, that both houses of the legislature be transferred out of Paris to the former royal château at Saint-Cloud, today a short walk from the end of a Metro line, but in the eighteenth century well beyond the city limits, across the Seine at the west edge of town, far removed from the

4 A. Schom, *Napoleon Bonaparte*, 208.

populous quartiers of eastern Paris that had traditionally furnished the crowds in the successful uprisings of the early Revolution.

Our shorthand for Napoleon's accession to power is 18 Brumaire, and most histories speak only of that day, but as Malcolm Crook has observed, 19 Brumaire was far more critical and more contentious.[5] Things went according to plan in the Council of Elders, which acquiesced to the proposals of Sieyès and Bonaparte with only a few murmurs about the constitution, but in the Council of Five Hundred Napoleon was greeted by cries of "Traitor!" and "Dictator!", and the meeting dissolved into a general tumult. Napoleon, surprisingly, faltered in the face of this resistance and nearly fainted at the front of the assembly. It was Lucien who saved the day, escorting his brother out of the meeting hall, and exhorting the troops gathered in the courtyard to support their general. Led by Joachim Murat, they stormed into the Council of Five Hundred. The terrified deputies, clad in togas, scrambled out the windows and fled across the gardens to the nearby woods as dusk fell. What Sieyès had hoped would be an orderly, and legal, transfer of power, had ended with a brazen assertion of military force.

Historians have interpreted the signficance of Brumaire in strikingly different ways. For Georges Lefebvre, it was a decidedly negative development: "That the French Revolution turned to dictatorship was no accident; it was driven there by inner necessity, and not for the first time either. Nor was it an accident that the Revolution led to the dictatorship of a general, but it so happened that this general was Napoleon Bonaparte .... " Martyn Lyons offers a much more sanguine view: "Brumaire, then, did not announce the end of the principles of the French Revolution. It signified rather that one particular institutional form of those revolutionary ideals had served out its usefulness, and succumbed to history .... The *coup* of Brumaire may best be interpreted not as a rupture with the immediate revolutionary past, but as a new attempt to secure and prolong the hegemony of the revolutionary bourgeoisie."[6] One might well wonder what it means to "succumb to history." The phrase suggests an element of inevitability, as does Lefebvre's mention of an

5 M. Crook, *Napoleon Comes to Power: Democracy and Dictatorship in Revolutionary France, 1795–1804* (Cardiff, University of Wales Press, 1998), 57. Chapter Three offers an excellent discussion of the events surrounding the Brumaire coup, and the book includes a valuable selection of documents in English. Another useful volume combining historical commentary and primary sources is R. Blaufarb, *Napoleon: A Symbol for an Age: A Brief History with Documents* (Boston, Bedford Books, 2007).

6 G. Lefebvre, *Napoleon* (London, Routledge and Kegan Paul, 1969), I, 60; M. Lyons, *Napoleon Bonaparte and the Legacy of the French Revolution* (New York, St. Martin's, 1994), 41–42. Both passages are cited in M. Crook, *Napoleon Comes to Power*, 102–3.

"inner necessity." Malcolm Crook, by contrast, stresses the contingency of the event, the possibility that the coup might have failed, and he points as well to a relative lack of popular support for it: "There had been little overt opposition, yet apathy and resignation were the order of the day; there was little enthusiasm for what was generally regarded as an unexceptional event and scant recognition that a turning point had been reached."[7] This view accords with the argument made by Lynn Hunt nearly thirty years ago, that it was the repudiation of representative democracy that made Brumaire possible: "Bonaparte brought together the different strands of this development; he became the ultimate Director – the legislature was reduced to impotence, parties lost their function with the abolition of elections, and the executive ruled without opposition .... As a consequence, the Revolution's internal mechanism – the mobilization of the political classes, however widely or narrowly defined – was finally destroyed."[8] Howard Brown, whose work we considered in the previous chapter, would agree with Lyons, that Brumaire was not much of a rupture, not because of continuity with the revolutionary past, but rather because the turn toward a "security state" had begun under the Directory itself and would not reach full fruition until 1804. Brumaire, for Brown, was just a stop along the way.[9]

How did Napoleon himself view Brumaire? From his earliest days as a general Bonaparte was self-conscious about how contemporaries and history would view his accomplishments, and he consistently tried to influence that view, by issuing what we today would call press releases on the spot, after military victories for example, and in the voluminous memoirs that he dictated to aides on St. Helena near the end of his life. In this instance we can look to the proclamation that he released to the public on 19 Brumaire, even before the success of the coup had been fully secured. He began: "On my return to Paris, I found division among all the authorities and agreement upon only one point, namely, that the Constitution was half-destroyed and unable to save liberty. All parties came to see me, and confided their plans to me, revealed their secrets, and requested my support; I refused to be the man of any party." The emphasis here is on political divisions and factions, above which Napoleon would rise, and on the unworkability of the existing constitution. He went on:

---

7 M. Crook, *Napoleon Comes to Power*, 70.

8 L. Hunt, D. Lansky, and P. Hanson, "The Failure of the Liberal Republic in France, 1795–1799: The Road to Brumaire," *Journal of Modern History* 51 (December 1979), 734–59. This article is also reprinted in T. C. W. Blanning, ed., *The Rise and Fall of the French Revolution* (Chicago, University of Chicago Press, 1996), 468–93.

9 H. Brown, *Ending the French Revolution: Violence, Justice, and Repression from the Terror to Napoleon* (Charlottesville, University of Virginia Press, 2006).

"The Council of Elders summoned me; I responded to its call. A plan of general restoration had been put together by men whom the nation is accustomed to regard as defenders of liberty, equality and property …."[10] Napoleon notes here the rectitude and probity of the Council of Elders, just as he would go on to emphasize the irresoluteness of the Council of Five Hundred, and the physical danger that he encountered in their meeting hall, along with those deputies devoted to the public good. Note, however, that in the passage above, the original bywords of the Revolution had been amended, to "liberty, equality and property." Fraternity has disappeared – there was no room in the political order that Napoleon's coup heralded for the radical fraternity embraced by the Parisian *sans-culottes* – and the commitment to property offered reassurance to the bourgeosie, that segment of society on whose support the early Directory had most depended. On the very day that this proclamation was issued, the Council of Elders revoked restrictions on financial settlements with contractors, and in the following week the surtax on the wealthy and the law of hostages were also repealed, followed by a law inviting the return of many *émigrés*. It remained to be seen what liberty and equality might mean in the Napoleonic regime that followed.

Napoleon in Power

Steven Englund has written that the "paradox of his relentlessly political life is that Napoleon successfully 'ended' politics – at least in the turbulent, partisan, daily sense that the French had practiced it during a decade of revolution." If one thinks of politics as the essence of the French Revolution, then, it would seem difficult to consider Napoleon its heir. But Englund goes on to observe that: "I was going to subtitle this life 'The Empire of Circumstance,' so great was the power of the French Revolution in determining Napoleon's rise and his enduring attainments."[11] There is paradox, then, in the figure of Napoleon Bonaparte. A product of the Revolution, he also ended it, some might say betrayed it; but at the end of a fifteen-year reign, one might also argue that among his most enduring achievements were institutions or initiatives that the revolutionaries, not he, had launched. Indeed, some of those revolutionaries, men who had weathered the tumultuous days of the Year II, became loyal supporters of Napoleon, even after he declared himself emperor. What did they see in his

---

10 M. Crook, *Napoleon Comes to Power*, 96.

11 S. Englund, *Napoleon: A Political Life* (Cambridge, MA, Harvard University Press, 2004), 471 and 472.

leadership and his policies that they found consistent with the ideals of 1789?

The first task confronting Napoleon and the other two consuls, Sieyès and Roger-Ducos, was to see to the drafting of a new constitution. This was entrusted to a commission of deputies drawn from the two houses of the existing legislature, working under the leadership of Pierre-Claude Daunou. In barely a month they produced a constitution, short and obscure as Napoleon preferred. Sieyès produced his own document, but was powerless to secure its adoption. In February 1800 the new constitution was submitted to the citizenry for approval in a plebiscite, in which all adult males were eligible to vote. This would be the only sense in which the Napoleonic regime could be said to embrace participatory politics – the citizenry would vote, when plebiscites were called on rare occasions, but there would be no meaningful elections. In this first plebiscite, preceded as would become custom by voluminous government propaganda, the constitution was approved by a margin of more than 3 million votes in favor to 1,500 against.

Napoleon now became First Consul, named to a term of ten years and granted extensive executive powers. Jean-Jacques-René Cambacérès and Charles-François Lebrun were named second and third consuls, though with advisory powers only, while Sieyès and Roger-Ducos were relegated to the newly created Senate. These four men were granted authority to name the first thirty-one members of the Senate, who would then name an additional twenty-nine members. The Senate, in turn, had the authority to name the 100 members of the Tribunate and the 300 members of the Corps Législatif, drawn from lists submitted by departmental electoral assemblies. The Council of State, composed of men appointed by Napoleon, initiated all legislation. The Tribunate had the power to discuss that legislation, but could not amend it before forwarding it to the Corps Législatif, which similarly had only the right to approve or reject. The Senate could effectively block legislation proposed by Napoleon, but within two years the First Consul had succeeded in naming another forty senators, which nullified its independence. The Consulate thus had the trappings of parliamentary government, but none of the substance.

Early in his term as First Consul Napoleon moved to resolve the most vexatious problem of the revolutionary decade, the split between the French government and the Catholic Church. After months of difficult, sometimes forced, negotiations, a Concordat was reached in late 1801 and announced to the public in April 1802, accompanied by a number of Organic Articles to which Pope Pius VII had not previously agreed. The Concordat effectively ended the endemic resistance that had festered in the Vendée since 1793, and would govern relations between Church and

State in France until 1905. By this agreement, Catholicism was recognized as "the religion of the majority of Frenchmen." Papal investiture of archbishops and bishops was restored, although these would be nominated to Rome by Napoleon, while the Gallican independence of the French church was also recognized, and reinforced by the Organic Articles, to the displeasure of the pope. All clergy would continue to be paid by the French state, and in return the pope renounced all claim to the properties confiscated from the church early in the Revolution and sold as *biens nationaux*. In this fashion peace was restored to church–state relations, but the Catholic Church would never regain the strength or influence in France that it had enjoyed under the Old Regime.

Isser Woloch has written that "Napoleon did not vault onto the imperial throne but moved toward dictatorship gradually. Each assertion of new power came gilded with a veneer of legality and a rhetoric of commitment to the principles of 1789."[12] However cautious Napoleon may have been, he moved resolutely in the direction of complete personal power. Among his first appointments was that of Joseph Fouché as minister of police, a post that the former deputy in the National Convention and ex-terrorist had held under the Directory. Fouché moved quickly to place suspected dissidents under surveillance and impose censorship. The proliferation of newspapers that had been a hallmark of the early Revolution, and a crucial element in mobilizing political activism, soon came to an end. Each *département* was allowed just a single newspaper, and only four newspapers continued publication in Paris. Napoleon had resisted suggestions after Brumaire, from Sieyès among others, that he arrest or exile potential enemies, but in December 1800 an attempted assassination at the Opera provided the pretext for just such steps. The *Moniteur*, the semi-official organ of the government, suggested in its initial report of the attack that those responsible were akin to the perpetrators of the 1792 September Massacres, raising the specter of opposition from the left. Fouché, for his part, was convinced that it was a royalist plot, a suspicion that he would eventually prove. But Napoleon was determined to move against ex-Jacobins, and although he encountered resistance among his advisers and the Council of State, in short order a decree was issued for the summary deportation of roughly one hundred thirty former militants and *sans-culottes*.[13] In 1802 Napoleon requested that the Senate name him First Consul for life, to secure the stability of the government. Although the Senate refused, the more pliant Council of State complied, and the customary plebiscite confirmed its proclamation by an overwhelming majority.

---

12 I. Woloch, *Napoleon and His Collaborators* (New York, W. W. Norton, 2001), 156.

13 Ibid., 69–80.

Having eliminated the remants of a Jacobin opposition, Napoleon soon dealt with potential royalist opponents. In 1803 Fouché lured Georges Cadoudal and General Pichegru from England to Paris, on the pretext of a clandestine meeting with royalist conspirators. Both were arrested – Cadoudal was executed and Pichegru died in prison. In March 1804 Fouché's men traveled to Germany to kidnap the Duc d'Enghien, an heir in the Condé family, and returned him to the château at Vincennes, where he was shot. Just two months later, in May 1804, once again on the pretext of security and stability, Napoleon persuaded the Senate to proclaim the Empire, ratified overwhelmingly by plebiscite shortly thereafter. Knowledge that there was an heir to the throne, Napoleon argued, would remove all incentive to potential assassins. In December he brought Pope Pius VII to Notre Dame Cathedral for his coronation, although to mark his independence from the Catholic Church he placed the crown on his own head, while the pope looked on from his place of honor. The cermony was captured on canvas by Jacques-Louis David, who had made the transition from ardent Jacobin and festival master of the Republic to official painter at the imperial court.

Were we to judge Napoleon purely by this steady path toward absolute political power, we could hardly see him as heir to the Revolution. As statebuilder and lawmaker, however, his connection to the ideals of 1789 remained discernible. The Civil Code was completed in 1804, even as Napoleon was declaring himself emperor, and remains today the basis of French civil law. It guaranteed equality before the law, and preserved, in slightly less radical form, the revolutionary commitment to equal inheritance, thereby ensuring the breakup of large estates. The Civil Code also confirmed the abolition of the seigneurial system and the sale of *biens nationaux*, thus securing Napoleon's popularity among the peasantry. Although political liberty was obviously curtailed under the Napoleonic regime, personal liberty was guaranteed, as was the right to due process. Freedom of religion was confirmed, and civil marriage was required, a tradition that survives in France today. In many aspects, the Civil Code enshrined the family as the basis of society, a patriarchal society. Divorce by mutual consent was allowed, though difficult to obtain, and those divorced could not remarry for three years. The Code strengthened the authority of fathers over children, and of husbands over wives. Women were not fully equal to men before the law, nor would they gain equal rights in France until well after World War II, later than in most other European countries. From the perspective of women's rights, Napoleon nullified what few gains they had made during the Revolution and perpetuated their status as second-class citizens.

Napoleon's regime carried forward many of the administrative reforms introduced under the Revolution. The basic administrative structure was retained, but departmental and district councils were now appointed rather than elected, as were mayors. The linchpin of the administrative bureaucracy was the newly created position of prefect, one per department. The prefects, who reported directly to the minister of the interior, oversaw all aspects of local administration, were responsible for maintaining order, and were expected to ensure political support for the regime. Reminiscent of the intendants of the Old Regime, they are the very symbol of the centralization of state power under Napoleon. Historians have differed in their assessment of how much credit, or blame, Napoleon deserves for this. De Tocqueville famously argued that in this regard the revolutionary decades had actually changed relatively little, that the centralization of power that so characterized the state of his day (mid-nineteenth century) had its origins in the reigns of Louis XIII and Louis XIV.[14] Geoffrey Ellis offers a strong dissent: "Such a view is mistaken in many of its details and also detracts from Napoleon's major contribution to the same process. 'Modern,' 'open to talents,' and 'meritocratic' his government may not always have been; but what he bequeathed to subsequent generations, whether they liked it or not, was a stronger and more efficient structure of State centralism than anything which had gone before."[15] Martyn Lyons would also accord Napoleon the distinction of being "the founder of the modern state."[16] Isser Woloch, while mindful of Napoleon's contributions to the creation of a "new regime" in France, insists upon crediting as well those men serving in the emperor's government who had previous experience in revolutionary politics and administration: "The ex-revolutionary collaborators in particular kept aloft the banner of liberal revolutionary principles, however selective, symbolic, or observed in the breach they may have become."[17] Administrative structures, the judicial system, taxation, primary and secondary education, public health and welfare programs – Napoleon put his stamp on all of these, but he built upon the reforms initiated by the governments of the Revolution, both the National Convention and the Directory.

It was in the area of military conscription, Woloch observes with a note of surprise, that Napoleon may have achieved his most singular administrative achievement. Throughout the 1790s young French men had resisted recruitment into the army, even in 1793–94 when patriotic fervor had reached its greatest pitch. Only in 1798, with the Jourdan Law, was conscription actually introduced, and it elicited a rise in resistance and desertion. But despite the unprecedented demand for military power that

14 A. de Tocqueville, *L'Ancien Régime et la révolution* (Paris, Lévy frères, 1856).
15 G. Ellis, *Napoleon: Profiles in Power* (London, Pearson Education, 1997), 235.
16 M. Lyons, *Napoleon Bonaparte and the Legacy of the French Revolution*, 295.
17 I. Woloch, *Napoleon and His Collaborators*, 240.

came after 1804, the incidence of overt resistance declined: "By Napoleon's choice, conscription constituted the ultimate frontier of state building, of the articulation of the administrative state projected by the Revolution." In the end, the "conscription machine" broke the back of draft evasion.[18]

Why was this so? How did Napoleon succeed in dramatically diminishing, if not quite eliminating, popular resistance to military service, and what does this tell us about the relationship between Napoleon and the Revolution? At its origins, we might recall, the Vendée rebellion was born in 1793 out of twin resentments: over military conscription and over the Civil Constititution of the Clergy. The Concordat with the Catholic Church had removed one of those resentments, and perhaps this allowed the peasantry to tolerate more easily the other. Perhaps young men were also more willing to march off to war for the glory, and plunder, that Napoleon's conquests promised than they had been for the more abstract ideals of the Revolution. We must also not forget the "security state" that Napoleon put in place, completing the work of the Directory, and the chilling effect that this had on resistance of any sort.

In his wide-ranging discussion of the new regime that the Revolution and Napoleon combined to put in place, Woloch observes that there were limits to the administrative centralization they introduced. The services and administrative reforms that were introduced generally extended no further than the departmental *chefs-lieux*, or the other large towns of the provinces. Village life was left largely untouched, with two or three exceptions. One was the sale of the confiscated church lands, although here one might argue that it was the bourgeois of provincial towns who were best positioned to purchase land at auction. The other two were taxes and conscription, which weighed more heavily on rural France than on the inhabitants of towns and cities.

There are two ironies in all of this, one of which Woloch addresses and the other that he does not. The first, implicit in his analysis, is that the countryside was shortchanged both during the Revolution and under Napoleon. This is hardly surprising. It is consistent with our sense of the Revolution, and the Enlightenment before it, as largely urban affairs, centered in the towns and cities of France. It is also consistent with the pattern one finds in virtually all societies embarking on industrialization, however gradual that may have been in the French case – in order for it to proceed, surplus food, material resources, and labor must all be shifted from rural areas to the growing urban centers. In terms of the reforms introduced in this period – whether in schooling, health care, or poor

18 I. Woloch, *The New Regime: Transformations of the French Civic Order, 1789–1820s* (New York, W. W. Norton, 1994), 433.

relief – their failure to reach the level of the villages was due both to budgetary constraints and the demands of war. In both senses, the peasantry gave more than they received. This leads to the second irony, which Woloch does emphasize, namely that "the Napoleonic conscription machine (with its tightly controlled safety valves of replacement and medical dispensations) arguably produced the most disastrous result of the French Revolution by virtue of the mass slaughter it facilitated through the disease, privation, and battle casualties of the Empire's extravagant military campaigns."[19] The popular support for the Napoleonic regime, in the form of cooperation with conscription, allowed the emperor to pursue the strategy of conquest that ultimately proved to be his undoing.

It is beyond the scope of this volume to consider Napoleon's military campaigns at length, but two points are worth examining briefly: the extent of French expansion under the Empire, and the ways in which that expansion exported revolutionary ideas to the rest of Europe; and the cost in human life of Napoleon's wars. A report on a recent conference in Germany on the theme of the Napoleonic wars and their impact began with this observation: "The military expansion of France ensured that hardly any part of Europe remained untouched by these revolutionary transformations."[20] Indeed, beginning with the second Italian campaign in 1805, Napoleon defeated the Austrians, Prussians, and Russians in successive years, so that by the Peace of Tilsit in July 1807 France was at peace with every European power save Great Britain. Satellite kingdoms were established in Italy, Naples, Holland, and Westphalia, and France annexed territory in Belgium, Holland, Piedmont, Savoy, Catalonia, and the Rhineland. Some areas, such as Belgium and the Italian states, welcomed French rule more than others – there was endemic guerrilla resistance on the Spanish peninsula, where Napoleon's brother Joseph was imposed as king in 1808, and a number of the German states also resisted French rule. But along with its armies, France exported the ideals of representative government and civil liberties, introduced the Napoleonic Code in the regions that it ruled, weakened the landed aristocracy and enlisted bourgeois elites as allies, thereby weakening feudalism in much of central and southern Europe, and planted the seeds of nationalism, whether through emulation of French institutions and ideals, or through the resistance that French troops elicited. One might well

19 Ibid., 432.

20 Report on the international and interdisciplinary conference: "Experience, Memory and Media: Transmitting the Revolutionary and Napoleonic Wars in 19th and 20th Century Europe," 11–13 October 2007, University of Mannheim. This report, posted on H-France on 27 December 2007, summarizes papers from the conference, which are projected to be published as a volume in the Palgrave series, "War, Culture and Society, 1750–1850."

argue, indeed, that Napoleon exported to much of the rest of Europe many of the revolutionary ideals that he betrayed at home.

Eventually Napoleon overreached his grasp. Steven Englund makes much of Napoleon's "will-to-power" in exploring his extraordinary life. That will-to-power, translated into ambition, may be what led him to the Russian campaign of 1812. Napoleon set off on the march to Moscow with an army of 500,000, many of them not French. Undone by the wiliness of Alexander I, an opposing army that refused to be engaged, and the harshness of the Russian winter, he limped back to Paris with barely 30,000 men. That catastrophic loss is indicative of the cost in human life over the course of Napoleon's rule. Between 1803 and 1814, approximately 86,500 men died in battle; another 300,000 died in hospital, and well over 500,000 either disappeared or were badly wounded, producing a total of just over 1 million French casualties. Yet despite that heavy toll, French population grew from roughly 26,000,000 in 1789 to 30,000,000 in 1815.[21] Still, the toll of Napoleon's wars exceeded that of the Terror and the Vendée rebellion combined.

The Russian campaign did not spell the end of Napoleon's rule. Thanks to that remarkable conscription machine, he would raise yet another army. But the coalition of allies, emboldened by the signs of Napoleon's vulnerability, reassembled their armies for a push onto French territory, forcing the emperor's abdication and exile to Elba, a small island off the coast of Italy. Louis XVIII, the brother of the ill-fated Louis XVI, returned to the throne, but the French citizenry was not eager to sacrifice its hard-won civil liberties to a Bourbon restoration, and Bonaparte escaped from Elba in March 1815 to embark upon One Hundred Days of "liberal" rule, only to be defeated once again at Waterloo. This time he was exiled far from Europe, nearly a thousand miles off the east coast of southern Africa on the island of St. Helena. There he spent his final years, dictating his memoirs to his aides in an effort to shape history's judgment of his reign and his military conquests.

There will likely never be a final, definitive judgment of Napoleon's achievements and his relation to the Revolution. Alan Schom, at the end of his often sympathetic treatment of Bonaparte, was quite scathing in his final analysis. Dismissing Napoleon's insistence that history would "have to give me my rightful due," he concludes:

> Clearly Napoleon had forgotten the hundreds of smoking villages he had bombarded or burned to the ground, from Moscow to Warsaw to Prussia,

---

21 O. Connelly, *French Revolution/Napoleonic Era*, 245. Connelly's figures are drawn from J. Houdaille, "Le problème des pertes de guerre," *Revue d'Histoire moderne et contemporaine* XVII (1970), 418.

> throughout northern and southern Italy, and sweeping across the plains and mountains of Iberia. He had forgotten the thousands of genuine POWs he had subsequently executed in cold blood. He had forgotten the hundreds of thousands of civilian refugees rendered homeless by his wars, the thousands upon thousands of old women and young girls raped by his Grande Armée, of the hundreds of towns and cities he had ruthlessly looted, the three million or so dead soldiers of all nations left rotting across the face of Europe, and the millions of wounded and permanently handicapped, the destroyed political institutions of a few hundred states and principalities – the shattered economies, the fear and dread he had left behind everywhere, France included. The memory of Genghis Khan paled in comparison.[22]

Steven Englund, though not ignoring Napoleon's transgressions, is rather more nuanced and generous in his final assessment: "Internationally, too, Napoleon's name swiftly claimed association with liberalism and national independence – incredibly, if one considers only the Empire's legacy of tyranny and does not give due measure to the power of myth around a charismatic personality." And further, "However, the republican tradition in France, though it long ago (in the 1840s) repudiated the Napoleonic tradition, yet retains a far profounder trace of that imprint than it cares to concede."[23]

There is one final controversy, one last debate, associated with Napoleon's final days on St. Helena. A quarter century ago Ben Weider and David Hapgood alleged that Napoleon had been murdered on St. Helena, poisoned with arsenic by one of his aides, the Comte de Montholon, acting in concert with the future Charles X, brother to Louis XVIII.[24] Traces of arsenic were found in hair from the emperor's head supposedly given by Napoleon to a close friend. Critics of this conspiracy theory point out that wallpaper in the eighteenth century often contained arsenic, and that Napoleon spent days confined to a single room where he might have ingested the poison simply by breathing. Where does the truth lie? Alan Schom is persuaded, and concludes that there can be no doubt that Napoleon was murdered. Steven Englund, reviewing the same body of literature, finds the forensic evidence inconclusive and claims that there is no archival evidence to support the allegations of murder.[25] And so, on this question, as with so much else in regard to Napoleon Bonaparte, the debate goes on.

---

22 A. Schom, *Napoleon Bonaparte*, 789.

23 S. Englund, *Napoleon: A Political Life*, 457, 460.

24 B. Weider and D. Hapgood, *The Murder of Napoleon* (New York, Congdon and Lattes, 1982). Four years earlier Weider published his theories in a coauthored book with Sten Forshufvud, the Swedish toxicologist who first put forward the argument about poisoning: *Assassination at St. Helena: The Poisoning of Napoleon Bonaparte* (Vancouver, Mitchell Press, 1978).

25 A. Schom, *Napoleon Bonaparte*, 779–86; S. Englund, *Napoleon: A Political Life*, 454–56.

9
Revolutionary Violence

Revolutions are, by definition, violent. So are wars. But revolutionary violence, by and large, has generated much more controversy and opprobrium over the years than the carnage visited upon people by wars, despite the fact that many more people have died as a result of warfare than have died as a result of revolution, even if one includes the victims of the Soviet gulag and those of the Chinese Great Leap Forward and Cultural Revolution. The excessses of revolutionary violence, it is often said, tarnish irredeemably the noble ideals of revolutionaries. Seldom is the same said of the violence of warfare, although wars, too, are often fought in the name of noble causes.

The violence of the French Revolution is no exception in this regard. Both popular violence and the violence of the Terror were the focus of political debate at the time, and historians and others have continued to argue right up to the present day about what, if any, of the violence of the Revolution was justified. In the epilogue to *Citizens*, Simon Schama wrote: "From the very beginning – from the summer of 1789 – violence was the motor of the Revolution." One page later he followed up that assertion with two questions: "Why was the French Revolution like this? Why, from the beginning, was it powered by brutality?"[1] The second question, it seems to me, clarifies the ambiguity left by the succinctness of the initial statement, which one might read as akin to Trotsky's assertion that war is the locomotive of history. But revolutionary violence, for Schama, is brutality, and by that characterization he seems to be portraying the revolutionaries themselves

1 S. Schama, *Citizens: A Chronicle of the French Revolution* (New York, A. Knopf, 1989), 859–60.

as less than civilized, to be claiming that violence is the very essence of the Revolution. We might take this assertion as illustrative of one extreme in the debate about violence in the French Revolution.

Jean-Clément Martin, current holder of the Chair of the French Revolution at the Sorbonne, has recently staked out a position at the opposite pole of the debate in his book *Violence et Révolution: Essai sur la naissance d'un mythe national* (*Violence and Revolution: Essay on the Birth of a National Myth*). Martin is not, as the book title might suggest, denying the reality or gravity of revolutionary violence, but he insists that we place it in its proper perspective, as suggested in the following passage: "Soon, however, the guillotine, like all the other real or fictional machines conceived during the period, escaped the control of its promoters, under the effect of the passions and the social struggles that were the motor of the French Revolution."[2]

The most obvious difference between these two positions is expressed in the final words of the quotation. For Schama, violence was the motor of the Revolution, whereas for Martin personal passion and social struggle were the motor. For Schama, violence is the starting point. For Martin it is a product of other forces. For Martin, violence is an essential part of revolution, while for Schama it is the very essence of revolution. Martin begins his observation, significantly, with the image of the guillotine, the instrument of the Terror (although not exclusively so), a machine of execution conceived as an agent of both humanity and equality. But as Martin suggests, it soon became one of the most powerful and emotional of the symbols of the Revolution, one that evoked horror and fear. For some, the guillotine became synonymous with the Revolution.

If we are to understand revolutionary violence, I would argue, it needs to be placed in context, not presented in isolation. Those who would condemn violence – whether it be revolutionary violence, or criminal violence, or the violence of terror – tend to isolate it, to give it primacy, in order to reject it. Who among us, after all, would defend violence in and of itself? But by isolating violence, and rejecting its legitimacy, we also come to fear it, and in that fear we lose our opportunity to understand it. In a historical perspective, this tendency to isolate violence leads to a caricature of it rather than a full picture.

Violence – or more precisely the fear of violence – ought to be considered in relationship to the concepts, or ideals, of order, liberty, and civilized society. We often think of violence as the negation of order, a betrayal of civilized society, but we might do well to remind ourselves of Max Weber's

2 J.-C. Martin, *Violence et Révolution: essai sur la naissance d'un mythe national* (Paris, Seuil, 2006), 80. Translation mine.

definition of the modern state, which rested crucially on the notion that the state enjoys a monopoly over the legitimate use of armed force, or violence. From that perspective, in the midst of a revolution in which the nature of the state, the definition of sovereignty, and the exercise of sovereignty were all being contested, the question of who might legitimately resort to violence would also, naturally, be a point of contestation. Indeed, the ability to marshal force in defense of a claim to sovereignty proved to be decisive at various points in the Revolution.

Similarly, those who asserted the universality of human rights in 1789 did so in the face of what they took to be a despotic state, whether they located the source of that despotism among the royal ministers or in the person of the king himself. The revolutionaries may have taken human rights to be natural and inalienable, but that does not mean that they expected them to be granted without a struggle, a potentially violent struggle. That expectation would be manifestly fulfilled in the first months of the Revolution: by Louis XVI's order for the massing of troops in the outskirts of Paris in late June, by the assault on the Bastille on 14 July responding to that threat, by the Great Fear that swept through much of provincial France in late July and August, triggered by rumors of aristocratic plots to destroy crops before they could be harvested.

The goal of this chapter will be to place revolutionary violence in its context, to try to come to terms not only with its impact but with its genesis. Was revolutionary violence the product of ideology, or of discourse as François Furet would have it, or did it emerge out of social tensions, individual passions, personal rivalries, even despair, as Jean-Clément Martin or Richard Cobb might argue? Were there moments in the Revolution, as the revolutionaries themselves claimed, when violence was salutary, and others when it became negative or counterproductive? Is it possible, from our perspective today, to speak of revolutionary violence in positive terms?

Let us be clear from the outset, however, that we cannot speak of a single "revolutionary violence." We must distinguish among a number of different types of violence and consider the relationship between them. One thinks first of popular violence – the storming of the Bastille, the heads on pikes being carried through the streets of Paris. This is the violence of the crowd, at times sanctioned by revolutionary leaders and at other times decried and suppressed. Then there was the guillotine, the state violence of the Terror. Was this an expression of the popular will, or a perversion of the people's desires? State violence did not end with 9 Thermidor and the fall of Robespierre, though. The repressive violence of the Directory regime was of a different sort, directed at different enemies, but it was violence all the same. As my initial remarks would suggest, if we are to deal comprehensively with the topic of violence in this period, we must consider the violence of war as well as these other forms of revolutionary violence. Was the revolutionary war of the early 1790s a qualitatively different phenomenon from the Napoleonic wars that came at decade's end? If, as Mao Zedong is reported to have said, "politics is war without bloodshed while war is politics with bloodshed," then was revolutionary war a logical outgrowth of revolutionary politics? And what of the civil war that raged within France? How are we to understand the brutal violence of the Vendée, on both sides? Can we equate the White Terror, the two waves of violent reprisals against ex-Jacobins (or ex-Terrorists), with the violence of the Terror that its perpetrators claimed to be avenging, or with the popular violence of the early Revolution? Or was it somehow fundamentally different? Finally, would a discussion of violence in the French Revolution be complete without considering the violence of hunger and deprivation? Some of the most egregious acts of popular violence were committed by those who had teetered on the brink of starvation in 1788 and 1789 – the rabble, *la canaille*, as their social betters called them. In 1795, when the propertied classes once again had their hands firmly in control of political power and the price controls of the Terror had been removed, the common people who had survived the early years of the Revolution once again found themselves on the brink of starvation. Many of them, indeed, would not survive the bitter winter of *nonante-cinq*, 1795. Was this not a form of violence, too?

Popular Violence

"Let *us* be terrible, to dispense the people from the need to be terrible themselves."[3] Thus spoke Georges Danton before the National Convention in the spring of 1793, urging the creation of a Revolutionary Tribunal so that France might be spared a repeat of the September Massacres of the previous fall. By that time, one might argue, the legitimacy of popular violence had been recognized by many of the deputies, even if they did not fully countenance it. They were about to institutionalize the people's justice, the justice of the crowd, by voting for a Revolutionary Tribunal, before which would appear not common criminals, but rather the enemies of the Revolution, by extension the enemies of the people. The link between popular violence, at least certain instances of popular violence, and the state violence of the Terror was thus explicitly asserted at this transitional moment of the Revolution.

3 N. Hampson, *Danton* (Oxford, Basil Blackwell, 1988), 102.

We must make a distinction here between political violence, such as the storming of the Bastille in July 1789, to which we shall turn in a moment, and public vengeance, such as the killing of Louis Bertier de Sauvigny and his father-in-law Joseph Foulon just eight days after the fall of the Bastille. Bertier de Sauvigny had been royal governor of Paris since 1776, while Foulon had succeeded Necker as controller general upon the latter's dismissal on July 12. In the midst of the popular tumult of mid-July Bertier tried to flee the capital, but was apprehended by a crowd, which then went to find Foulon. Both men were suspected of manipulating grain supplies, either for their own profit or to worsen the plight of the poor. Having shown no sympathy for the crowd, they now received none. They were beaten to death, decapitated, and their heads paraded through the streets of Paris, Foulon's mouth stuffed full with the straw that he allegedly had suggested the people eat. Many were horrified by these brutal deaths. But when the deputy Lally-Tollendal condemned the killings before the Assembly at Versailles, Antoine Barnave uttered his famous riposte, "Was their blood, then, so pure?"

What are we to make of such violence? Consider the following perspective offered by Jack Censer and Lynn Hunt:

> Popular violence defined the French Revolution. Without crowds of lower-class people, there would have been no fall of the Bastille, no overthrow of the monarchy, no arrest of the Girondins, no spectacle of the guillotine. The middle-class deputies who led the French Revolution depended on popular support, which inevitably meant popular violence, but they also feared that violence, felt repulsed by it, and constantly maneuvered to get a handle on it. Popular violence pushed the Revolution forward, but it also threatened to dissolve it altogether in an acid wash of blood, political vengeance, and anarchic disorder.[4]

How does this characterization differ from the succinct view of Simon Schama, cited above, that "violence was the motor of the Revolution?" There are several differences, I would argue. First, by degree of emphasis: Schama's statement implies that violence "powered" the Revolution, whereas Censer and Hunt point to the "middle-class deputies who led the French Revolution." While those deputies depended on popular violence at times, they were ambivalent about it, were even "repulsed" by it

---

4 J. Censer and L. Hunt, "Imaging the French Revolution: Depictions of the French Revolutionary Crowd," *American Historical Review* 110, no. 1 (February 2005), 38–45. The quotation is the opening passage in this essay, which introduces both a set of images and a series of essays, most of them focusing on violence and images of violence, all available on-line at http://chnm.gmu.edu/revolution/imaging/home.html.

in certain instances. Second, Schama's characterization of violence in the Revolution is overwhelmingly negative, whereas for Censer and Hunt, "popular violence pushed the Revolution forward ...." They acknowledge the negative aspects, the danger that popular violence might devolve into "political vengeance, and anarchic disorder," but this is the risk of such violence, not its essence. Indeed, without that popular violence, the Bastille would not have fallen, the monarchy would not have been overthrown. For Censer and Hunt, the gains of the Revolution, at least many of them, depended on violence, while Schama sees the Revolution as wallowing in violence.

This more judicious appraisal of popular violence does overstep on one count, I would argue. Censer and Hunt assert that the deputies' dependence on popular support "inevitably meant popular violence." They also note among their examples "the arrest of the Girondins" on 2 June 1793. This is perhaps the best example, however, of a revolutionary *journée* on which massive popular support did not end in popular violence. Some 80,000 people surrounded the National Convention on 2 June, demanding the proscription of the leading Girondin deputies, but that goal was achieved without violence. The *threat* of violence was there, to be sure, but it did not occur.[5]

There were numerous instances of popular violence in the first years of the Revolution, in the provinces as well as in Paris. Some took the form of large-scale popular protests, as with the assault on the Bastille, the popular insurrections that often led to municipal revolutions in provincial towns during the summer of 1789, certain manifestations of the Great Fear that swept across central France in July and August 1789, the women's march to Versailles on 5–6 October 1789, and the assault on the Tuileries palace on 10 August 1792 that brought the fall of the monarchy. There were also many cases similar to the killing of Foulon and Bertier, instances in which the crowd was intent on exacting vengeance, or popular justice, rather than being engaged in political protest. Such was the case in September 1792, when Parisian militants invaded the makeshift prisons of the capital, seized suspected traitors and counterrevolutionaries, conducted summary trials in the streets and courtyards, and ultimately massacred as many as 1,400 of those prisoners. This marked a turning point, at once the most massive episode of popular violence in the Revolution and also very nearly the last, at least on such a scale. There would be a few instances of the crowd exercising popular justice in the years ahead, both in the provinces and in Paris (most

---

5 P. R. Hanson, *The Jacobin Republic under Fire: The Federalist Revolt in the French Revolution* (University Park, Pennsylvania State University Press, 2003), 59–62.

notably the Prairial riots of May 1795), but as early as the fall of 1792 and culminating in the spring of 1793 the institutions of revolutionary justice were put in place – popular violence would give way to state violence. Each of these examples of popular violence has drawn the attention, and debate, of historians, and each merits some further discussion here.

The fall of the Bastille is perhaps the most widely recognized event of the French Revolution, made so in part by the fact that since the late nineteenth century Bastille Day, 14 July, has been the French national holiday. But news of the fall of the Bastille resonated throughout France and across Europe almost immediately, hailed by most as a great victory for the people. If the National Assembly had asserted the sovereignty of the nation at Versailles on 17 June, the people of Paris seemingly secured it by force of arms on 14 July. News of the dismissal of Jacques Necker, along with reports of royal troops gathering outside Paris, prompted the mobilization of the crowd, which by late afternoon may have numbered as many as 80,000. Relatively few died in this uprising – only a half dozen soldiers, and 98 of the besiegers – but the governor of the Bastille, Bernard-René de Launey, lost his life and his head at the hands of the angry crowd before authorities could safely imprison him at the Hôtel de Ville.

What was the significance of this event? First, it brought an end to the king's apparent plan to turn back the rising tide of revolution by armed force. On 17 July Louis XVI traveled from Versailles to Paris to accept the revolutionary cockade and recognize the new municipal authorities. But the fall of the Bastille had a far greater symbolic impact, even if that symbolism ultimately proved to be overdrawn and contested. In the popular imagination the fortress stood, 30 meters high, as a symbol of royal despotism. Earlier in the century its inmates had included such literary luminaries as Voltaire, but in July 1789 its walls held only seven prisoners, and its most celebrated recent inmate had been the Marquis de Sade, hardly a firebrand for either literary or political freedom. As news of its fall spread, however, it inspired similar uprisings in provincial cities, ranging from Caen to Marseille, which in turn led to the ousting from office of royal officials and their replacement by new municipal councils.[6] In this way the popular revolution spread throughout France. The legitimacy of popular violence in this instance seemed clear to most – the vanquishers of the

---

6 For an account of the assault on the château in Caen see P. R. Hanson, *Provincial Politics in the French Revolution: Caen and Limoges, 1789–1794* (Baton Rouge, Louisiana State University Press, 1989), 31–34; for Marseille see R. Reichardt, "Prises et démolition des Bastilles Marseillaises," in C. Badet, ed., *Marseille en Révolution* (Marseille, Editions Rivage, 1989), 53–67. See L. Hunt, "Committees and Communes: Local Politics and National Revolution in 1789," *Comparative Studies in Society and History* XVIII (July 1976), 321–46, for an account of the municipal revolutions of summer 1789.

Bastille would soon be recognized as national heroes. But not all shared that view: "From one moment to the next, the people of Paris turned into a tribe of cannibals," wrote one royalist lawyer.[7]

Popular violence also spread to the French countryside in the summer of 1789, most notably in the wave of rural panic known as the Great Fear. Georges Lefebvre traced the seven distinct currents of the Great Fear, which moved with astonishing rapidity throughout most of central and south-central France in the weeks following the fall of the Bastille. The movement grew in part out of the anxiety produced by the poor harvests of 1788, but was triggered by rumors that the aristocracy was paying brigands to go into the fields to cut the grain before it had fully ripened, thereby throwing the peasantry into even deeper economic crisis and thwarting the popular movement for reform. As the rumors spread, peasants attacked the châteaux of local seigneurs, drinking the lord's wine and sometimes seizing and destroying the records of the hated seigneurial dues. Considerable property damage resulted, but very few lives were lost in this violence. While Lefebvre's work showed well the social and economic context of this violence, the more recent scholarship of Clay Ramsey yields insight into popular attitudes and the ideological content of the Great Fear. Ramsey argues that the protests grew less out of a sense of "class" conflict, and more out of the traditional peasant suspicion of outsiders, heightened in some areas by the incursion of the market into rural France. His analysis also underscores the great regional diversity of the provinces.[8]

Anxiety about food supply combined with unsettling political news to produce a third major instance of popular violence in 1789, the march of Parisian market women to Versailles on 5 October. Grain and bread prices continued to escalate as the new harvest was being brought in, and at Versailles Louis XVI was refusing to sign both the Declaration of the Rights of Man and Citizen and the decrees abolishing seigneurial dues that the Constituent Assembly had passed following the Night of 4 August. As we saw in Chapter Two, the women's march ended in violence and an unruly invasion of the queen's bedchamber, and in the wake of this terrifying incident the king agreed not only to return to Paris with his family but to sign the legislation that had lain on his desk now for weeks. Once again,

---

7 J. Godechot, *The Taking of the Bastille, July 14th 1789* (New York, Scribner, 1970); H. J. Lusebrink and R. Reichardt, *The Bastille: A History of a Symbol of Despotism and Freedom* (Durham, Duke University Press, 1997), 63 for the quotation.

8 G. Lefebvre, *The Great Fear of 1789: Rural Panic in Revolutionary France* (New York, Vintage Books, 1973); C. Ramsey, *The Ideology of the Great Fear: The Soissonnais in 1789* (Baltimore, Johns Hopkins University Press, 1992).

then, popular violence had "pushed the Revolution forward," in the words of Censer and Hunt. But this incident differed from the earlier examples in two significant ways. First, and most obviously, the vast majority of those participating were women. Some suggested at the time, and nineteenth-century historians perpetuated this view, that there were men dressed as women among the leaders of the crowd, but Olwen Hufton and others have refuted that myth. This was a women's march and protest, unique among the many *journées* of the Revolution. In Hufton's words, "the women were intent upon a particular kind of demonstration which the men might have ruined ...."[9] In marching to Versailles the women followed an Old Regime tradition, the market fishwives visiting the queen's bedchamber on the occasion of a royal birth, but as Elizabeth Colwill has argued, in this instance the women transformed that practice into something quite different, a political act that was neither deferential nor solicitous. A second novel aspect of this incident was the almost immediate public condemnation of the real and threatened violence. Was this because the protesters were female? In any case, there were those who charged that the women had been paid by Mirabeau or the Duc d'Orléans in a plot to depose Louis XVI. Eyewitnesses reported having heard some of the more disreputable women threaten "to kill the Austrian whore." Reports such as these prompted the Châtelet court to order a judicial investigation, and the public mood seemed to shift in regard to the legitimacy of popular protest. For the next year the streets of Paris would be remarkably calm.[10]

10 August 1792 stands alongside 14 July 1789 as the second momentous popular insurrection of the Revolution. With the war against Austria and Prussia going badly, and the king recalcitrant on the emotional issues of aristocratic *émigrés* and non-juring clergy, the people of Paris, joined by volunteers from the provinces, rose up in an assault on the Tuileries Palace that would topple Louis XVI from the throne. There was nothing spontaneous about this uprising. Indeed, there had been a failed insurrection on 20 June, so a month and a half of planning and mobilization led up to 10 August, which was as much a military exercise as it was a popular upheaval. As with nearly all of the successful Parisian insurrections, bourgeois leadership combined with support from the *sans-culottes*,

9 O. Hufton, *Women and the Limits of Citizenship in the French Revolution* (Toronto, University of Toronto Press, 1992), 14.

10 G. Rudé, *The Crowd in the French Revolution* (Oxford, Oxford University Press, 1959); E. Colwill, "Rites of Subjection, Bonds of Sex: The Women's March to Versailles," unpublished manuscript; B. Shapiro, *Revolutionary Justice in Paris, 1789–90* (Cambridge, Cambridge University Press, 1993).

moblized through the clubs and section assemblies of the capital. Both Robespierre and Danton called for insurrection, and the Cordelier Club, of which Danton was a leader, played a particularly important role. As historians have made clear, these uprisings were not the work of the mob, of *la canaille*, but were rather composed largely of respectable citizens. Women once again played a substantial role in mobilizing neighborhood support, and in the aftermath of the uprising the *fédérés* from Marseille voted civic crowns to three activist women who were wounded in the fighting: Théroigne de Méricourt, Louise-Reine Audu, and Claire Lacombe. Six hundred Swiss Guards died in the assault on the Tuileries, and nearly four hundred of the besiegers were killed or wounded.[11]

Robespierre would soon characterize 10 August as a triumph of "the people," and one of the important consequences of this insurrection, in addition to the fall of the monarchy and the creation of the first French republic, was the adoption of universal manhood suffrage for the elections that fall and winter. The old distinction between "active" and "passive" citizen was now dropped, a casualty, it would seem, of popular violence. Within weeks, however, another violent episode occurred that would tarnish the victory that the people had achieved at the Tuileries. Between 2 and 6 September 1792, militant *sans-culottes* invaded the prisons of Paris and massacred more than a thousand prisoners, goaded to this macabre act by reports of Prussian troops advancing toward the capital, fearful that the traitors in the prisons would rise up to attack the defenders of the city from behind.

The September Massacres would soon become a politically charged debating point, with deputies on the left defending the executions as an extension of 10 August, while those on the right, and even moderate republicans, condemned them as acts of wanton violence, cynically manipulated by men such as Robespierre, Danton, and Marat, who sought to gain positions of political power on the shoulders of the popular movement. Marat may have been the only revolutionary to champion the massacres with enthusiasm, calling for further exemplary executions of the people's enemies. But it is striking that for some weeks virtually no one condemned the killings. Jean-Marie Roland, then minister of the interior and a supporter of the Girondins, described the massacres as a regrettable but necessary measure, "over which perhaps a veil must be drawn." As the political opposition between Girondins and Montagnards grew

---

11 The classic account of 10 August remains G. Rudé, *The Crowd in the French Revolution*, 95–108; but see also N. Hampson, *Danton*, 71–79; D. P. Jordan, *The King's Trial* (Berkeley, University of California Press, 1979), 34–42; and D. Godineau, *The Women of Paris and Their French Revolution* (Berkeley, University of California Press, 1998), 110–14.

more bitter, however, those who had either participated in or supported the massacres came to be denounced as *septembriseurs,* as "drinkers of blood," or as anarchists. There would be no mark of heroism accorded to those who participated in this act of popular violence, as there had been to those who stormed the Bastille or who joined in the assault on the Tuileries palace.[12]

Brian Singer argues that there were two striking differences between the popular violence of the September Massacres and that of earlier incidents in the Revolution: the absence of public spectacle on the one hand, and the element of popular justice that was an integral part of the prison massacres. He notes, following Rudé, that while acts of violence such as the killings of Foulon and Bertier were relatively moderate in quantitative terms, they were maximized as spectacle, following a highly ritualized scenario with roots in both Old Regime popular culture and royal justice. In the September Massacres, by contrast, the executions took place away from public view, secluded in the courtyards of the prisons. One sees here, Singer argues, a transition from "popular violence" to "popular justice" – in most cases popular tribunals were set up and summary justice was passed prior to the executions, even as the perpetrators ignored or denied the authority of both the Paris Commune and the Legislative Assembly, an assertion of direct democracy and popular sovereignty.

Singer offers an additional interesting insight in regard to the violence of the September Massacres. One of the seminal contributions of George Rudé's work was to make clear that the revolutionary crowd was not composed of the rabble, of the *gens sans aveu*, as contemporary opponents alleged and as conservative historians would argue up into the twentieth century. The same was true of the September Massacres, so far as we know. Those carrying out the violence were militants from the sections and clubs of Paris, workers, artisans, and small shopkeepers. Their victims, however, despite the professed agenda of eliminating political enemies, were predominantly common criminals, drawn precisely from the population of *gens sans aveu* that bourgeois and aristocrats traditionally identified as scapegoats at times of popular disorder. In this instance the *sans-culottes* had adopted the prejudice of their social betters.[13]

12 P. Caron, *Les Massacres de septembre* (Paris, Maison du livre français, 1935); F. Bluche, *Septembre 1792: logiques d'un massacre* (Paris, Robert Laffont, 1986); M. Dorigny, "Violence et Révolution: Les Girondins et les massacres de septembre," in A. Soboul, ed., *Girondins et Montagnards* (Paris, Société des études robespierristes, 1980), 103–20.

13 B. Singer, "Violence in the French Revolution: Forms of Ingestion/Forms of Expulsion," in F. Fehér, ed., *The French Revolution and the Birth of Modernity* (Berkeley, University of California Press, 1990), 150–73.

The September Massacres were not entirely devoid of public spectacle, however. Among the victims was Marie-Thérèse-Louise de Savoie-Carignan, the Princesse de Lamballe, a close companion at Versailles of Queen Marie-Antoinette. As Antoine de Baecque recounts, Lamballe was taken from La Force prison, executed, and beheaded, her head later displayed before the windows of the Temple, where the queeen and her family were being held. De Baecque makes clear that the contemporary accounts of her dismemberment, sexual humiliation, the roasting of her heart, etc., were contradicted by the official record of her death. Those accounts, though, circulated widely at the time and persist to the present day, clear evidence of the capacity of the popular imagination to exaggerate the brutality of popular violence, in this case and others. Still, the death of Lamballe clearly resembles the public vengeance of killings such as those of Foulon and Bertier, and stands in contrast to the popular justice of the vast majority of the September Massacres, carried out behind the walls of the prison courtyards.[14]

State Violence: The Terror

> For two hundred years, the Terror has haunted the imagination of the West. The descent of the French Revolution from rapturous liberation into an orgy of apparently pointless bloodletting has been the focus of countless reflections on the often malignant nature of humanity and the folly of revolution.[15]

This paragraph illustrates well the challenge in trying to understand the Terror in the French Revolution. Everyone comes to the topic with preconceptions, generally molded in some fashion by popular representations drawn from literature or film. Those preconceptions are generally negative, not surprisingly so, for as Mona Ozouf and Bronislaw Baczko have both pointed out, the interpretation of the Terror began as soon as it was over, and the imperative for the Thermidorians was to discredit the

---

14 A. de Baecque, "The Princesse de Lamballe; or, Sex Slaughtered," in de Baecque, *Glory and Terror: Seven Deaths under the French Revolution* (New York, Routledge, 2003), 61–84. De Baecque appears not to have read Singer's essay, and suggests that many of the other killings of September were similarly public. For the classic account of the ritual character of executions under the Old Regime, whether royal or popular, see M. Foucault, *Discipline and Punish* (New York, Vintage Books, 1979).

15 D. Andress, *The Terror: The Merciless War for Freedom in Revolutionary France* (New York, Farrar, Straus, and Giroux, 2005). The quotation is the lead paragraph from the inside flap of the bookjacket.

policies of those they had overthrown while at the same time preserving the revolutionary project.[16]

Thus, as in the quotation above, one sees the dichotomy drawn between "rapturous liberation" and "an orgy of apparently pointless bloodletting …." One notes the choice of the adjective "malignant" in the next sentence, implicitly linking Terror to a cancer, and the final reference to the "folly of revolution," seemingly concluding at the outset that the Terror nullified whatever the revolutionaries might have achieved prior to the Year II.

Despite these preconceptions, shared by nearly all, the Terror continues to fascinate us. In addition to the books by Martin and Andress, already noted, three other substantial works on revolutionary terror have appeared within the past decade: Arno Mayer's *The Furies: Violence and Terror in the French and Russian Revolutions*; Graeme Fife's *The Terror: The Shadow of the Guillotine*; Sophie Wahnich's *La Liberté ou la mort: essai sur la Terreur et le terrorisme*; and Eli Sagan's *Citizens and Cannibals: The French Revolution, the Struggle for Modernity, and the Origins of Ideological Terror.*[17] Since 2001, indeed, the "war on terror" has generated a whole new body of literature focusing on Islamic terrorism. Terror and terrorism are, of course, two quite different things, but much of the literature seems to share the assumption that both are the work of ideological fanatics.[18]

For many years this has been a central point of contention among those writing about the French Terror. Even before it occurred, Edmund Burke saw the Terror as the inevitable result of revolutionary ideas. In François Furet's view, "the Revolution invented formidable enemies for itself, for every Manichean creed needs to overcome its share of eternal evil."[19] For Keith Baker, by the "constitutional decisions taken by the National Assembly in mid-September 1789," in particular the decisions to adopt a unicameral legislature and to grant the king only a suspensive veto,

---

16 M. Ozouf, "The Terror after the Terror: An Immediate History," and B. Baczko, "The Terror before the Terror? Conditions of Possibility, Logic of Realization," in K. M. Baker, ed., *The Terror* (Oxford, Pergamon, 1994), 3–18, 19–38.

17 A. Mayer, *The Furies: Violence and Terror in the French and Russian Revolutions* (Princeton, Princeton University Press, 2000); G. Fife, *The Terror: The Shadow of the Guillotine: France, 1792–1794* (New York, St. Martin's Press, 2004); S. Wahnich, *La Liberté ou la mort: essai sur la Terreur et le terrorisme* (Paris, La Fabrique Editions, 2003); E. Sagan, *Citizens and Cannibals: The French Revolution, the Struggle for Modernity, and the Origins of Ideological Terror* (New York, Rowman and Littlefield, 2001).

18 A search on Amazon.com for books under the heading of "The Terror," produces a list of titles such as *Terror in the Name of God*; *Armageddon, Oil and Terror*; *The Age of Sacred Terror*; and *Unholy Terror*, and no titles, at least on the first page, on the French Terror.

19 F. Furet, *Interpreting the French Revolution* (Cambridge, Cambridge University Press, 1981), 54.

"in the long run, it was opting for the Terror."[20] These interpretations are not identical, but each points to revolutionary ideology, or discourse, and ultimately the political philosophy of Jean-Jacques Rousseau as the root cause of the Terror.

By contrast, a number of historians over the years, principally on the left, have emphasized social factors and circumstances in explaining the violence of the Terror. Alphonse Aulard, for example, portrayed the Terror as a kind of national self-defense against the challenges of foreign war and counterrevolution.[21] Georges Lefebvre, writing in a Marxist vein, viewed the Terror more as the product of social conflict: the bourgeois revolutionaries defending their gains in the face of aristocratic opposition.[22] Historians such as Albert Mathiez, Albert Soboul, and Richard Cobb, who focused more on the *sans-culottes* and the urban poor, presented an economic explanation for the Terror, pointing to the imposition of price controls and the mobilization of "people's armies" to ensure the delivery of grain to urban markets.[23] R. R. Palmer, whose *Twelve Who Ruled* still stands as one of the best comprehensive studies of the Committee of Public Safety and the year of the Terror, also emphasizes the difficult circumstances in which the French Republic found itself, given both the foreign war and widespread revolt within France, but sees the Terror as a defense of republican ideals, on the one hand, and as an important period for the institutional creation of the modern state on the other.[24] David Andress, whose work has already been cited, in the end concludes that the "problem of the Terror was that its unrelenting quest to preserve and protect the fragile flower of personal liberty was also the engine of the destruction of that very thing."[25]

We have already addressed in Chapter Six some of these broader interpretive debates in regard to the Terror, but how do they speak to the

---

20 K. Baker, *Inventing the French Revolution* (Cambridge, Cambridge University Press, 1990), 305.

21 A. Aulard, *The French Revolution: A Political History, 1789–1804* (London, T. F. Unwin, 1910).

22 G. Lefebvre, *The French Revolution* (New York, Columbia University Press, 1962). W. B. Kerr, *The Reign of Terror: 1793–94: The Experiment of the Democratic Republic, and the Rise of the Bourgeoisie* (Toronto, University of Toronto Press, 1927) makes a very similar argument.

23 A. Mathiez, *La Vie chère et le mouvement social sous la terreur* (Paris, Payot, 1927); A. Soboul, *The Parisian Sans-culottes and the French Revolution, 1793–94* (Oxford, Clarendon Press, 1964); R. C. Cobb, *The People's Armies: Instrument of the Terror in the Departments* (New Haven, Yale University Press, 1987); and *The Police and the People: French Popular Protest, 1789–1820* (Oxford, Clarendon Press, 1970).

24 R. R. Palmer, *Twelve Who Ruled: The Year of the Terror in the French Revolution* (Princeton, Princeton University Press, 1941).

25 D. Andress, *The Terror*, 373.

narrower question, our focus here, of violence in the Terror? Generally speaking, those who view the Terror in ideological terms condemn the violence as unjustified, undermining, in effect, the entire revolutionary project. Those who see the Terror as the result of social conflict, or the product of circumstances, tend to interpret the violence as regrettable but necessary, or as with Andress, and to some degree Palmer, as ultimately harming the Revolution itself. Whereas those on the right would condemn the Terror in its entirety, historians more sympathetic to the Revolution have sometimes distinguished the early Terror from the Great Terror of spring 1794.

One approach to placing the Terror in perspective has been to examine it in statistical terms, most notably in the study published by Donald Greer in the 1930s. Greer placed the total number of executions between March 1793 and August 1794 (what some would consider a narrow chronological definition of the Terror) at just under 17,000, but these included only those who were executed following a trial, which leaves out between 30,000 and 40,000 either executed without trial (as in the drownings in Nantes or the mass executions in Toulon) or who died in jail awaiting trial. It also excludes the many deaths in the repression of the Vendée rebellion, which some include among the victims of the Terror, but which I would consider to be victims of civil war, to which we shall turn shortly. Based on his statistical study, Greer reached two significant conclusions. First, noting that the greatest number of executions occurred either in Paris, in frontier departments close to theatres of war, or in regions of rebellion or civil war within France, he concluded that the Terror should be understood not in ideological terms, but rather as a political weapon wielded against the enemies of the Revolution. Second, based upon his social analysis of the executions, he argued that the Terror could not be interpreted in class terms, since just over 8 percent of the victims were aristocrats, while nearly 25 percent were bourgeois and 28 percent were peasants. As Louis Henry later observed, however, the aristocracy represented less than 1 percent of the French population, while the peasantry represented more than 70 percent, so that in statistical terms the former were under-represented among the victims of the Terror while the latter were over-represented, which qualifies, rather than nullifies, Greer's conclusion.[26]

The geographic distribution of the Terror also tends to support the argument that war and counterrevolution were the principal causal

26 D. Greer, *The Incidence of the Terror during the French Revolution* (Cambridge, MA, Harvard University Press, 1935). See also R. Louis, "The Incidence of the Terror: A Critique of Statistical Interpretation," *French Historical Studies* 3 (Spring 1964), 379–89.

factors, rather than ideology. 90 percent of the executions occurred in thirteen departments (out of eighty-four in the country) plus Paris, 70 percent in just five. A third of the departments saw fewer than ten executions and a handful saw no executions at all. Very few women counted among the victims of the guillotine, though several prominent women did march to the scaffold. It would be an exaggeration, then, to say that Frenchmen everywhere lived in fear of the Terror in 1793–94. One might debate, at any rate, the degree to which an atmosphere of Terror was pervasive throughout France.

Those who challenge this view point to what is commonly referred to as the Great Terror, the three months prior to the fall of Robespierre. By this time, April 1794, the war abroad was going well, the centers of federalist revolt had all been pacified, and the rebellion in the Vendée was at least temporarily subdued. Yet the pace of the Terror increased, trials and executions became more centralized in Paris, and the law of 22 Prairial (10 June 1794) streamlined judicial procedures and left juries with just two possible verdicts: innocence or death.[27] More than thirty people a day went to the guillotine in Paris in June and July. During this period, then, the Terror seemed to target political enemies within the revolutionary fold more than counterrevolutionaries. This trend had begun, some would argue, with the trial of the Girondins in October 1793, followed by the trials of the Hébertistes and Dantonists in March/April 1794.[28]

The paramount symbol of the Terror, of course, is the guillotine. It was proposed by Dr. Joseph Guillotin in January 1790, adopted by the Constituent Assembly as the instrument for capital punishment on 25 September 1791, and first used in April 1792. It was adopted in the name of humanity and equality. Under the Old Regime executions were generally slow and painful, and only aristocrats were entitled to be executed by the sword. The guillotine, argued its namesake, would be quick and painless, and more sure than the sword. In most cases it was, but to many observers it seemed overwhelmingly impersonal, machine-like in its operation. And

27 Patrice Gueniffey, a student of François Furet, takes up the question of the Prairial Laws in *La Politique de la Terreur: essai sur la violence révolutionnaire, 1789–1794* (Paris, Fayard, 2000), 277–315. Although Gueniffey rejects an interpretation of the Terror as a response to circumstances, he views it as a product of revolutionary politics rather than ideology or discourse. Thus, the Great Terror is explained principally in terms of Robespierre's pursuit of political power.

28 David Bell is critical of Arno Mayer, who emphasizes war and counterrevolution as causal factors, for not addressing the Great Terror in *The Furies*. See D. Bell, "Violence, Terror, and War: A Comment on Arno Mayer's *The Furies*," *French Historical Studies* 24 (Fall 2001), 559–67. This issue also includes comments by Mary Nolan and Timothy Tackett, and a response from Mayer.

at the height of the Terror, in late 1793 early 1794, its efficiency seemed unequal to the task. In Lyon Jean-Marie Collot d'Herbois and Joseph Fouché lined federalist rebels up in front of cannons to hasten their executions, a method that proved entirely unsatisfactory, while in Nantes Jean-Baptiste Carrier and the local terrorists sent hundreds of Vendéen rebels to their deaths by drowning in the Loire River.

It is the image of the guillotine, though, more than anything else, that captured the popular imagination at the time and that continues to linger in our mind's eye today. It is not an image of humanity. For the crowd, the guillotine was initially an object of fascination. Was the victim conscious of his or her own death? Did the severed head retain consciousness for a few instants after its separation from the body? But executions by guillotine, at least in most cases, lacked the drama of those carried out under the Old Regime. They were over in an instant – once the blade dropped, the deed was done. And as Daniel Arasse has argued, "the excessively frequent spectacle of the guillotine was alienating the people ...." In June 1794, as the pace of the Terror in Paris quickened, the National Convention ordered the scaffold moved from the Place de la Révolution to a more obscure square on the eastern edge of the capital.[29]

If the Terror began, to return to the words of Danton, as an effort to bring popular violence to an end – "let *us* be terrible, to dispense the people from the need to be terrible themselves" – as an effort to leave behind popular vengeance and replace it with the rule of law, by the summer of 1794 the representatives of the people, and the people themselves, had grown weary of the Terror. Far from aiding in the regeneration of the people, as some Jacobin deputies had promised, the violence of the Terror seemed to be debasing the people, with no end in sight. 9 Thermidor, and the fall of Robespierre, did bring the Terror to an end, but it did not bring an end to state violence. The Thermidorian regime, the Directory, and Napoleon's Consulate, too, all felt a need to employ repressive measures against the enemies of the regime. How did that violence, especially under the Directory, compare to the violence of the Terror?

State Violence: The Directory

"Any effort to understand the violence unleashed for and against the Revolution cannot end with Robespierre but must follow France's tortuous journey from a bloody reign of virtue to an even bloodier reign of

---

29 D. Arasse, *The Guillotine and the Terror* (London, Penguin Books, 1989), 94, 107.

military prowess."[30] Howard Brown, in his important and provocative recent book, argues that the emergence of what he terms a "security state" in France under the Directory marked the triumph of Hobbes over Rousseau in the French Revolution. What does he mean by this? Whether one sees the Terror as the product of circumstance or ideology, one cannot deny that the leading Jacobins of the Year II, most notably Robespierre and St. Just, defended revolutionary terror as a means for the achievement of republican virtue. By 1795, Brown argues, France had fallen into such a state of social disorder that the pursuit of the Rousseauean general will had given way to a Directory regime determined to establish its own legitimacy by the restoration, through repression, of public order. Liberty was sacrificed by the French people not for equality, as de Tocqueville famously argued, but for security.

Brown draws a contrast between the Directory and the Jacobin Republic, on the one hand, and the Napoleonic regime of the Consulate, on the other. He argues that the state violence of the Terror was too often arbitrary and seemingly without purpose, and that it targeted particular social groups. Directorial repression, by contrast, had at least the veneer of constitutionality and targeted people based on individual criminal or politically seditious acts. Not everyone would agree with this argument. Greer's statistical evidence, for example, challenges the notion that the Terror was directed against particular social groups, and Alan Forrest has argued persuasively that whatever the Terror may have been, however great its excesses, it was in the end legal. The National Convention passed legislation defining acts of counterrevolution and established revolutionary tribunals, however cursory their judicial proceedings may have been.[31]

What one does clearly see under the Directory was the militarization of state repression. France was divided into twenty-six military districts in this period, and on average there were seventy generals stationed in the interior throughout the Directory regime. Military commissions were set up to try and sentence the accused when it became clear that civil juries were reluctant to convict those accused of crimes that might be interepreted as civil disobedience. Local loyalties often prevailed against the mandates of national law. Given the political instability of the period, the

30 H. G. Brown, *Ending the French Revolution: Violence, Justice, and Repression from the Terror to Napoleon* (Charlottesville, University of Virginia Press, 2006), 3.

31 A. Forrest, "The Local Politics of Repression," in K. M. Baker, ed., *The Terror*, 81–98. Forrest also emphasizes the importance of considering local context in intepreting the violence of the Terror. The National Convention might pass laws, but it could not control how they were implemented at the local level.

Directory used the state of siege as a tool to manipulate electoral results, as in the Floréal coup of 1798. While the level of state violence may not have equaled that under the Terror, criminal courts under the Directory sentenced more than 550 people to death each year. All of this evidence, Brown argues, shows that it was under the Directory, rather than under Napoleon, that the French state moved decisively in the direction of a security state that denied its citizens civil liberties that the revolutionaries of 1789 had championed, in the name of restoring civil order. Napoleon, by contrast, would offer them glory.[32]

Jean-Clément Martin also addresses state violence under the Directory, arguing that the most striking difference, as compared to the violence of the Terror, was the degree to which national elites came to exercise centalized control and their willingness to use force against their political opponents. By contrast, the violence of the Terror reflected a delicate negotiation between legislation and policy emanating from Paris, and the local tensions, individual rivalries, and personal ambitions that were responsible for many of the excesses in the provinces. In his view, the Prairial legislation of late spring 1794 marked not so much the culmination of the Terror (as an ideological interpretation might see it) but rather a desire to curb local excesses and deviations by centralizing the machinery of state violence, a trend that the Directory regime would continue.[33]

One final aspect of Howard Brown's argument about Directorial violence merits discussion here. He introduces a chapter on "Liberal Authoritarianism" with this observation: "That the French Revolution did not end in 1799 is made abundantly clear by the high levels of civil strife that continued well thereafter, especially in the west and south."[34] This, it seems to me, comes perilously close to Schama's assertion that "violence was the motor of the Revolution," to defining revolution purely in terms of violence. Once violence came to an end, so did the Revolution. But it was not only violence that disappeared under the "security state" imposed by Napoleon: so, too, did the experiment with liberal republicanism initiated by the Jacobins and continued under the Directory. One might argue that participatory politics, rather than violence, was the motor of the Revolution, that this began to disappear under the "liberal authoritarianism" of the Directory and was finally put to rest by Bonaparte.

---

32 H. G. Brown, *Ending the French Revolution*, 126–29, 163, 208–9. Michael Sibalis prefers the term "police state" to "security state." See M. Sibalis, "Napoleonic Police State," in P. Dwyer, ed., *Napoleon and Europe* (New York, Longman, 2001).

33 J.-C. Martin, *Violence et Révolution*, especially pages 188–93, 195–201, 215–20, and 267–70. Martin's insistence on the importance of local factors in understanding the violence of the Terror is shared by A. Forrest in the essay cited above.

34 H. G. Brown, *Ending the French Revolution*, 235.

The Violence of War

How can one compare the violence of war to either popular violence or the violence of the Terror? On the one hand one might explore the issue of magnitude, which is a relatively straightforward proposition. We have seen above that the victims of the Terror may have numbered as many as 50,000, leaving aside the deaths in the Vendée. Colin Jones breaks down the fatalities of the revolutionary wars into two periods: roughly 203,000 (mostly men, but a few women who disguised themselves as men in order to fight) died between 1792 and 1794, while 235,000 died between 1795 and 1799. Were we to include the Napoleonic wars between 1799 and 1815 the death toll would slightly more than double.[35] In simple numerical terms, then, very nearly ten times as many people died on the battlefield during the revolutionary decade as died on the guillotine. Some would argue that those wars were largely defensive, perhaps, but of course there are those who have argued that the Terror was also defensive violence carried out against those who attacked the Revolution.

We might also consider, however, the ways in which revolutionary violence and the violence of war were linked to each other. The September Massacres, for example, came just days after news reached Paris that the fortress at Verdun was in peril, amidst fears that Austrian and Prussian troops would soon be threatening the capital. Similarly, news that Toulon had been handed over to the British appears to have contributed to passage of the Law of Suspects in September 1793.[36] Clearly the foreign war was seen by political leaders, if not by Louis XVI, as a *revolutionary* war, a dicey proposition when one considered that the army was still led by a predominantly aristocratic officer corps. To fail on the battlefield was to risk being seen as opposed to the Revolution, and more than a few generals paid with their heads for their incompetence, viewed by the Jacobins as treason. While the war was initially popular at home, this was not universally true, particularly in the west of France where protests and resistance to

---

35 C. Jones, *The Longman Companion to the French Revolution* (London, Longman, 1988), 288; M. Lyons, *Napoleon Bonaparte and the Legacy of the French Revolution* (New York, St. Martin's Press, 1994), 46.

36 Mona Ozouf found, however, that there was very little rhetoric in the National Convention, as reported in *Le Moniteur* at the time of the September Massacres, linking the prison killings to the war news, and she finds the rhetoric at the time of the fall of Toulon to be ambiguous in this regard. It is historians, she argues, who have drawn the connection between war and the Terror. M. Ozouf, "War and Terror in French Revolutionary Discourse (1792–1794)," *Journal of Modern History* 56 (December 1984), 579–97.

recruitment must be counted among the causes of the Vendée rebellion in the spring of 1793. Here is one instance, then, in which the violence of war, or perhaps more properly the stresses of war, had a clear impact on domestic violence. One other way in which the foreign war can be seen to have had an impact on revolutionary politics is in the popular movement in Paris. Albert Soboul has argued that the patriotism shown by the *sans-culottes* of the capital in volunteering for the army sapped participation in the sectional assemblies and clubs during the Year II and explains, at least in part, the failure of the Parisian *sans-culottes* to rise up in support of Robespierre on 9 Thermidor.[37] We have already remarked on the policy under the Directory to station generals in the interior, in charge of preserving or restoring order in the twenty-six military districts. One wonders as well if discharged soldiers might not have brought home with them the hardened mentality of the battlefield, if the brigandage of the late 1790s might perhaps have reflected in the crimes of ordinary people the violence of war. Along this same line of thinking, Alan Forrest has examined the relationship between desertion and counterrevolution.[38]

Arno Mayer links the violence of foreign war to the domestic violence during the Revolution, making a point very similar to that with which I began this chapter: "The murderous dragonnades of the Vendée are a black page in the history of France, but not the deadly battles of the *Grande Armée*, which are grandiosely, not to say shamelessly, exalted, mythologized, and memorialized ...." While Mayer calls into question the glorification of war, he also sees the revolutionary wars, and the wars of Napoleon for that matter, as carried out in defense of the Revolution, much as the Terror, in his view, was a defense against counterrevolution, an argument with which David Bell takes issue.[39]

Civil War and Counterrevolution

France was riven by civil war, of varying degrees of intensity, from the spring of 1793 until the early years of Napoleon's rule. One might look back as early as the spring of 1790 to the *bagarre* of Nîmes, or similar violence in Montauban at about the same time, both pitting Protestant supporters of the Revolution against Catholic opponents, but while these

---

37 A. Soboul, *The Sans-Culottes* (Princeton, Princeton University Press, 1980), 251–64. This is an abridged version of the first English translation of Soboul's work, cited above.
38 A. Forrest, *Conscripts and Deserters: The Army and French Society during the Revolution and Empire* (Oxford, Oxford University Press, 1989), 146–68.
39 A. Mayer, *The Furies*, 600, cited in D. Bell, "Violence, Terror and War," 564–65.

conflicts both featured pitched battles the violence was not sustained over any extended period.[40] Similarly, the first Camp de Jalès brought together as many as 25,000 potential counterrevolutionaries on a remote plain on the southeastern Massif Central in August 1790, but the assemblage was intermittent over the following years and amounted to little more than a thorn in the side of the revolutionary government. Only with the Vendée uprising in the spring of 1793 did resistance to the government in Paris assume truly serious proportions, and with the federalist revolts of June and July four major provincial cities also declared their opposition to the Jacobin regime, raising the very real possibility of true civil war.

The first point to make is that this violence was seen at the time as fratricidal, which made the repression of the rebellions particularly brutal, both the military engagements and the executions of captured rebels that followed, as in Nantes in the west and the federalist city of Lyon in the east. By autumn 1793 it was clear that the Vendée rebels had entered negotiations with the British for arms, a treasonous act.[41] But even before this, most French citizens viewed the Vendée rebellion as counterrevolutionary. Both Caen and Bordeaux, two of the federalist cities, sent contingents of volunteers to do combat in the Vendée at the very moment that they were also preparing armed forces to contest what they viewed as the illegal proscription of Girondin deputies from the National Convention. This opposition to Paris, then, was of a different sort from that in the Vendée, which even supporters of the federalist protest viewed as simply beyond the pale. Consider, for example, this letter from a Bordeaux municipal officer, serving with a volunteer force in the Vendée in the fall of 1793: "Brothers and friends, I hasten to inform you that the brigands of the Vendée are destroyed. 40,000 brigands have drunk from the big cup. We pursued them to the banks of the Loire, and although a number of the cowardly slaves tried to save themselves by surrendering, as soon as they fell into our hands we dispatched them to the realm of the moles."[42] There is no sense of regret here, no note of apology for this complete annihilation of a rebel force.

---

40 J. Hood, "Revival and Mutation of Old Rivalries in Revolutionary France," *Past and Present* LXXXII (February 1979), 82–115.

41 D. Sutherland emphasizes the significance of this betrayal in "The Vendée: Unique or Emblematic?," in K. M. Baker, ed., *The Terror*, 99–114. This is one of the best, succinct essays discussing the violence of the Vendée and its relation to the Terror.

42 Letter dated 24 November 1793, contained in the Departmental Archives of the Gironde, 12L1. For a discussion of the contingents sent from Caen and Bordeaux to the Vendée see P. R. Hanson, *The Jacobin Republic under Fire: The Federalist Revolt in the French Revolution* (University Park, Pennsylvania State University Press, 2003), Chapter 3.

In this regard the Vendée rebellion was quite different from the federalist revolt. Only in Lyon did federalism end with a massive siege and substantial battlefield casualties. In Bordeaux, Marseille, and Caen, although the national government sent troops to put down the rebellion, there was little serious resistance and very few casualties in the military engagements. In the Vendée, though, the civil war went on for years, and atrocities were committed on both sides, including the killing of women and children. By national decree, anyone apprehended bearing arms against the Republic was declared an outlaw, subject to execution on the spot. We have already noted above the drownings of captured rebels ordered by Jean-Baptiste Carrier in October–November 1793 in Nantes, where some 3,000 men and women were executed. Following the defeat of the main rebel force at Savenay in December, General Louis-Marie Turreau, newly appointed commander of the Army of the West, adopted a "scorched earth" policy in order to eliminate what remained of the rebel forces. General Turreau organized his soldiers into two armies of twelve columns each, the *colonnes infernales*, positioned them at the eastern and western extremes of the rebel zone, and ordered them to proceed toward each other, putting to the bayonet all those they encountered who had taken up arms, and putting to the torch all villages and towns, except for thirteen designated as patriotic. Wide swaths of countryside were laid waste, and thousands were killed. It is impossible to make an accurate estimate – some have put the figure at 200,000, others have asserted that over the decade (since the rebellion would not be fully suppressed until after the Concordat of 1801) roughly one-third of the population of the west perished.

For a great many years the full scope of the violence in the Vendée went unremarked, since so much of the killing was undocumented and the carnage on both sides represented a national embarrassment. On the eve of the Bicentennial, however, Reynald Secher published a book asserting that the repression of the Vendée rebellion amounted to genocide, imposing an ideological interpretation on the violence.[43] Secher's book generated a firestorm of debate, in political as well as academic circles, and his thesis has been generally discredited. He is scarcely the only historian, however, to emphasize the violent repression of the Vendée rebellion. Donald Sutherland's work has long made the case for taking seriously counterrevolution in the history of the Revolution, not only in the west but across France; while Jean-Clément Martin, the preeminent historian

43 R. Secher, *Le Génocide Franco-Français: La Vendée-vengé* (Paris, Presses Universitaires de France, 1986). In the context of contemporary French politics, Secher's allegation constitutes a riposte to those on the left who have condemned the Vichy regime for complicity with the Nazi genocide of the Holocaust.

of the Vendée in France, has stressed the need to consider local factors in interpreting a conflict that took on considerable national magnitude.[44]

Among the provocative observations made by Jean-Clément Martin in his recent book on violence is that while the term "Vendée" became virtually synonymous with counterrevolution in the 1790s, despite the fact that much of the bloodshed in the west took place outside of the Vendée proper, no similar label emerged during the Revolution to characterize the virtually endemic violence up and down the Rhône Valley between 1790 and 1815. Why, he asks, did one region become mythified for its violence, while the other did not?[45] This is not to say that the violence of the Rhône Valley and the Midi has been ignored by historians. Hubert Johnson dealt at length with political violence in the Midi during the early years of the Revolution; Colin Lucas has published a very insightful article on popular violence in the region, stressing its roots in traditional blood feuds and personal rivalries, extending back into the Old Regime; and Gwynne Lewis has studied the violence of the 1790s, extending forward into the nineteenth century, in what he characterized as a "second Vendée."[46]

As we have seen in previous chapters, the fear of conspiracy played a major role in the current of revolutionary politics, from the Great Fear to the Flight to Varennes and the rumors of *émigré* plots against the Republic. The fear of counterrevolutionary plots has often been presented as an essential element of Jacobin ideology and a potent ingredient in the genesis of the Terror. While the fear of conspiracy may have been exaggerated, particularly in the Year II, a new collection of essays makes it very clear that this was not simply a figment of the Jacobin imagination, and that conspiratorial plots of various stripes were sprinkled throughout the revolutionary decade. The fear of conspiracy was an important element in popular culture long before 1789, blossomed once again

44 D. M. G. Sutherland, *France, 1789–1815: Revolution and Counterrevolution* (Oxford, Oxford University Press, 1985); and *The French Revolution and Empire: The Quest for a Civic Order* (Oxford, Blackwell, 2003); J.-C. Martin, *La Vendée de la mémoire, 1800–1980* (Paris, Editions du Seuil, 1989); *La Vendée et la France* (Paris, Editions du Seuil, 1987); *Blancs et Bleus dans la Vendée déchirée* (Paris, Gallimard, 1986); *Une Guerre interminable: La Vendée deux cents ans après* (Nantes, Reflets du passé, 1985).

45 J.-C. Martin, *Violence et Révolution*, 156–62.

46 H. C. Johnson, *The Midi in Revolution: A Study of Regional Political Diversity, 1789–1793* (Princeton, Princeton University Press, 1986); C. Lucas, "Themes in Southern Violence after 9 Thermidor," in G. Lewis and C. Lucas, eds., *Beyond the Terror: Essays in French Regional and Social History* (Cambridge, Cambridge University Press, 1983), 152–94; G. Lewis, *The Second Vendée: The Continuity of Counterrevolution in the Department of the Gard, 1789–1815* (Oxford, Clarendon Press, 1978).

amidst the food shortages and political unrest of 1789, and played an important role in urban politics all across France in the early years of the Revolution.[47]

Between 1795 and 1800 there were entire regions of the country that were beyond the control of the state because of endemic popular violence. Sporadic resistance to the government of the Directory continued in the Vendée, although repression by the army, commanded by General Hoche, was considerably less draconian than that which occurred in 1794. To the north, Lower Normandy and Brittany were afflicted by *chouannerie*, royalist peasant rebellions that extended across ten departments, but which never coalesced into a unified military campaign as had the Vendée rebellion. The *chouans* operated in small bands, a modified guerrilla movement, capturing grain convoys, persecuting local officials and constitutional priests, and particularly after 1795 targeting men who had been Jacobin club members or who were associated in some way with the policies of the Terror.[48] The violence of the Rhône Valley in 1795 is sometimes referred to as the first wave of the White Terror (the second wave coming in 1815 with the fall of Napoleon), and like the attacks of the *chouans* was directed principally against former Jacobins, especially in and around Lyon and Marseille. This violence could certainly be compared to the popular violence of the early Revolution. It had a political meaning, although counterrevolutionary rather than revolutionary, and its perpetrators could be said in most cases to be acting out of a sense of vengeance or popular justice. By contrast, much of the violence of this period was essentially brigandage, or highway robbery. While the brigands not infrequently claimed a political intent upon apprehension, in order to curry sympathy with juries or with local authorities who they hoped might turn a blind eye to their transgressions, one might question whether their actions had an explicit political intent, however much the spread of such brigandage may have undermined the authority of the Directory regime.[49]

---

47 P. R. Campbell, T. E. Kaiser, and M. Linton, eds., *Conspiracy in the French Revolution* (Manchester, Manchester University Press, 2007).

48 D. Sutherland, *The Chouans: The Social Origins of Popular Counterrevolution in Upper Brittany, 1770–1796* (Oxford, Clarendon Press, 1982); M. Hutt, *Chouannerie and Counterrevolution: Puisaye, the Princes and the British Government of the 1790s*, 2 vols. (Cambridge, Cambridge University Press, 1983).

49 While Howard Brown acknowledges this distinction in his description of popular violence under the Directory, I do not feel that he incorporates it sufficiently into his analysis of the repression of brigandage in the south and east as compared to the repression of *chouannerie* and the lingering outbreaks of resistance in the Vendée in the west. H. Brown, *Ending the French Revolution*, especially Chapters 9–11.

Violence of Hunger and Deprivation

As Gyanendra Pandey has observed, "the actions of politically disadvantaged, or unrepresented, people are commonly labeled violent; the acts of those in power, the authorities and the arms of the state, less frequently so."[50] We have already remarked on the distinction between popular violence and state violence in the French Revolution, but we should also take note of the more "routine violence" of hunger and deprivation that was sometimes imposed upon the people by government policy. The peasant rebellions and the urban riots of 1789 were of course responses to hunger and deprivation, seen by the people as due to the failings of the Old Regime monarchy. Throughout the early years of the Revolution, authorities did all they could to ensure the grain supply, to keep the markets provisioned, in part simply to preserve public order but also to see to the needs of the people, despite the fact that the right to subsistence was not among those declared by the National Assembly. Part of the legislative machinery of the Terror was the imposition of price controls, the *maximum*, imposed first on grains in the spring of 1793 and then on other staple goods in the autumn of that year under pressure from the *sans-culottes*. After 9 Thermidor, with the end of the Terror, the price controls were repealed as well, and in the face of the coldest winter of the century in 1795, hunger and deprivation once again returned. People starved and froze to death in the back alleys of Paris, prompting some to regret the execution of Robespierre, lamenting that while heads may have fallen during the Terror at least there was bread in the bakeries. This misery led ultimately to the last desperate popular insurrections of the Revolution, the riots of Germinal and Prairial in the spring of 1795.

Richard Cobb, always sensitive to the poor and to the quirky anecdotes that enliven history, devoted a small book to the death and misery in Paris in those years, in which he examined the records from the morgue for some 404 people whose bodies were recovered from the streets and alleyways of the city, or from the Seine River, into which they had thrown themselves to commit suicide.[51] Their deaths were instances of routine violence, and this study is on the one hand a kind of collective social history, an exploration of the circumstances and lived experience of a group of misfortunate common people, people who played no prominent role in the political drama of the French Revolution, but whose lives were nonetheless affected by it. But

---

50 G. Pandey, *Routine Violence: Nations, Fragments, Histories* (Stanford, Stanford University Press, 2006), 3.

51 R. Cobb, *Death in Paris, 1795–1801* (Oxford, Oxford University Press, 1978).

Cobb's study also attempts to restore to these suicides and accidental anonymous deaths their identity, their individualism. This is what violence does ultimately. It depersonalizes, it denies its victims' individuality, their humanity. In our study of revolutionary violence, then, it is essential that we acknowledge not only the differences between varying modes, or expressions, of violence – whether it be popular violence or state violence, revolutionary violence or counterrevolutionary violence, or quite ordinary violence – but that we also restore to the victims of violence their humanity. It was for the achievement of universal human rights, after all, that many of them gave their lives.

10

Legacy of the Revolution

What is the legacy of the French Revolution here in the first decade of the twenty-first century? There are several ways we might approach that question. One would be simply to ask: "What changed in France? How much of an impact did the Revolution really have?" For much of the latter twentieth century the *Annales* school exercised a powerful influence on historical scholarship in France, and that tradition emphasized underlying long-term forces for change – the *longue durée* – and dismissed the history of events – *l'histoire événementielle* – of which the French Revolution would certainly be exemplary. For historians of the *Annales* school, the upheaval of the Revolution was of only passing interest. François Furet, although not an *Annaliste* strictly speaking, once wrote that "nothing resembled French society under Louis XVI more than French society under Louis Philippe," ruler of France as the first Orleanist king between 1830 and 1848.[1] Had nothing really changed? Or, how had life changed, we might ask, for a typical French man or woman, if such a person ever existed, waking up on a fine spring morning in 1820? If the revolutionaries sought to "regenerate" France, to what degree did they succeed in that endeavor?

We might also ask: "What is the legacy of 1789 for us as students of the French Revolution?" Why study the French Revolution? For those approaching the topic in the nineteenth century, even well into the twentieth, there would have been a sense of immediacy or urgency in answering that question. One studied the French Revolution because its lessons were still applicable to the political and social struggles of the day. There was

1 F. Furet, *Interpreting the French Revolution* (Cambridge, Cambridge University Press, 1981), 24.

unfinished business to be addressed. For the French, to be sure, the legacy of the Revolution lived on in 1830, 1848, 1871, and even 1968. But by 1989, with the Bicentennial of the Revolution and the fall of the Berlin Wall, there were those who argued that the French Revolution was finally over, that the dream of popular revolution that had been passed from the Jacobins of 1789 to the Bolsheviks of 1917 was a thing of the past. There would be no revolutions in the future of the representative democracies of North America and Europe.

But even if that were true – and there are those who would dispute it – might we not examine the ideals of the French Revolution and ask if they have meaning for us still today? What did the French revolutionaries mean when they proclaimed "Liberty, Equality, and Fraternity" to be their motto, and do they mean the same things to us today? Are human rights more secure in our society than they were in France at the end of the eighteenth century? Are freedom of expression, and freedom of religion, still the inalienable rights asserted by the deputies of the Constituent Assembly and the drafters of the American Bill of Rights more than two hundred years ago? Are there other rights, unimagined or discarded by the revolutionaries of France, being claimed by people today?

Yet another frame within which to consider the legacy of the French Revolution is the perspective of peoples beyond Europe and North America. Among the most poignant papers delivered at the International Congress on the History of the French Revolution in Washington, D.C. in 1989 was that of Professor Zhilian Zhang, from Beijing University, on "The French Revolution and the Chinese Revolution." The date was 4 May, the 200th anniversary of the opening of the Estates General at Versailles. As Professor Zhang spoke there were a million students gathered on Tiananmen Square in Beijing. He began his paper by recalling his father, who had sat for the very last imperial exam given in China in 1905, a grueling three-day ordeal in which aspirants for official positions were expected to write an "eight-legged essay" on an assigned topic, drawing on their knowledge of the Confucian classics. Imperial China teetered on the brink of revolution, and in his essay, which Professor Zhang had saved at great peril through the upheaval of the Cultural Revolution, his father made reference to Montesquieu and Rousseau, expressing his hope that their ideas about representative government might finally be adopted in China. Eighty-four years later Professor Zhang expressed his own hope that the young people of China might finally bring liberty to their nation. In his words, "On va faire une révolution française en 1989 en Chine." One month later the tanks rolled into Tiananmen Square.

We might consider the influence of 1789 not only on other revolutions around the world but on movements for national independence as well.

A starting point here will be to look at the history of Haiti since 1804, the immediate impact of the French Revolution on the island having already been considered in Chapter Four. France lost its colony of Saint-Domingue during the revolutionary decade, but over the next century it claimed, often by conquest, a colonial empire extending from the Caribbean to Africa and on to East Asia and the Pacific, second in size and expanse only to the British Empire. In the aftermath of World War II many of those colonies claimed their independence in movements often led by young people who had studied in Paris, where they read the essays of Rousseau and Montesquieu, and learned about the storming of the Bastille. Those independence movements, too, must be counted as part of the legacy of the French Revolution.

Finally, we must consider the legacy of the French Revolution in the context of its own historiography. If the Marxist interpretation has been laid to rest, where does the field stand today? Can we still speak of the French Revolution as a bourgeois revolution? If yes, in what sense? If not, is there any emerging consensus among historians as to how we might envision, or interpret, the Revolution? What are the currents of research among historians writing about the Revolution today, and what awaits the next generation of researchers?

What Changed in France?

In 1815 Louis XVIII ascended the Bourbon throne (for the second time, the first having been cut short by Napoleon's return from Elba and his final Hundred Days) and ruled France for ten years in what history records as the Restoration. By its very title this period suggests an effort on the part of the monarchy to restore the Old Regime. To what degree did it succeed? Or alternatively, in what measure had the Revolution changed French society irrevocably?

Viewed from the perspective of the monarchy itself, one would have to conclude that the Restoration was a failure, almost from the beginning. Louis XVIII ruled in accordance with a Charter, introduced at his first return to the throne but retained throughout his reign. This in effect made the Restoration a constitutional monarchy, although Louis was careful not to call the Charter a constitution, and also explicitly repudiated the idea of popular sovereignty. While the electorate was restricted to the wealthy elite, as it had been under the Directory, the king ruled in concert with an elected parliament, and the Charter granted the people many of the civil liberties first claimed by the Declaration of the Rights of Man and Citizen. Furthermore, when Louis' brother, Charles X, assumed the throne in 1824 and attempted to undo key elements of the Charter in an effort to reassert absolutist rule, his efforts were met with widespread hostility and ultimately a revolutionary uprising in 1830, bringing the Restoration to an end and forcing Charles X to flee to England.

Completely apart from the fate of the monarchy, however, the legacy of the Revolution lived on in nineteenth-century France in a number of ways. For starters, the administrative map created by the deputies of the Constituent Assembly endured. Indeed, although French borders have expanded somewhat since 1815, to the east and southeast, and population growth has led to the creation of several new *départements* in the Paris basin, the map of France today resembles very closely the map of 1790. The prefects created by Napoleon continued to serve under the Bourbon and Orleanist monarchies, as they would in the governments of the Second and Third Republics, down to the present day.

The map of the Old Regime was itself a symbol of the privilege that was the very basis of that society, and privilege, too, went by the wayside after 1789. Old aristocratic families would be recognized as such for generations – old habits of social deference die hard – but the Bourbon monarchy made no effort to restore the privileges of the hereditary nobility. France would remain a country of citizens enjoying equal legal rights, even if most of those citizens did not enjoy political rights until after 1830, with universal manhood suffrage not restored, in a meaningful way, until 1870.

As Lynn Hunt has observed, even if the French people did not retain their political rights after 1815 (or even under the Napoleonic regime), they did not forget the experience of participatory politics: "Thousands of men and even many women gained firsthand experience in the political arena: they talked, read, and listened in new ways; they voted; they joined new orgnizations; and they marched for their political goals. Revolution became a tradition, and republicanism an enduring option."[2] Not until the Third Republic would republicanism take firm root in France, and even then it would be severely challenged during the Vichy years of World War II, when "Liberty, Equality, Fraternity" were replaced by "Work, Family, *Patrie*." But the political experience of the Revolution established the terms, or the framework, within which French politics would be contested for the next two centuries. As Julian Jackson has written, "the conflicts of occupied France can be seen as a continuation of what have been called the 'Franco-French wars' – between those who accepted the legacy of the Revolution and those who did not." Not only were the fault lines during the Vichy era largely conceived in terms resonant of

2 L. Hunt, *Politics, Culture, and Class in the French Revolution* (Berkeley, University of California Press, 1984), 221.

revolutionary divisions, at war's end, in July 1945, an "Estates General" of the French Resistance convened in Paris to present grievance lists outlining the aspirations of the French people for post-war society.[3]

Republicanism was not the only political ideology to emerge from the French Revolution. Liberalism and conservatism grew out of the political alignments of the first revolutionary assemblies, and our modern conceptions of left and right on the political spectrum quite literally have their origins in the seating arrangements of the National Convention. Nationalism, socialism, and even communism all had their roots in the ideals and political struggles of the 1790s and would dominate European politics through the end of the twentieth century. The political legacy of the French Revolution, then, although a contentious one, can hardly be denied.

The social and economic legacy of the Revolution, by contrast, remains a subject of considerable debate. For Lynn Hunt, "the social and economic changes brought about by the Revolution were not revolutionary."[4] That is to say, while the aristocracy ceased to exist as a privileged order, most nobles families managed to retain much of their property and resumed positions of influence in local society. Land changed hands through the sale of *biens nationaux*, but France remained for several more generations a country in which landed money had more status than industrial capital, and to the degree that the peasantry managed to buy those properties, the process perpetuated a society in which small-scale agriculture predominated. This is not necessarily to say, however, that social change was not part of the legacy of the French Revolution. Hunt's point addresses most explicitly the classic Marxist intepretation of the Revolution: it did not introduce wholesale social and economic change clearing the way so that industrial capitalism might flourish. Rather, it fostered the persistence of a predominantly agrarian society and an industrial sector based on artisanal production. One might argue, though, that this was inherent in the revolutionary vision of the *sans-culottes*, that for them liberty and equality meant that production would remain on a human scale, that no one would control more property than they might work, or manage, themselves.[5] The persistence of small-scale agriculture in France, what some historians have labeled *la voie paysanne*, may not have been a revolutionary social achievement, but it is a distinctive characteristic of modern French society to which the Revolution certainly contributed. One might consider this issue, as well, from the perspective of the comparative study

3 J. Jackson, *France, The Dark Years, 1940–1944* (Oxford, Oxford University Press, 2001), 23, 594.

4 L. Hunt, *Politics, Culture, and Class*, 221.

5 See W. H. Sewell, Jr., *Work and Revolution in France: The Language of Labor from the Old Regime to 1848* (Cambridge, Cambridge University Press, 1980), for an argument in this vein.

of revolutions. In so many subsequent revolutions – the Russian, Mexican, and Chinese to take only three examples – the issue of land reform looms large. In those cases the aspiration, seldom met, was to put land in the hands of the producers. In France, by contrast, the peasantry already had land, to a considerable degree, either as owners or as renters. The Revolution allowed them to keep it.

Peter McPhee, focusing on the lived experience of ordinary French people during this period, takes a position contrary to Hunt's: "No French adult alive in 1799 was in any doubt that they had lived through a revolutionary upheaval, willingly or resentfully, and that the society in which they lived was fundamentally different."[6] McPhee goes on to delineate a number of areas in which change was substantial: a shift in self-identity, or mentality, from "subject" to "citizen" and a corresponding decline in social deference, remarked upon by contemporaries at the time; the disappearance of privileges and their replacement by rights, already noted in the discussion above; a shift from a society in which vertical links prevailed to one in which horizontal social ties were more important, broadly reflective of the revolutionary ideal of equality. Some of these changes might be more properly viewed as cultural, or political, as when McPhee emphasizes the importance of the experience of voting on popular attitudes. But as he observes, "the meanings of this new political culture varied by class, gender, and region," and it is important to recognize that politics would be contested in social terms, indeed in class terms, throughout the nineteenth century. McPhee quotes a peasant from a small village in the Gard in the aftermath of the 1848 revolution: "If a majority of us were republicans, it was in memory of our beautiful Revolution of 1793, of which our fathers had inculcated the principles which still survive in our hearts. Above all, we were children of the Revolution."[7] Note, however, that for this young man it was the memory of 1793 more than 1789 that endured.

In McPhee's view, it was the abolition of seigneurial dues and obligations that constituted the most important social legacy of the Revolution: "This is the single most important 'social fact' of the French Revolution."[8] This change effectively meant a reduction in income for those families who owned *seigneuries* under the old Regime, and a corresponding increase in income for those peasants who worked their lands. Some land did exchange hands, as well, but today's estimate that it represented

6 P. McPhee, *Living the French Revolution, 1789–1799* (New York, Palgrave Macmillan, 2006), 202.
7 Ibid., 205.
8 Ibid., 210.

perhaps as little as 10 percent of the total is lower than it once was, and research is ongoing on this topic.[9] Donald Sutherland takes a less sanguine view of the impact of the Revolution in rural France, emphasizing the degree to which counterrevolutionary sentiments prevailed among much of the peasantry (particularly in the west and Brittany), as well as the weight of peasant tradition that in his view proved impervious to the reforms emanating from Paris.[10] Eugen Weber, although not a historian of the Revolution, has similarly argued that the persistence of local dialects and regional culture on through the nineteenth century was such that the peasantry did not truly coalesce into a French nation until after the experience of World War I.[11]

The Revolution had certain negative impacts on France as well, of course. The textile industry would never recover its former vitality, especially in the west and the northeast, although its decline was apparent already before 1789. The loss of Saint-Domingue crippled France's trans-Atlantic trade, which was also hurt by the two decades of war with Great Britain – neither Bordeaux nor Nantes would ever recover the lustre that they had achieved in the eighteenth century. If the merchants of Atlantic seaports suffered, however, so did the urban and rural poor. Despite the best intentions of the Jacobins and the legislation passed both in the Year II and under the Directory, none of the revolutionary regimes nor the Napoleonic government succeeded in marshaling the resources to fund poor relief or other social programs. The gap left by the collapse of church resources devoted to assisting the destitute would not be filled for decades to come.[12] Nor would the role that the Catholic Church played in French society prior to 1789 ever be resumed. Monastic orders largely disappeared, of course, but the persecution of the church that followed passage of the Civil Constitution of the Clergy led not only to the emigration of substantial numbers of clergy but to a serious decline in recruitment into the priesthood that persisted into the nineteenth century. It is difficult to be precise in assigning responsibility for the drop in natality that occurred in France during and after the Revolution, but the decline in clerical influence on birth control practices and the legislation of the 1790s mandating partible inheritance likely contributed to the declining birth

---

9 B. Bodinier and E. Teyssier, "Les biens nationaux en France: Etat de la question," in M. Lapied and C. Peyrard, eds., *La Révolution française au carrefour des recherches* (Aix-en-Provence, Publications de l'Université de Provence, 2003), 87–99.

10 D. Sutherland, *France, 1789–1815: Revolution and Counterrevolution* (Oxford, Oxford University Press, 1985.

11 E. Weber, *Peasants into Frenchmen: The Modernization of Rural France, 1870–1914* (Stanford, Stanford University Press, 1976).

12 A. Forrest, *The French Revolution and the Poor* (Oxford, Blackwell, 1981).

rate and stagnant population growth.[13] Once the most populous nation in Europe, France would fall behind Germany, Great Britain, and Russia in the nineteenth century, and eventually Italy as well, with devastating consequences for its ability to compete militarily with Germany from 1870 through the two world wars of the twentieth century.

The Impact of the Revolution on the World

For two hundred years after 1789 it was almost impossible to contemplate revolution without thinking about the French Revolution. The Bolsheviks compared themselves to the Jacobins, as did historians of the Russian Revolution. Mao Zedong read Rousseau, Kant, and Hegel in his cave in Yanan in the 1940s as he contemplated the challenge of unifying China and leading the Red Army and Chinese Communist Party to victory in 1949. When the Sandinistas designed a flag to symbolize their revolution in Nicaragua in the 1980s, the red sun rising above Lake Managua took the shape of a phrygian cap, itself an ancient symbol that the Parisian *sans-culottes* had borrowed from the Romans. Revolutionaries around the world looked to the French Revolution – its successes and its failures – as a model for their own. The fact that France was a predominantly agrarian society in the eighteenth century, ruled by a monarchy, and dominated by a landowning aristocracy, made its revolution applicable to many Third World countries in the twentieth century. The ideals embodied in "Liberty, Equality, and Fraternity" were both malleable and universal, and the principles expressed in the Declaration of the Rights of Man and Citizen could be translated into many languages and adapted to many cultures. The fact that France was the most powerful nation in Europe at the time of the Revolution, the palace at Versailles the very symbol of absolute monarchy, gave hope to revolutionaries everywhere who were struggling against powerful, oppressive regimes. Rousseau's observation that "man, born free, finds himself everywhere in chains" had been translated by Marx and Engels into "Workers of the World unite, you have only your chains to lose," and for people around the world the image that best evoked that sentiment was of Parisians storming the Bastille.

Does the French Revolution still speak to people around the globe today? As I write these words, the people of Pakistan are reeling from the recent assassination of Benazir Bhutto, a candidate for president in the elections that have now been postponed. Commentators wonder how the nation will respond and have worried about the propensity for violence

13 P. McPhee, *Living the French Revolution*, 222–23.

and the danger of emotional reaction in a country in which the literacy rate is under 50 percent. That was the literacy rate in France in 1789 – roughly 50 percent. Technology has changed enormously since then, of course, and the power of the internet and television to broadcast images to millions of people brings a new dimension to the spread of news, and rumors. Let us not forget, however, how rapidly news radiated out into the neighborhoods of Paris from the Palais Royal in 1789, nor how astonishing was the speed with which the Great Fear spread through the countryside later that summer. We should also be mindful that the power of governments to control, and censor, communications has also increased, as has their military power to suppress popular movements. But Benazir Bhutto represented above all the promise that democracy can bring change, and she expressed as well the importance of separating politics from religion. These are messages that both radiate from the French Revolution, and they are messages that are little altered by new technology or the increase in the repressive power of governments.

Among the many conferences around the world in 1989 was one sponsored by the Woodrow Wilson Center in Washington, D.C. on the global impact of the French Revolution. Conference papers addressed central and eastern Europe, Russia, the Caribbean and Latin America, the Arab world, the Middle East, sub-Saharan Africa, China, and North America.[14] The list of regions *not* mentioned might be shorter. The many observations and insights offered can scarcely be summarized here, but three broad points might be suggested regarding the continuing influence of the French Revolution around the world. First, the struggle for human rights is an ongoing one, and people in many different countries continue to interrogate and be inspired by the claims put forward in the Declaration of the Rights of Man and Citizen. Today women and children assert their rights more vociferously than was the case in 1789, as do people in the gay, lesbian, bisexual, and transgendered communities. Many advocates in the developing world ask why the French revolutionaries neglected the right to subsistence, while enshrining the right to own property. And in both Europe and the United States, the increase in immigrant communities has raised new questions about the universality of proclaimed human rights. If, as Lynn Hunt argues, the origin of human rights lies in the emergence of the capacity for empathy, how in the twenty-first century will we find the empathy that will allow us to respect the human rights of those whom we fear?

Secondly, it is important to recognize the inherent tension, even contradiction, in the legacy of the French Revolution for other parts of the

14 J. Klaits and M. H. Haltzel, eds., *The Global Ramifications of the French Revolution* (Cambridge, Cambridge University Press, 1994).

world. Even in the 1790s as the ideals of the Revolution spread across Europe, and more glaringly as the revolutionary and Napoleonic armies began to expand French boundaries, liberation was accompanied by conquest. In the nineteenth and twentieth centuries the French established a worldwide empire, propounding as they went the values of their culture even as they exploited the colonial peoples economically and denied them both self-rule and the civil rights that their own forebears had declared to be universal back in the eighteenth century. As that French empire largely collapsed in the decades following World War II, revolutionaries and leaders of independence movements in the colonies – from Vietnam to Morocco, Algeria, and the Ivory Coast – were both inspired on the one hand by the ideals of 1789 and the people who had conceived them, and repelled by the hypocrisy of the nation that had imposed colonial rule on their countries. But there is another lesson from the French Revolution for those peoples attempting to establish independence and constitutional rule in today's world, and that is that it is a slow process. The United States, proud of its long constitutional tradition, is often impatient as its government attempts to "export," or "impose," democracy in other parts of the world. The French, historians remind us, drafted four constitutions in the 1790s alone, and proceeded in fits and starts through nearly two centuries until republican stability was finally achieved in 1958, just as the French empire began to unravel.

Thirdly, there is the case of the first piece of the French empire to be lost in the wake of the French Revolution. We have touched briefly in this volume on the impact of 1789 in Saint-Domingue, and the lessons from that experience will resonate more widely as research continues and the teaching of global history expands. Two aspects of its legacy are worth noting here. Haiti is today the poorest nation in the western hemisphere, and it would seem hard not to attribute that reality, at least in part, to the economic and diplomatic policies adopted by France, Great Britain, and the United States over the past two centuries toward the country in which the first, and only, successful slave revolt in modern history occurred. On the other hand, had Napoleon not failed to reimpose French rule on the island in 1802 he might not have sold Louisiana to the United States, and the subsequent history of North America and the Caribbean might have been quite different.

The Legacy of the French Revolution in its Historiography

Essays have been devoted to this topic in recent years, and the reader will find them referenced in the accompanying bibliography. Let me here pose only the central question in the recent debates about the history of the

French Revolution: Was it a bourgeois revolution? It was not, I would argue, in the strict Marxist sense with its implicit emphasis on economic determinism, despite Henry Heller's recent effort to revivify that interpretation.[15] But neither am I persuaded by Sarah Maza's recent argument that the bourgeoisie was nothing more than a myth.[16] The French bourgeoisie may have been an amorphous lot – hardly the capitalist class that Marx imagined – but it seems reasonable to think of the propertied elite of the Third Estate, which included large landowners, lawyers, and merchants, as a bourgeoisie. As Timothy Tackett has compellingly argued, the deputies of the Third Estate did feel a strong sense of social difference from and resentment toward the aristocratic deputies of the Second Estate.[17] One cannot understand the oppositions of 1789–91 in purely political terms. The French Revolution may have been a political revolution, but it was a revolution with a social basis and social consequences. There can be little doubt that the Revolution principally benefitted the propertied classes of France, and that in the nineteenth century property came to be controlled by a bourgeoisie increasingly conscious of itself as a class.

In a 1989 essay for the *New York Review of Books*, Robert Darnton proposed the term "possibilism" to evoke the essence of the French Revolution, a "sense of boundless possibility" that was not divorced from the violence of the event, but rooted in it. "Out of the destruction," Darnton wrote, "they created a new sense of possibility – not just of writing constitutions nor of legislating liberty and equality, but of living by the most difficult of revolutionary values, the brotherhood of man."[18] This may be the most important legacy of the French Revolution, the "sense of possibility," not only expressed but realized at the time – a conviction that ordinary people, working together, could rise up and change their world. Out of that conviction, and energy, emerged the inspiring ideals of "Liberty, Equality, and Fraternity," the assertion of human rights, but also the regime of the Terror and the dictatorship of Napoleon.

The lack of a new paradigm to take the place of the Marxist interpretation of the French Revolution may be troubling to some, but for me it is

---

15 H. Heller, *The Bourgeois Revolution in France, 1789–1815* (New York, Berghahn Books, 2006); see also G. C. Comninel, *Rethinking the French Revolution: Marxism and the Revisionist Challenge* (London, Verso, 1987).

16 S. Maza, *The Myth of the French Bourgeoisie: An Essay on the Social Imaginary, 1750–1850* (Cambridge, MA, Harvard University Press, 2003).

17 T. Tackett, *Becoming a Revolutionary: The Deputies of the French National Assembly and the Emergence of a Revolutionary Culture, 1789–1790* (Princeton, Princeton University Press, 1996).

18 R. Darnton, "What Was Revolutionary about the French Revolution?," *New York Review of Books* (19 January 1989), 3–10.

the richness of this decade of crisis, its multifaceted quality, that makes it so compelling and continually relevant. Constitutional principles, state-building, civil liberties, civil war, women's rights, the abolition of slavery, religion and politics, popular culture, music and theatre, science and technology, the plight of the weak and powerless – all of those issues, and more, are there to be explored in the history of the French Revolution. At the heart of it all, however, of that era of "possibility" that gave birth to modern democracy, lies this central and enduring question: How does one prevent a politics of hope from degenerating into a politics of fear?

Bibliography

Aftalion, F., *The French Revolution: An Economic Interpretation* (Cambridge, Cambridge University Press, 1990).

Agulhon, M., *Marianne into Battle: Republican Imagery and Symbolism in France, 1789–1880* (Cambridge, Cambridge University Press, 1981).

Andress, D., *French Society in Revolution, 1789–1799* (Manchester, Manchester University Press, 1999).

Andress, D., *Massacre at the Champ de Mars: Popular Dissent and Political Culture in the French Revolution* (Suffolk, The Boydell Press, 2000).

Andress, D., *The Terror: The Merciless War for Freedom in Revolutionary France* (New York, Farrar, Straus, and Giroux, 2005)

Andrews, R. M., "Paris of the Great Revolution, 1789–1796," in G. Brucker, ed., *Peoples and Communities in the Western World* (Homewood, IL, Dorsey Press, 1979), v.2, 56–116.

Andrews, R. M., "Social Structures, Political Elites and Ideology in Revolutionary Paris, 1792–94: A Critical evaluation of Albert Soboul's *Les Sans-Culottes Parisiens en l'an II*," *Journal of Social History* 19 (1985), 71–112.

Applewhite, H. B., *Political Alignment in the French National Assembly, 1789–1791* (Baton Rouge, Louisiana State University Press, 1993).

Arasse, D., *The Guillotine and the Terror* (London, Penguin Books, 1989).

Aulard, A., *La Société des Jacobins: recueil de documents pour l'histoire du Club des Jacobins de Paris* (Paris, Jouaust, 1889–97), 6 vols.

Aulard, A., *Recueil des actes du Comité de salut public avec la correspondance officielle des représentants en mission et le registre du Conseil exécutif provisoire* (Paris, Imprimerie nationale, 1889–99), 36 vols.

Aulard, A., *Histoire politique de la Révolution française* (Paris, A. Colin, 1903).

Aulard, A., *La Révolution française et les congrégations* (Paris, E. Cornely, 1903).

Aulard, A., *The French Revolution: A Political History, 1789–1804* (London, T. F. Unwin, 1910).

Baczko, B., *Ending the Terror: The French Revolution after Robespierre* (Cambridge, Cambridge University Press, 1994).

Baecque, A. de, ed., *L'An I des droits de l'homme* (Paris, Presses du CNRS, 1988).

Baecque, A. de, *The Body Politic: Corporeal Metaphor in Revolutionary France, 1770–1800*, trans. C. Mandell (Stanford, Stanford University Press, 1997).

Baecque, A. de, *Glory and Terror: Seven Deaths under the French Revolution* (New York, Routledge, 2003).

Baker, K. M., *Condorcet: From Natural Philosophy to Social Mathematics* (Chicago, University of Chicago Press, 1975).

Baker, K. M., ed., *The Political Culture of the Old Regime* (Oxford, Pergamon, 1987).

Baker, K. M., "Public Opinion at the end of the Old Regime," *Journal of Modern History* 60 (September, 1988), S1–S21.

Baker, K. M., *Inventing the French Revolution* (Cambridge, Cambridge University Press, 1990).

Baker, K. M., ed., *The Terror* (Oxford, Pergamon, 1994).

Barber, E. G., *The Bourgeoisie in 18th-Century France* (Princeton, Princeton University Press, 1973).

Barber, E. G., *Jean-Jacques Rousseau dans la Révolution française 1789–1801* (Paris, Les Belles Lettres, 1995).

Barnard, H. C., *Education and the French Revolution* (Cambridge, Cambridge University Press, 1969).

Beik, P, *The French Revolution Seen from the Right: Social Theories in Motion, 1789–1799* (New York, Howard Fertig, 1970).

Bell, D. A., *Lawyers and Citizens: The Making of a Political Elite in Old-Regime France* (New York, Oxford University Press, 1994).

Bell, D. A., *The Cult of the Nation in France: Inventing Nationalism, 1689–1800* (Cambridge, MA, Harvard University Press, 2001).

Bell, D. A., "Violence, Terror, and War: A Comment on Arno Mayer's *The Furies*," *French Historical Studies* 24 (Fall 2001), 559–67.

Bell, D. A., *The First Total War: Napoleon's Europe and the Birth of Warfare as We Know It* (Boston, Houghton Mifflin, 2007).

Bellanger, C. et al., *Histoire Générale de la presse française* (Paris, Presses Universitaires de France, 1969).

Benoit, B., ed., *Ville et Révolution française* (Lyon, Presses Universitaires de Lyon, 1994).

Bergeron, L., *France under Napoleon*, trans. R. R. Palmer (Princeton, Princeton University Press, 1981).

Bertaud, J.-P., *The Army of the French Revolution: From Citizen Soldiers to Instruments of Power* (Princeton, Princeton University Press, 1988).

Biard, M., *Missionaires de la République* (Paris, Comité des Travaux Historiques et Scientifiques, 2002).

Biard, M. and P. Dupuy, *La Révolution française: dynamiques, influences, débats, 1787–1804* (Pairs, A. Colin, 2005).

Bienvenu, R. T., *The Ninth of Thermidor: The Fall of Robespierre* (New York, Oxford University Press, 1968).

Blanning, T. C. W., *The French Revolutionary Wars: 1787–1802* (New York, Arnold Publishers, 1996).

Blanning, T. C. W., ed., *The Rise and Fall of the French Revolution* (Chicago, University of Chicago Press, 1996).

Blanning, T. C. W., *The French Revolution: Class War or Culture Clash?* (New York, Palgrave Macmillan, 1997).

Blaufarb, R., *Napoleon: A Symbol for an Age: A Brief History with Documents* (Boston, Bedford Books, 2007).

Bluche, F., *Septembre 1792: logiques d'un massacre* (Paris, Robert Laffont, 1986).

Blum, C., *Rousseau and the Republic of Virtue: The Language of Politics in the French Revolution* (Ithaca, Cornell University Press, 1986).

Bosher, J. F., *French Finances, 1770–1795: From Business to Bureaucracy* (Cambridge, Cambridge University Press, 1970).

Bossenga, G., *The Politics of Privilege: Old Regime and Revolution in Lille* (Cambridge, Cambridge University Press, 1991).

Bossenga, G., "Rights and Citizens in the Old Regime," *French Historical Studies* 20 (1997), 217–43.

Bouloiseau, M., *La République jacobine: 10 août 1792–9 thermidor an II* (Paris, Editions du Seuil, 1972).

Bouton, C., *The Flour War: Gender, Class and Community in late Ancien Régime Society* (University Park, Pennsylvania State University Press, 1993).

Brinton, C., *The Jacobins: An Essay in the New History* (New York, Macmillan, 1930).

Brown, H. G. and J. A. Miller, eds., *Taking Liberties: Problems of a New Order from the French Revolution to Napoleon* (Manchester, Manchester University Press, 2002).

Brown, H. G., *Ending the French Revolution: Violence, Justice, and Repression from the Terror to Napoleon* (Charlottesville, University of Virginia Press, 2006).

Burke, E., *Reflections on the Revolution in France* (New York, Oxford University Press, 1999).

Burstin, H., *L'Invention du sans-culotte: regard sur le Paris révolutionnaire* (Paris, Odile Jacob, 2005).

Burstin, H., *Une révolution à l'oeuvre: le faubourg Saint-Marcel, 1789–1794* (Seyssel, Champ Vallon, 2005).

Calhoun, C., ed., *Habermas and the Public Sphere* (Cambridge, MA, MIT Press, 1992).

Campbell, P. R., ed., *The Origins of the French Revolution* (New York, Palgrave Macmillan, 2006).

Campbell, P. R., T. E. Kaiser, and M. Linton, eds., *Conspiracy in the French Revolution* (Manchester, Manchester University Press, 2007).

Caron, P., *Les Massacres de septembre* (Paris, Maison du livre français, 1935).

Censer, J. R., *Prelude to Power: The Parisian Radical Press, 1789–1791* (Baltimore, Johns Hopkins University Press, 1976).

Censer, J. R., "The Coming of a New Interpretation of the French Revolution," *Journal of Social History* 21 (1987), 295–309.

Censer, J. R., "Commencing the Third Century of Debate," *American Historical Review* 94 (1989), 1309–25.

Censer, J. R., ed., *The French Revolution and Intellectual History* (Chicago, The Dorsey Press, 1989).

Censer, J. R., "Social Twists and Linguistic Turns: Revolutionary Historiography a Decade after the Bicentennial," *French Historical Studies* 22 (1999), 139–67.

Censer, J. R. and L. Hunt, *Liberty, Equality, Fraternity: Exploring the French Revolution* (University Park, Pennsylvania State University Press, 2001).

Censer, J. R. and L. Hunt, "Imaging the French Revolution: Depictions of the French Revolutionary Crowd," *American Historical Review* 110, no. 1 (February 2005), 38–45.

Chartier, R., *Les Origines culturelles de la Révolution française* (Paris, Seuil, 1990).

Chaumié, J., "Les Girondins et les Cent Jours," *Annales historiques de la Révolution française* XLIII (1971), 329–65.

Chaumié, J., "Les Girondins," in A. Soboul, ed., *Actes du colloque Girondins et Montagnards* (Paris, Société des études robespierristes, 1980), 19–60.

Chaussinand-Nogaret, G., *The French Nobility in the Eighteenth Century: From Feudalism to Enlightenment*, trans. W. Doyle (Cambridge, Cambridge University Press, 1985).

Chisick, H., *The "Ami du Roi" of the Abbé Royou: The Production, Distribution and Readership of a Conservative Journal of the Early French Revolution* (Philadelphia, American Philosophical Society, 1992

Cobb, R. C., *The Police and the People: French Popular Protest, 1789–1820* (Oxford, Clarendon Press, 1970).

Cobb, R. C., *Reactions to the French Revolution* (Oxford, Oxford University Press, 1972).

Cobb, R. C., *Death in Paris, 1795–1801* (Oxford, Oxford University Press, 1978).

Cobb, R. C., *The People's Armies: Instrument of the Terror in the Departments* (New Haven, Yale University Press, 1987).

Cobb, R. C. and C. Jones, eds., *Voices of the French Revolution* (Topsfield, MA, Salem House Publishers, 1988).

Cobban, A., *The Social Interpretation of the French Revolution* (Cambridge, Cambridge University Press, 1964).

Collins, J. B., *The Ancien Régime and the French Revolution* (Toronto, Wadsworth, 2002).

Colwill, E., "Just Another Citoyenne? Marie-Antoinette on Trial, 1790–1793," *History Workshop* 28 (1989), 63–87.

Comninel, G., *Rethinking the French Revolution: Marxism and the Revisionist Challenge* (London, Verso, 1987).

Connelly, O., *French Revolution/Napoleonic Era* (New York, Holt, Rinehart, and Winston, 1979).

Cousin, B., ed., *Les Fédéralismes: réalités et représentations, 1789–1874* (Aix-en-Provence, Publications de l'Université de Provence, 1995).

Cowans, J., *To Speak for the People: Public Opinion and the Problem of Legitimacy in the French Revolution* (New York, Routledge, 2001).

Cox, M. R., ed., *The Place of the French Revolution in History* (Boston, Houghton Mifflin, 1998).

Crook, M., *Toulon in War and Revolution* (Manchester, Manchester University Press, 1991).

Crook, M., *Elections in the French Revolution: An Apprenticeship in Democracy, 1789–1799* (Cambridge, Cambridge University Press, 1996).

Crook, M., *Napoleon Comes to Power: Democracy and Dictatorship in Revolutionary France, 1795–1804* (Cardiff, University of Wales Press, 1998).

Crouzet, F., *Britain Ascendant: Comparative Studies in Franco-British Economic History*, trans. Martin Thom (Cambridge, Cambridge University Press, 1990).

Crouzet, F., *La Grande Inflation: la monnaie en France de Louis XVI à Napoléon* (Paris, Fayard, 1993).

Crow, T., *Emulation: Making Artists for Revolutionary France* (New Haven, Yale University Press, 1997).

Cubells, M., *Les Horizons de la Liberté: naissance de la révolution en Provence, 1787–1789* (Aix-en-Provence, Edisud, 1987).

Darnton, R., "The High Enlightenment and the Low-Life of Literature in Pre-Revolutionary France," *Past and Present* 51 (May 1971), 81–115.

Darnton, R., "In Search of the Enlightenment: Recent Attempts to Create a Social History of Ideas," *Journal of Modern History* 43 (1971), 113–32.

Darnton, R., *The Business of Enlightenment: A Publishing History of the Encyclopédie, 1775–1800* (Cambridge, MA, Harvard University Press, 1979).

Darnton, R., *The Literary Underground of the Old Regime* (Cambridge, MA, Harvard University Press, 1982).

Darnton, R., *The Great Cat Massacre and other Episodes in French Cultural History* (New York, Basic Books, 1984).

Darnton, R., "What was revolutionary about the French Revolution?," *New York Review of Books* (19 January 1989), 3–10.

Darnton, R. and D. Roche, eds., *Revolution in Print: The Press in France, 1775–1800* (Berkeley, University of California Press, 1989).

Darnton, R., *The Kiss of Lamourette: Reflections in Cultural History* (New York, W. W. Norton, 1990).

Darnton, R., *The Forbidden Best-Sellers of Pre-Revolutionary France* (New York, W. W. Norton, 1995).

Davies, P., *The Debate on the French Revolution* (Manchester, Manchester University Press, 2006).

Desan, S., "The Rhetoric of Religious Revival during the French Revolution," *Journal of Modern History* 60 (1988), 1–27.

Desan, S., *Reclaiming the Sacred: Lay Religion and Popular Politics in Revolutionary France* (Ithaca, Cornell University Press, 1990).

Desan, S., "'War Between Brothers and Sisters': Inheritance Law and Gender Politics in Revolutionary France," *French Historical Studies* 20 (1997), 597–634.

Desan, S., "What's after Political Culture? Recent French Revolutionary Historiography," *French Historical Studies* 23 (2000), 163–96.

Desan, S., *The Family on Trial in Revolutionary France* (Berkeley, University of California Press, 2004).

Dorigny, M., "Violence et Révolution: Les Girondins et les massacres de septembre," in A. Soboul, ed., *Girondins et Montagnards* (Paris, Société des études robespierristes, 1980), 103–20.

Dorigny, M., *Montesquieu dans la Révolution française* (Paris, EDHS, 1990).

Doyle, W., "The Parlements of France and the Breakdown of the Old Regime," *French Historical Studies* 6 (1970), 415–48.

Doyle, W., "Was There an Aristocratic Reaction in Pre-Revolutionary France?," *Past and Present* 57 (November 1972), 97–122.

Doyle, W., *The Parlement of Bordeaux and the End of the Old Regime, 1771–1790* (London, E. Benn, 1974).

Doyle, W., *Origins of the French Revolution* (Oxford, Oxford University Press, 1980).

Doyle, W., *The Oxford History of the French Revolution* (Oxford, Oxford University Press, 1989).

Doyle, W., *The French Revolution: A Very Short Introduction* (Oxford, Oxford University Press, 2001).

Dowd, D. L., *Pageant-Master of the Republic: Jacques-Louis David and the French Revolution* (Lincoln, University of Nebraska Press, 1948).

Dubois, L., *Les Esclaves de la République: l'histoire oubliée de la première émancipation, 1789–1794*, trans. J.-F. Chaix (Paris, Calmann-Lévy, 1998).

Dubois, L., *Avengers of the New World* (Cambridge, MA, Harvard University Press, 2004).

Dubois, L., *A Colony of Citizens: Revolution and Slave Emancipation in the French Caribbean, 1787–1804* (Chapel Hill, University of North Carolina Press, 2004).

Duckworth, C., *The d'Antraigues Phenomenon: The Making and Breaking of a Revolutionary Royalist Espionage Agent* (Newcastle upon Tyne, Avero Publications, 1986).

Dunn, S., *The Deaths of Louis XVI: Regicide and the French Political Imagination* (Princeton, Princeton University Press, 1994).

Duprat, C., *Le Temps de philanthropes: la philanthropie parisienne des Lumières à la monarchie de Juillet* (Paris, Editions du CTHS, 1993), 2 vols.

Dupuy, R. and M. Morabito, eds., *1795: pour une République sans Révolution* (Rennes, Presses Universitaires de Rennes, 1996).

Dwyer, P. G., *Talleyrand: Profiles in Power* (London, Pearson Education, 2002).

Dwyer, P. G., *Napoleon: The Path to Power* (New Haven, Yale University Press, 2008).

Echeverria, D., *The Maupeou Revolution: A Study in the History of Libertarianism, 1770–1774* (Baton Rouge, Louisiana State University Press, 1985).

Edmonds, W. D., *Jacobinism and the Revolt of Lyon, 1789–1793* (Oxford, Clarendon Press, 1990).

Egret, J., *La Révolution des Notables: Mounier et les Monarchiens, 1789* (Paris, A. Colin, 1950).

Egret, J., *Louis XV et l'opposition parlementaire, 1715–1774* (Paris, A. Colin, 1970).

Egret, J., *Necker, ministre de Louis XVI (1776–1790)* (Paris, Honoré Champion, 1975).

Ellis, G., *Napoleon: Profiles in Power* (London, Pearson Education, 1997).

Englund, S., *Napoleon: A Political Life* (Cambridge, MA, Harvard University Press, 2004).

Farge, A., *The Vanishing Children of Paris: Rumor and Politics before the French Revolution*, trans. Claudia Miéville (Cambridge, MA, Harvard University Press, 1991).

Farge, A., *Fragile Lives: Violence, Power and Solidarity in Eighteenth-Century Paris*, trans. Carol Shelton (Cambridge, MA, Harvard University Press, 1993).

Farge, A., *Subversive Words: Public Opinion in Eighteenth-Century France*, trans. Rosemary Morris (University Park, Pennsylvania State University Press, 1995).

Fauré, C., *Democracy without Women: Feminism and the Rise of Liberal Individualism in France* (Bloomington, Indiana University Press, 1991).

Fehér, F., ed., *The French Revolution and the Birth of Modernity* (Berkeley, University of California Press, 1990).

Félix, J., *Les Magistrats du parlement de Paris, 1771–90* (Paris, SEDOPOLS, 1980).

Fick, C., *The Making of Haiti: The Saint-Domingue Revolution from Below* (Knoxville, University of Tennessee Press, 1990).

Fife, G., *The Terror: The Shadow of the Guillotine: France, 1792–1794* (New York, St. Martin's Press, 2004).

Fitzsimmons, M., *The Parisian Order of Barristers and the French Revolution* (Cambridge, MA, Harvard University Press, 1987).

Fitzsimmons, M., *The Remaking of France: The National Assembly and the Constitution of 1791* (Cambridge, Cambridge University Press, 1994).

Fitzsimmons, M., *The Night the Old Regime Ended: August 4, 1789, and the French Revolution* (University Park, Pennsylvania State University Press, 2003).

Ford, F. L., *Robe and Sword: The Regrouping of the French Aristocracy after Louis XIV* (Cambridge, MA, Harvard University Press, 1953).

Forrest, A., *Society and Politics in Revolutionary Bordeaux* (Oxford, Oxford University Press, 1975).

Forrest, A., *The French Revolution and the Poor* (Oxford, Blackwell, 1981).

Forrest, A., *Conscripts and Deserters: The Army and French Society during the Revolution and Empire* (Oxford, Oxford University Press, 1989).

Forrest, A., *Soldiers of the French Revolution* (Durham, Duke University Press, 1990).

Forrest, A. and P. Jones, eds., *Reshaping France: Town, Country and Region during the French Revolution* (Manchester, Manchester University Press, 1991).

Forrest, A., *The French Revolution* (Oxford, Blackwell, 1995).

Forrest, A., *Revolution in Provincial France: Acquitaine, 1789–1799* (Oxford, Clarendon Press, 1996).

Forrest, A., *Paris, the Provinces and the French Revolution* (London, Arnold Publishers, 2004).

Francesco, A. de, "Popular Sovereignty and Executive Power in the Federalist Revolt of 1793," *French History* 5 (1991), 74–101.

Friedland, P., *Political Actors: Representative Bodies and Theatricality in the Age of the French Revolution* ((Ithaca, Cornell University Press, 2002).

Furet, F., "Le catéchisme de la Révolution française," *Annales: Economies, Sociétés, Civilisation* XXVI (1971), 255–89.

Furet, F., *Penser la Révolution française* (Paris, Gallimard, 1978), trans. by Elborg Forster as *Interpreting the French Revolution* (Cambridge, Cambridge University Press, 1981).

Furet, F., *Marx and the French Revolution* (Chicago, University of Chicago Press, 1988).

Furet, F. and M. Ozouf, eds., *A Critical Dictionary of the French Revolution*, trans. Arthur Goldhammer (Cambridge, MA, Harvard University Press, 1989).

Furet, F. and R. Halévi, eds., *Orateurs de la Révolution française* (Paris, Gallimard, 1989).

Furet, F., "A Commentary," *French Historical Studies* 16 (Fall 1990), 792–802.

Furet, F. and M. Ozouf, eds., *La Gironde et les Girondins* (Paris, Editions Payot, 1991).

Furet, F., *Revolutionary France, 1770–1880*, trans. A. Nevill (Oxford, Oxford University Press, 1995).

Furet, F. and R. Halévi, *La monarchie républicaine: La Constitution de 1791* (Paris, Fayard, 1996).

Gainot, B., *1799, un noveau jacobinisme?: la démocratie représentative, une alternative à brumaire* (Paris, Editions du CTHS, 2001).

Garden, M., *Lyon et les Lyonnais au XVIIIe siècle* (Paris, Les Belles Lettres, 1970).

Garrigus, J. D., *Before Haiti: Race and Citizenship in French Saint-Domingue* (New York, Palgrave Macmillan, 2006).

Garrioch, D., *Neighborhood and Community in Paris, 1740–1790* (Cambridge, Cambridge University Press, 1986).

Garrioch, D., *The Formation of the Parisian Bourgeoisie, 1690–1830* (Cambridge, MA, Harvard University Press, 1996).

Garrioch, D., *The Making of Revolutionary Paris* (Berkeley, University of California Press, 2002).

Gaspar, D. B. and D. P. Geggus, eds., *A Turbulent Time: The French Revolution and the Greater Caribbean* (Bloomington, Indiana University Press, 1997).

Gauchet, M., *La Révolution des droits de l'homme* (Paris, Gallimard, 1989).

Gauchet, M., *La Révolution des pouvoirs: la souveraineté, le peuple et la représentation, 1789–1799* (Paris, Gallimard, 1995).

Gauthier, F., *La Voie paysanne dans la Révolution française: l'exemple de la Picardie* (Paris, F. Maspero, 1977).

Geggus, D., *Slavery, War and Revolution: The British Occupation of Saint-Domingue, 1793–1798* (Oxford, Oxford University Press, 1982).

Geggus, D., *Haitian Revolutionary Studies* (Bloomington, Indiana University Press, 2002).

Gelbart, N. R., *Feminine and Opposition Journalism in Old Regime France: The 'Journal des Dames'* (Berkeley, University of California Press, 1987).

Gendron, F., *The Gilded Youth of Thermidor* (Montreal, McGill-Queen's University Press, 1993).

Gershoy, L., *Bertrand Barère: A Reluctant Terrorist* (Princeton, Princeton University Press, 1962).

Gilroy, P., *The Black Atlantic: Modernity and Double-Consciousness* (Cambridge, MA, Harvard University Press, 1993).

Godechot, J., *Les Institutions de la France sous la Révolution et l'Empire* (Paris, Presses Universitaires de France, 1951).

Godechot, J., *The Taking of the Bastille, July 14th 1789* (New York, Scribner, 1970).

Godechot, J., *La Grande nation: l'expansion révolutionnaire de la France dans le monde de 1789 à 1799* (Paris, Aubier Montaigne, 1983).

Godineau, D., *The Women of Paris and their French Revolution* (Berkeley, University of California Press, 1998).

Goldstone, J. A., ed., *Revolutions: Theoretical, Comparative, and Historical Studies* (New York, Harcourt Brace Jovanovich, 1986).

Goodman, D., ed., *Marie-Antoinette: Writings on the Body of a Queen* (New York, Routledge, 2003).

Gordon, D., *Postmodernism and the Enlightenment: New Perspectives in Eighteenth-Century French Intellectual History* (London, Routledge, 2001).

Gottschalk, L. R., *Jean Paul Marat: A Study in Radicalism* (New York, Benjamin Blom, 1927).

Goubert, P., *The Ancien Regime: French Society, 1600–1750* (New York, Harper Torchbooks, 1973).

Gough, H., *The Terror in the French Revolution* (London, Macmillan Press, 1998).

Greer, D., *The Incidence of the Terror during the French Revolution* (Cambridge, MA, Harvard University Press, 1935).

Greer, D., *The Incidence of the Emigration during the French Revolution* (Cambridge, MA, Harvard University Press, 1951).

Griffiths, R., *Le Centre Perdu: Malouet et les "monarchiens" dans la Révolution française* (Grenoble, Presses Universitaires de Grenoble, 1988).

Gross, J.-P., *Fair Shares for All: Jacobin Egalitarianism in Practice* (Cambridge, Cambridge University Press, 1997).

Gueniffey, P., *Le Nombre et la raison: La Révolution française et les élections* (Paris, Editions de l'EHESS, 1993).

Gueniffey, P., *La Politique de la Terreur: essai sur la violence révolutionnaire, 1789–1794* (Paris, Fayard, 2000).

Guérin, D., *Class Struggle in the First French Republic: Bourgeois and Bras Nus, 1793–95*, trans. Ian Patterson (London, Pluto Press, 1977).

Guilhaumou, J., *La Langue politique et la Révolution française* (Paris, Méridiens Klincksieck, 1989).

Guilhaumou, J., *La Mort de Marat* (Bruxelles, Editions Complexe, 1989).

Guilhaumou, J., *Marseille républicaine (1791–1793)* (Paris, Presses de la Fondation Nationale des Sciences Politiques, 1992).

Guilhaumou, J., *L'Avènement des porte-parole de la République (1789–1792)* (Lille, Presses Universitaires du Septentrion, 1998).

Guilhaumou, J., *Sieyès et l'ordre de la langue: l'invention de la politique moderne* (Paris, Editions Kimé, 2002).

Gutwirth, M., *The Twilight of the Goddesses: Women and Representation in the French Revolutionary Era* (New Brunswick, NJ, Rutgers University Press, 1992).

Habermas, J., *The Structural Transformation of the Public Sphere: An Inquiry into a Category of Bourgeois Society*, trans. Thomas Burger (Cambridge, MA, MIT Press, 1992).

Hampson, N., *A Social History of the French Revolution* (London, Routledge and Kegan Paul, 1963).

Hampson, N., *The Life and Opinions of Maximilien Robespierre* (London, Duckworth, 1974).

Hampson, N., *Will and Circumstance: Montesquieu, Rousseau and the French Revolution* (London, Duckworth, 1983).

Hampson, N., *Danton* (Oxford, Basil Blackwell, 1988).

Hampson, N., *Prelude to Terror: The Constituent Assembly and the Failure of Consensus, 1789–1791* (Oxford, Basil Blackwell, 1988).

Hampson, N., *Saint-Just* (Oxford, Basil Blackwell, 1991).

Hanson, P. R., *Provincial Politics in the French Revolution: Caen and Limoges, 1789–1794* (Baton Rouge, Louisiana State University Press, 1989).

Hanson, P. R., "The Federalist Revolt: An Affirmation or Denial of Popular Sovereignty?," *French History* 6 (1992), 335–55.

Hanson, P. R., "Monarchist Clubs and the Pamphlet Debate over Political Legitimacy in the Early Years of the French Revolution," *French Historical Studies* 21 (Spring 1998), 299–324.

Hanson, P. R., *The Jacobin Republic under Fire: The Federalist Revolt in the French Revolution* (University Park, Pennsylvania State University Press, 2003).

Hanson, P. R., *Historical Dictionary of the French Revolution* (Lanham, MD, Scarecrow Press, 2004).

Hardman, J., *Louis XVI* (New Haven, Yale University Press, 1993).

Hardman, J., *Louis XVI: The Silent King* (London, Arnold, 2000).

Harris, R. D., *Necker, Reform Statesman of the Ancien Régime* (Berkeley, University of California Press, 1979).

Haydon, C. and W. Doyle, eds., *Robespierre* (Cambridge, Cambridge University Press, 1999).

Heller, H., *The Bourgeois Revolution in France, 1789–1815* (New York, Berghahn Books, 2006).

Hesse, C., *The Other Enlightenment: How French Women Became Modern* (Princeton, Princeton University Press, 2001).

Heuer, J. N., *The Family and the Nation: Gender and Citizenship in Revolutionary France, 1789–1830* (Ithaca, Cornell University Press, 2005).

Higonnet, P., *Class, Ideology, and the Rights of Nobles during the French Revolution* (Oxford, Clarendon Press, 1981).

Higonnet, P., "The Social and Cultural Antecendents of Revolutionary Discontinuity: Montagnards and Girondins," *English Historical Review* 100 (1985), 513–44.

Higonnet, P., *Sister Republics* (Cambridge, MA, Harvard University Press, 1988).

Higonnet, P., *Goodness beyond Virtue: Jacobins during the French Revolution* (Cambridge, MA, Harvard University Press, 1998).

Hobsbawm, E. J., *Echoes of the Marseillaise: Two Centuries Look Back on the French Revolution* (New Brunswick, NJ, Rutgers University Press, 1990).

Hood, J., "Protestant–Catholic Relations and the Roots of the First Popular Counterrevolutionary Movement in France," *Journal of Modern History* 43 (June 1971), 245–75.

Hood, J., "Revival and Mutation of Old Rivalries in Revolutionary France," *Past and Present* LXXXII (February 1979), 82–115.

Houdaille, J., "Le problème des pertes de guerre," *Revue d'Histoire moderne et contemporaine* XVII (1970), 418.

Huet, M. H., *Rehearsing the Revolution: The Staging of Marat's Death, 1793–1797* (Berkeley, University of California Press, 1982).

Hufton, O., *Bayeux in the Late Eighteenth Century* (Oxford, Clarendon Press, 1967).

Hufton, O., *Women and the Limits of Citizenship in the French Revolution* (Toronto, University of Toronto Press, 1992).

Hunt, L., "Committees and Communes: Local Politics and National Revolution in 1789," *Comparative Studies in Society and History* XVIII (July 1976), 321–46.

Hunt, L., *Revolution and Urban Politics in Provincial France: Troyes and Reims, 1786–1790* (Stanford, Stanford University Press, 1978).

Hunt, L., D. Lansky, and P. Hanson, "The Failure of the Liberal Republic in France, 1795–1799: The Road to Brumaire," *Journal of Modern History* 51 (December 1979), 734–59.

Hunt, L., *Politics, Culture, and Class in the French Revolution* (Berkeley, University of California Press, 1984).

Hunt, L., *The Family Romance of the French Revolution* (Berkeley, University of California Press, 1992).

Hunt, L., ed., *The French Revolution and Human Rights: A Brief Documentary History* (Boston, Bedford Books, 1996).

Hunt, L., *Inventing Human Rights: A History* (New York, W. W. Norton, 2007).

Hutt, M., *Chouannerie and Counterrevolution: Puisaye, the Princes and the British Government of the 1790s* (Cambridge, Cambridge University Press, 1983), 2 vols.

Hyslop, B. F., *French Nationalism in 1789 According to the General Cahiers* (New York, Octagon Books, 1968).

Hyslop, B. F., *A Guide to the General Cahiers of 1789* (New York, Octagon Books, 1968).

James, C. L. R., *The Black Jacobins: Toussaint L'Ouverture and the San Domingo Revolution* (New York, Vintage Books, 1989, 2nd ed.).

Jaume, L., *Le Discours jacobin et la démocratie* (Paris, Fayard, 1989).

Jessenne, J.-P., *Révolution et Empire, 1783–1815* (Paris, Hachette, 1993).

Johnson, C., *Revolutionary Change* (Boston, Little, Brown, 1966).

Johnson, H. C., *The Midi in Revolution: A Study of Regional Political Diversity, 1789–1793* (Princeton, Princeton University Press, 1986).

Johnson, H. J., *Listening in Paris: A Cultural History* (Berkeley, University of California Press, 1996).

Jones, C., *The Longman Companion to the French Revolution* (London, Longman, 1988).

Jones, C., "Bourgeois Revolution Revivified: 1789 and Social Change," in C. Lucas, ed., *Rewriting the French Revolution* (Oxford, Clarendon Press, 1991), 69–118.

Jones, C., "The Great Chain of Buying: Medical Advertisement, the Bourgeois Public Sphere, and the Origins of the French Revolution," *American Historical Review* 101 (February 1996), 13–40.

Jones, P. M., *The Peasantry in the French Revolution* (Cambridge, Cambridge University Press, 1988).

Jones, P. M., *Reform and Revolution in France: The Politics of Transition, 1774–1791* (Cambridge, Cambridge University Press, 1995).

Jones, P., *Liberty and Locality in Revolutionary France: Six Villages Compared, 1760–1820* (Cambridge, Cambridge University Press, 2003).

Jordan, D. P., *The King's Trial* (Berkeley, University of California Press, 1979).

Jordan, D. P., *The Revolutionary Career of Maximilien Robespierre* (Chicago, University of Chicago Press, 1989).

Kafker, F. A., J. M. Laux, and D. G. Levy, eds., *The French Revolution: Conflicting Interpretations* (Malabar, FL, Krieger, 2002).

Kaiser, T. E., "This Strange Offspring of *Philosophie*: Recent Historiographical Problems in Relating the Enlightenment to the French Revolution," *French Historical Studies* 15 (1988), 549–62.

Kaiser, T. E., "Who's Afraid of Marie-Antoinette? Diplomacy, Austrophobia, and the Queen," *French History* 14 (2000), 241–71.

Kaiser, T. E., "From the Austrian Committee to the Foreign Plot: Marie-Antoinette, Austrophobia, and the Terror," *French Historical Studies* 26 (2003), 579–617.

Kaplan, S. L., *The Historians' Feud, France, 1789/1989* (Ithaca, Cornell University Press, 1996), originally published in French as *Adieu 89* (Paris, Fayard, 1993).

Kaplow, J., *Elbeuf during the Revolutionary Period: History and Social Structure* (Baltimore, Johns Hopkins University Press, 1964).

Kaplow, J., ed., *New Perspectives on the French Revolution: Readings in Historical Sociology* (New York, John Wiley and Sons, 1965).

Kates, G., *The "Cercle Social," the Girondins, and the French Revolution* (Princeton, Princeton University Press, 1985).

Kates, G., ed., *The French Revolution: Recent Debates and New Controversies* (London, Routledge, 1998).

Kelly, G. A., *Victims, Authority, and Terror: The Parallel Deaths of d'Orléans, Custine, Bailly, and Malesherbes* (Chapel Hill, University of North Carolina Press, 1982).

Kennedy, E., *A Cultural History of the French Revolution* (New Haven, Yale University Press, 1989).

Kennedy, M. L., *The Jacobin Clubs in the French Revolution: The First Years* (Princeton, Princeton University Press, 1982).

Kennedy, M. L., *The Jacobin Clubs in the French Revolution: The Middle Years* (Princeton, Princeton University Press, 1988).

Kennedy, M. L., *The Jacobin Clubs in the French Revolution, 1793–1795* (New York, Berghahn Books, 2000).

Kerr, W. B., *The Reign of Terror: 1793–94: The Experiment of the Democratic Republic, and the Rise of the Bourgeoisie* (Toronto, University of Toronto Press, 1927).

Kessel, P., *La Nuit du 4 août 1789* (Paris, Arthaud, 1969).

Klaits, J. and M. H. Haltzel, eds., *The Global Ramifications of the French Revolution* (Cambridge, Cambridge University Press, 1994).

Kors, A., ed., *Encyclopedia of the Enlightenment* (Oxford, Oxford University Press, 2003).

Kuscinski, A., *Dictionnaire des conventionnels* (Paris, F. Rieder, 1916–19).

Kwass, M., *Privilege and the Politics of Taxation in Eighteenth-Century France: Liberté, Egalité, Fiscalité* (Cambridge, Cambridge University Press, 2000).

Labrousse, C. E., *Esquisse du mouvement des prix et des revenus en France au XVIIIe siècle* (Paris, Librairie Dalloz, 1933).

Labrousse, C. E., *La Crise de l'économie française à la fin de l'Ancien Régime et au début de la Révolution* (Paris, Presses Universitaires de France, 1944).

Landes, J. B., *Women and the Public Sphere in the Age of the French Revolution* (Ithaca, Cornell University Press, 1988).

Landes, J. B., *Visualizing the Nation: Gender, Representation, and Revolution in Eighteenth-Century France* (Ithaca, Cornell University Press, 2001).

Lapied, M. and C. Peyrard, eds., *La Révolution française au carrefour des recherches* (Aix-en-Provence, Publications de l'Université de Provence, 2003).

Lefebvre, G., *Les Paysans du Nord pendant la Révolution française* (Lille, O. Marquant, 1924)

Lefebvre, G., *The Coming of the French Revolution*, trans. R. R. Palmer (Princeton, Princeton University Press, 1947).

Lefebvre, G., *The French Revolution* (New York, Columbia University Press, 1962).

Lefebvre, G., *The Thermidorians* (New York, Vintage Books, 1964).

Lefebvre, G., *Napoleon* (London, Routledge and Kegan Paul, 1969).

Lefebvre, G., *The Great Fear of 1789: Rural Panic in Revolutionary France*, trans. J. White (New York, Vintage Books, 1973).

Leith, J., *The Idea of Art as Propaganda in France, 1750–1799: A Study in the History of Ideas* (Toronto, University of Toronto Press, 1965).

Leith, J., *Media and Revolution* (Toronto, University of Toronto Press, 1968).

Lemay, E. H., *Dictionnaire des constituants, 1789–1791* (Paris, Universitas, 1991).

Lemay, E. H. and A. Patrick, *Revolutionaries at Work: The Constituent Assembly, 1789–1791* (Oxford, Voltaire Foundation, 1996).

Levy, D. G., H. B. Applewhite, and M. D. Johnson, *Women in Revolutionary Paris, 1789–1795* (Urbana, University of Illinois Press, 1979).

Levy, D. G., *The Ideas and Careers of Simon-Nicolas-Henri Linguet* (Urbana, University of Illinois Press, 1980).

Lewis, G., *The Second Vendée: The Continuity of Counterrevolution in the Department of the Gard, 1789–1815* (Oxford, Clarendon Press, 1978).

Lewis, G. and C. Lucas, eds., *Beyond the Terror: Essays in French Regional and Social History* (Cambridge, Cambridge University Press, 1983).

Lewis, G., *The French Revolution: Rethinking the Debate* (London, Routledge, 1993).

Lewis-Beck, M. S., A. Hildreth, and A. B. Spitzer, "Was There a Girondin Faction Within the National Convention?," *French Historical Studies* 15 (Spring 1988), 519–36.

Ligou, D., *Montauban à la fin de l'Ancien Régime et aux débuts de la Révolution, 1787–1794* (Paris, M. Rivière, 1958).

Ligou, D., *Jeanbon Saint-André* (Paris, Messidor/Editions Sociales, 1989).

Linton, M., *The Politics of Virtue in Enlightenment France* (New York, Palgrave Macmillan, 2001).

Linton, M., "Fatal Friendships: The Politics of Jacobin Friendship," *French Historical Studies* 31 (Winter 2008), 51–76.

Livesey, J., *Making Democracy in the French Revolution* (Cambridge, MA, Harvard University Press, 2001).

Louis, R., "The Incidence of the Terror: A Critique of Statistical Interpretation," *French Historical Studies* 3 (Spring 1964), 379–89.

Lucas, C., *The Structure of the Terror: The Example of Javogues and the Loire* (Oxford, Clarendon Press, 1973).

Lucas, C., "Nobles, Bourgeois, and the Origins of the French Revolution," *Past and Present* 60 (August 1973), 84–126.

Lucas, C., ed., *The Political Culture of the French Revolution* (Oxford, Pergamon Press, 1988).

Lusebrink, H. J. and R. Reichardt, *The Bastille: A History of a Symbol of Despotism and Freedom* (Durham, Duke University Press, 1997).

Luttrell, B., *Mirabeau* (Carbondale, Southern Illinois University Press, 1990).

Lynn, J. A., *The Bayonets of the Republic: Motivation and Tactics in the Army of Revolutionary France, 1791–1794* (Urbana, University of Illinois Press, 1984).

Lyons, M., *France under the Directory* (Cambridge, Cambridge University Press, 1975).

Lyons, M., *Napoleon Bonaparte and the Legacy of the French Revolution* (New York, St. Martin's Press, 1994).

Marand-Fouquet, C., *La Femme au temps de la Révolution* (Paris, Stock/Laurence Pernoud, 1989).

Margadant, T., *Urban Rivalries in the French Revolution* (Princeton, Princeton University Press, 1992).

Margerison, K., *Pamphlets and Public Opinion: The Campaign for a Union of Orders in the Early French Revolution* (West Lafayette, IN, Purdue University Press, 1998).

Markham, F., *Napoleon and the Awakening of Europe* (New York, Macmillan, 1965).

Markoff, J., *The Abolition of Feudalism: Peasants, Lords, and Legislators in the French Revolution* (University Park, Pennsylvania State University Press, 1996).

Martin, J.-C., *Une Guerre interminable: La Vendée deux cents ans après* (Nantes, Reflets du passé, 1985).

Martin, J.-C., *Blancs et Bleus dans la Vendée déchirée* (Paris, Gallimard, 1986).

Martin, J.-C., *La Vendée et la France* (Paris, Editions du Seuil, 1987).

Martin, J.-C., *La Vendée de la mémoire, 1800–1980* (Paris, Editions du Seuil, 1989).

Martin, J.-C., ed., *Religion et Révolution* (Paris, Anthropos, 1994).

Martin, J.-C., *Contre-Révolution, Révolution et Nation en France, 1789–1799* (Paris, Editions du Seuil, 1998).

Martin, J.-C., *La Révolution à l'oeuvre: perspectives actuelles dans l'histoire de la Révolution française* (Rennes, Presses Universitaires de Rennes, 2005).

Martin, J.-C., *Violence et Révolution: essai sur la naissance d'un mythe national* (Paris, Seuil, 2006).

Maslan, S., *Revolutionary Acts: Theater, Democracy, and the French Revolution* (Baltimore, Johns Hopkins University Press, 2005).

Mason, H. T., ed., *The Darnton Debate: Books and Revolution in the Eighteenth Century* (Oxford, Voltaire Foundation, 1998).

Mason, L., *Singing the French Revolution: Popular Culture and Politics, 1787–1799* (Ithaca, Cornell University Press, 1996).

Mason, L. and Tracey Rizzo, eds., *The French Revolution: A Document Collection* (Boston, Houghton Mifflin, 1999).

Mathias, P. and P. O'Brien, "Taxation in Britain and France, 1715–1810: A Comparison of the Social and Economic Incidence of Taxes Collected for the Central Governments," *Economic History* 5, no. 3 (Winter, 1976), 601–50.

Mathiez, A., *La Vie chère et le mouvement social sous la Terreur* (Paris, Payot, 1927).

Mathiez, A., *After Robespierre: The Thermidorian Reaction* (New York, Grosset and Dunlap, 1931).

May, G., *Madame Roland and the Age of Revolution* (New York, Columbia University Press, 1970).

Mayer, A., *The Furies: Violence and Terror in the French and Russian Revolutions* (Princeton, Princeton University Press, 2000).

Maza, S., *Servants and Masters in Eighteenth-Century France: The Uses of Loyalty* (Princeton, Princeton University Press, 1983).

Maza, S., *Private Lives and Public Affairs: The Causes Célèbres of Pre-Revolutionary France* (Berkeley, University of California Press, 1993).

Maza, S., *The Myth of the French Bourgeoisie: An Essay on the Social Imaginary, 1750–1850* (Cambridge, MA, Harvard University Press, 2003).

Mazauric, C., *Sur la Révolution française: contributions à l'histoire de la révolution bourgeoise* (Paris, Editions sociales, 1970).

McDonald, J., *Rousseau and the French Revolution, 1762–91* (London, Athlone Press, 1965).

McMahon, D., *Enemies of the Enlightenment: The French Counter-Enlightenment and the Making of Modernity* (Oxford, Oxford University Press, 2001).

McManners, J., *The French Revolution and the Church* (New York, Harper and Row, 1970).

McPhee, P., *Revolution and Environment in Southern France: Peasants, Lords, and Murder in the Corbières, 1780–1830* (Oxford, Oxford University Press, 1999).

McPhee, P., *The French Revolution, 1789–1799* (Oxford, Oxford University Press, 2002).

McPhee, P., *Living the French Revolution, 1789–99* (New York, Palgrave Macmillan, 2006).

Melzer, S. E. and L. W. Rabine, eds., *Rebel Daughters: Women and the French Revolution* (Oxford, Oxford University Press, 1992).

Michelet, J., *Histoire de la Révolution française* (Paris, Editions de la Librairie de l'humanité, 1922–27), 8 vols.

Miller, J., *Rousseau: Dreamer of Democracy* (New Haven, Yale University Press, 1984).

Mitchell, C. J., *The French Legislative Assembly of 1791* (Leiden, E. J. Brill, 1988).

Monnier, R., *L'Espace public démocratique: essai sur l'opinion à Paris de la Révolution au Directoire* (Paris, Editions Kimé, 1994).

Monnier, R., *Républicanisme, patriotisme et Révolution française* (Paris, L'Harmattan, 2005).

Moore, L., *Liberty: The Lives and Times of Six Women in Revolutionary France* (New York, Harper Collins, 2007).

Mornet, D., *Les Origines intellectuelles de la Révolution française* (Paris, A. Colin, 1933).

Norberg, K., "The French Fiscal Crisis of 1788 and the Financial Origins of the Revolution of 1789," in P. T. Hoffman and K. Norberg, eds., *Fiscal Crises, Liberty, and Representative Government, 1450–1789* (Stanford, Stanford University Press, 1994).

O'Brien, P. and C. Keyder, *Economic Growth in Britain and France, 1780–1914: Two Paths to the Twentieth Century* (London, Allen and Unwin, 1978).

Offen, K., "The New Sexual Politics of French Revolutionary Historiography," *French Historical Studies* 16 (1990), 909–22.

Orr, L., *Headless History: Nineteenth-Century French Historiography of the Revolution* (Ithaca, Cornell University Press, 1990).

Outram, D., *The Body and the French Revolution: Sex, Class and Political Culture* (New Haven, Yale University Press, 1989).

Ozouf, M., "War and Terror in French Revolutionary Discourse (1792–1794)," *Journal of Modern History* 56 (December 1984), 579–97.

Ozouf, M., *Festivals and the French Revolution*, trans. A. Sheridan (Cambridge, MA, Harvard University Press, 1988).

Ozouf, M., *L'Homme régénéré: essais sur la Révolution française* (Paris, Gallimard, 1989).

Ozouf-Marignier, M.-V., *La Formation des Départements* (Paris, Editions EHESS, 1989).

Paine, T., *The Rights of Man* (New York, Oxford University Press, 1998).

Palmer, R. R., *Twelve Who Ruled: The Year of the Terror in the French Revolution* (Princeton, Princeton University Press, 1941).

Palmer, R. R., *The Age of the Democratic Revolution: A Political History of Europe and America, 1760–1800* (Princeton, Princeton University Press, 1959–64), 2 vols.

Palmer, R. R., *The Improvement of Humanity: Education and the French Revolution* (Princeton, Princeton University Press, 1985).

Palmer, R. R., *From Jacobin to Liberal: Marc-Antoine Jullien, 1775–1848* (Princeton, Princeton University Press, 1993).

Pandey, G., *Routine Violence: Nations, Fragments, Histories* (Stanford, Stanford University Press, 2006).

Pariset, F. G., ed., *Bordeaux au XVIIIe siècle* (Bordeaux, Fédération historique du Sud-Ouest, 1968).

Patrick, A., *The Men of the First French Republic: Political Alignments in the National Convention of 1792* (Baltimore, Johns Hopkins University Press, 1972).

Paulson, R., *Representations of Revolution (1789–1820)* (New Haven, Yale University Press, 1983).

Perrot, J. C., *Genèse d'une ville moderne: Caen au XVIIIe siècle* (Paris, La Haye: Mouton, 1975).

Popkin, J. D., *The Right-Wing Press in France, 1792–1800* (Chapel Hill, North Carolina University Press, 1980).

Popkin, J. D. and J. Censer, eds., *Press and Politics in Pre-Revolutionary France* (Berkeley, University of California Press, 1987).

Popkin, J. D., *News and Politics in the Age of Revolution: Jean Luzac's 'Gazette de Leyde'* (Ithaca, Cornell University Press, 1989).

Popkin, J. D., *Revolutionary News: The Press in France, 1789–1799* (Durham, Duke University Press, 1990).

Popkin, J. D., *A Short History of the French Revolution* (Upper Saddle River, NJ, Pearson Prentice Hall, 1995).

Préclin, E., *Les Jansénistes du dix-huitième siècle et la Constitution civile du clergé* (Paris, Imprimerie les presses modernes, 1929).

Price, M., *The Road from Versailles: Louis XVI, Marie Antoinette, and the Fall of the French Monarchy* (New York, St. Martin's Press, 2003).

Putnam, R., *Making Democracy Work: Civic Traditions in Modern Italy* (Princeton, Princeton University Press, 1993).

Ragan, B. T. and E. A. Williams, eds., *Re-creating Authority in Revolutionary France* (New Brunswick, NJ, Rutgers University Press, 1992).

Ramsey, C., *The Ideology of the Great Fear: The Soissonnais in 1789* (Baltimore, Johns Hopkins University Press, 1992).

Reichardt, R., "Prises et démolition des Bastilles Marseillaises," in C. Badet, ed., *Marseille en Révolution* (Marseille, Editions Rivage, 1989), 53–67.

Reinhard, M., *La Chute de la Royauté* (Paris, Gallimard, 1969).

Revel, J. R., *The Contested Parterre: Public Theater and French Political Culture, 1680–1791* (Ithaca, Cornell University Press, 1999).

Rials, S., *La Déclaration des droits de l'homme et du citoyen* (Paris, Hachette, 1988).

Richet, D., "Autour des origines idéologiques lointaines de la Révolution française: élites et despotismes," *Annales: Economies, Sociétés, Civilisation* XXIV (1969), 1–23.

Roche, D., *The People of Paris: An Essay in Popular Culture in the 18th Century* (Berkeley, University of California Press, 1987).

Roche, D., *France in the Enlightenment* (Cambridge, MA, Harvard University Press, 1998).

Rosanvallon, P., *The Demands of Liberty: Civil Society in France since the Revolution*, trans. A. Goldhammer (Cambridge, MA, Harvard University Press, 2007).

Rose, R. B., *The Enragés: Socialists of the French Revolution?* (Cambridge, Cambridge University Press, 1965).

Rose, R. B., *Gracchus Babeuf: The First Revolutionary Communist* (Stanford, Stanford University Press, 1978).

Rose, R. B., *The Making of the Sans-Culottes* (Manchester, Manchester University Press, 1983).

Rose, R. B., *Tribunes and Amazons: Men and Women of Revolutionary France, 1789–1871* (Paddington, Australia, Macleay Press, 1998).

Rudé, G., *The Crowd in the French Revolution* (Oxford, Clarendon Press, 1959).

Rudé, G., *Robespierre: Portrait of a Revolutionary Democrat* (New York, Viking Press, 1975).

Rudé, G., *The French Revolution: Its Causes, its History, and its Legacy after 200 Years* (New York, Grove Weidenfeld, 1988).

Sa'adah, A., *The Shaping of Liberal Politics in Revolutionary France: A Comparative Perspective* (Princeton, Princeton University Press, 1990).

Sagan, E., *Citizens and Cannibals: The French Revolution, the Struggle for Modernity, and the Origins of Ideological Terror* (New York, Rowman and Littlefield, 2001).

Schama, S., *Citizens: A Chronicle of the French Revolution* (New York, Alfred A. Knopf, 1989).

Schecter, R., *Obstinate Hebrews: Representations of Jews in France, 1715–1815* (Berkeley, University of California Press, 2003).

Schom, A., *Napoleon Bonaparte* (New York, Harper Collins, 1997).

Scott, J. A., *The Defense of Gracchus Babeuf before the High Court of Vendôme* (Boston, University of Massachusetts Press, 1967).

Scott, J. W., *Only Paradoxes to Offer: French Feminists and the Rights of Man* (Cambridge, MA, Harvard University Press, 1996).

Scott, S., *The Response of the Royal Army to the French Revolution* (Oxford, Clarendon Press, 1978).

Scott, S. and B. Rothaus, eds., *Historical Dictionary of the French Revolution* (Westport, CT, Greenwood Press, 1985).

Scott, W., *Terror and Repression in Revolutionary Marseille* (London, Macmillan, 1973).

Secher, R., *Le Génocide Franco-Français: La Vendée-vengé* (Paris, Presses Universitaires de France, 1986).

Seligman, E., *La Justice en France pendant la Révolution, 1791–1793* (Paris, Plon-Nourrit, 1901).

Sepinwall, A. G., *The Abbé Grégoire and the French Revolution: The Making of Modern Universalism* (Berkeley, University of California Press, 2005).

Sewell, W. H., *Work and Revolution in France: The Language of Labor from the Old Regime to 1848* (Cambridge, Cambridge University Press, 1980).

Sewell, W. H., *A Rhetoric of Bourgeois Revolution: The Abbé Sieyès and "What is the Third Estate?"* (Durham, Duke University Press, 1994).

Sewell, W. H., *Logics of History: Social Theory and Social Transformation* (Chicago, University of Chicago Press, 2005).

Shapiro, B., *Revolutionary Justice in Paris, 1789–90* (Cambridge, Cambridge University Press, 1993).

Shapiro, B., "Self-Sacrifice, Self-Interest, or Self-Defense?: The Constituent Assembly and the 'Self-Denying Ordinance' of May 1791," *French Historical Studies* 25 (Fall 2002), 625–56.

Shapiro, G. and J. Markoff, *Revolutionary Demands: A Content Analysis of the Cahiers de Doléances of 1789* (Stanford, Stanford University Press, 1998).

Sibalis, M., "Napoleonic Police State," in P. Dwyer, ed., *Napoleon and Europe* (New York, Longman, 2001).

Singer, B. C. J., *Society, Theory and the French Revolution* (New York, St. Martin's Press, 1986).

Skocpol, T., *State and Social Revolutions: A Comparative Analysis of France, Russia, and China* (Cambridge, Cambridge University Press, 1979).

Slavin, M., *The French Revolution in Miniature: Section Droits-de-l'Homme, 1789–1795* (Princeton, Princeton University Press, 1984).

Slavin, M., *The Making of an Insurrection: Parisian Sections and the Gironde* (Cambridge, MA, Harvard University Press, 1986).

Smith, J. M., *Nobility Reimagined: The Patriotic Nation in Eighteenth-Century France* (Ithaca, Cornell University Press, 2005).

Soboul, A., *Les Sans-culottes parisiens en l'an II: mouvement populaire et gouvernement révolutionnaire, 2 juin 1793–9 thermidor an II* (Paris, Clavreuil, 1958).

Soboul, A., *The Parisian Sans-culottes and the French Revolution, 1793–94* (Oxford, Clarendon Press, 1964).

Soboul, A., *The French Revolution*, trans. Alan Forrest and Colin Jones (New York, Vintage Books, 1975).

Soboul, A., *The Sans-culottes* (Princeton, Princeton University Press, 1980).

Soboul, A., *Comprendre la Révolution française: problèmes politiques de la Révolution française, 1789–1797* (Paris, F. Maspero, 1981).

Soboul, A., *Problémes paysans de la Révolution, 1789–1848* (Paris, François Maspero, 1983).

Soboul, A., ed., *Dictionnaire Historique de la Révolution française* (Paris, Presses Universitaires de France, 1989).

Sonenscher, M., "The Sans-culottes of the Year II: Rethinking the Language of Labour in Revolutionary France," *Social History* 9 (1984), 301–28.

Sonenscher, M., *Work and Wages: Natural Law, Politics, and the Eighteenth-Century French Trades* (Cambridge, Cambridge University Press, 1989).

Sonenscher, M., *Before the Deluge: Public Debt, Inequality, and the Intellectual Origins of the French Revolution* (Princeton, Princeton University Press, 2007).

Starobinski, J., *Jean-Jacques Rousseau: Transparency and Obstruction*, trans. A. Goldhammer (Chicago, University of Chicago Press, 1988).

Steinbrugge, L., *The Moral Sex: Woman's Nature in the French Enlightenment* (Oxford, Oxford University Press, 1992).

Stephens, H. M., *Orators of the French Revolution* (Oxford, Clarendon Press, 1892), 2 vols.

Stone, B., *The Parlement of Paris, 1774–1789* (Chapel Hill, University of North Carolina Press, 1981).

Stone, B., *The French Parlements and the Crisis of the Old Regime* (Chapel Hill, University of North Carolina Press, 1986).

Stone, B., *The Genesis of the French Revolution: A Global-Historical Interpretation* (Cambridge, Cambridge University Press, 1994).

Sutherland, D. M. G., *The Chouans: The Social Origins of Popular Counterrevolution in Upper Brittany, 1770–1796* (Oxford, Clarendon Press, 1982).

Sutherland, D. M. G., *France, 1789–1815: Revolution and Counterrevolution* (Oxford, Oxford University Press, 1985).

Sutherland, D. M. G., *The French Revolution and Empire: The Quest for a Civic Order* (London, Blackwell, 2003).

Swanson, S. G., "The Medieval Foundations of John Locke's Theory of Natural Rights: Rights of Subsistence and the Principle of Extreme Necessity," *History of Political Thought* (Fall, 1997), 1–66.

Swenson, J., *On Jean-Jacques Rousseau* (Stanford, Stanford University Press, 2000).

Sydenham, M. J., *The Girondins* (London, University of London Press, 1961).

Sydenham, M. J., *The French Revolution* (New York, Capricorn Books, 1965).

Sydenham, M. J., "The Republican Revolt of 1793: A Plea for Less Localized Local Studies," *French Historical Studies* 11 (1981), 120–38.

Sydenham, M. J., *Léonard Bourdon: The Career of a Revolutionary, 1754–1807* (Waterloo, Canada, Wilfried Laurier University Press, 1999).

Tackett, T., *Priest and Parish in Eighteenth-Century France: A Social and Political Study of the Curés in a Diocese of Dauphiné, 1750–1791* (Princeton, Princeton University Press, 1977).

Tackett, T., "The West in France in 1789: The Religious Factor in the Origins of the Counterrevolution," *Journal of Modern History* 54 (December 1982), 715–45.

Tackett, T., *Religion, Revolution, and Regional Culture in Eighteenth-Century France: The Ecclesiastical Oath of 1791* (Princeton, Princeton University Press, 1986).

Tackett, T., *Becoming a Revolutionary: The Deputies of the French National Assembly and the Emergence of a Revolutionary Culture, 1789–1790* (Princeton, Princeton University Press, 1996).

Tackett, T., *When the King took Flight* (Cambridge, MA, Harvard University Press, 2003).

Taine, H., *Les Origines de la France contemporaine* (Paris, Hachette, 1876–94).

Talmon, J. L., *The Origins of Totalitarian Democracy* (London, Secker and Warburg, 1952).

Taylor, G. V., "Types of Capitalism in Eighteenth-Century France," *English Historical Review* 79 (1964), 478–97.

Taylor, G. V., "Noncapitalist Wealth and the Origins of the French Revolution," *American Historical Review* 72 (1967), 469–96.

Taylor, G. V., "Revolutionary and Nonrevolutionary Content in the *Cahiers* of 1789: An Interim Report," *French Historical Studies* 7 (1972), 479–502.

Thomas, Chantal, *The Wicked Queen: The Origins of the Myth of Marie-Antoinette*, trans. J. Rose (New York, Zone Books, 2001).

Thompson, J. M., *Robespierre* (Oxford, Basil Blackwell, 1935).

Thompson, J. M., *The French Revolution* (New York, Basil Blackwell, 1943).

Tilly, C., *The Vendée* (Cambridge, MA, Harvard University Press, 1964).

Tilly, C., "How Protest Modernized in France," in W. O. Aydelotte et al., eds., *Dimensions of Quantitative Research in History* (Oxford, Oxford University Press, 1972).

Tilly, L., "The Food Riot as a Form of Political Conflict in France," *Journal of Interdisciplinary History* II, no. 1 (1971), 23–57.

Tocqueville, A. de, *L'Ancien régime et la révolution* ((Paris, Lévy frères, 1856), trans. by S. Gilbert as *The Old Regime and the French Revolution* (Garden City, NY, Doubleday, 1955).

Van Kley, D., "New Wine in Old Wineskins: Continuity and Rupture in the Pamphlet Debate of the French Prerevolution," *French Historical Studies* 17 (1991), 448–65.

Van Kley, D., ed., *The French Idea of Freedom: The Old Regime and the Declaration of Rights of 1789* (Stanford, Stanford University Press, 1994).

Van Kley, D., *The Religious Origins of the French Revolution: From Calvin to the Civil Constitution, 1560–1791* (New Haven, Yale University Press, 1996).

Viguerie, J. de, *Christianisme et Révolution* (Paris, Nouvelles éditions latines, 1988).

Vovelle, M., *La Chute de la monarchie, 1787–1792* (Paris, Editions du Seuil, 1972).

Vovelle, M., *Piété baroque et déchristianisation en Provence au XVIIIe siècle* (Paris, Plon, 1973).

Vovelle, M., *Religion et Révolution: La Déchristianisation de l'an II* (Paris, Hachette, 1976).

Vovelle, M., *La Mentalité révolutionnaire* (Paris, Editions Sociales, 1985).

Vovelle, M., *La Révolution française: images et récits, 1789–1799* (Paris, Messidor, 1986), 5 vols.

Vovelle, M., "L'Historiographie de la Révolution française à la veille du bicentenaire," *Annales historiques de la Révolution française* 60 (1988), 113–26, 306–15.

Vovelle, M., *La Révolution contre l'Eglise: de la Raison à l'Etre suprême* (Bruxelles, Editions Complexe, 1988).

Vovelle, M., ed., *Paris et la Révolution* (Paris, Publications de la Sorbonne, 1989).

Vovelle, M., *Les Colloques du Bicentenaire* (Paris, Editions La Découverte, 1991).

Vovelle, M., *Recherches sur la Révolution: un bilan des travaux scientifiques du Bicentenaire* (Paris, La Découverte, 1991).

Vovelle, M., *Combats pour la Révolution française* (Paris, Editions La Découverte, 1993).

Wahnich, S., *L'Impossible citoyen: l'étranger dans le discours de la Révolution française* (Paris, A. Michel, 1977).

Wahnich, S., *La Liberté ou la mort: essai sur la Terreur et le terrorisme* (Paris, La Fabrique Editions, 2003).

Waldinger, R., P. Dawson, and I. Woloch, eds., *The French Revolution and the Making of Citizenship* (Westport, CT, Greenwood Press, 1993).

Wallon, H., *Les Représentants du peuple en mission et la justice révolutionnaire dans les départements en l'an II (1793–1794)* (Paris, Hachette, 1889–1890), 5 vols.

Walzer, M., *Regicide and Revolution: Speeches at the Trial of Louis XVI* (New York, Columbia University Press, 1992).

Weber, E., *Peasants into Frenchmen: The Modernization of Rural France, 1870–1914* (Stanford, Stanford University Press, 1976).

Weider, B. and S. Forshufvud, *Assassination at St. Helena: The Poisoning of Napoleon Bonaparte* (Vancouver, Mitchell Press, 1978).

Weider, B. and D. Hapgood, *The Murder of Napoleon* (New York, Congdon and Lattes, 1982).

Weiss, P. A., *Gendered Community: Rousseau, Sex, and Politics* (New York, New York University Press, 1993).

Whaley, L., *Radicals: Politics and Republicanism in the French Revolution* (Phoenix, AZ, Sutton Press, 2000).

Williams, G. A., *Artisans and Sans-culottes* (New York, W. W. Norton, 1969).

Woloch, I., *Jacobin Legacy: The Democratic Movement under the Directory* (Princeton, Princeton University Press, 1970).

Woloch, I., *The New Regime: Transformations of the French Civic Order, 1789–1820s* (New York, W. W. Norton, 1994).

Woloch, I., *Napoleon and His Collaborators* (New York, W. W. Norton, 2001).

Zizek, S., *Virtue and Terror: Maximilien Robespierre* (New York, Verso, 2007).

Index

Note: note numbers in brackets indicate the location of quotations by people not named in the text.